Karrabing Film Collective. Wonderland

A Reader

Karrabing Film Collective. Wonderland

A Reader

HAUS DER KUNST

DISTANZ

Karrabing Film Collective.
Wonderland
A Reader

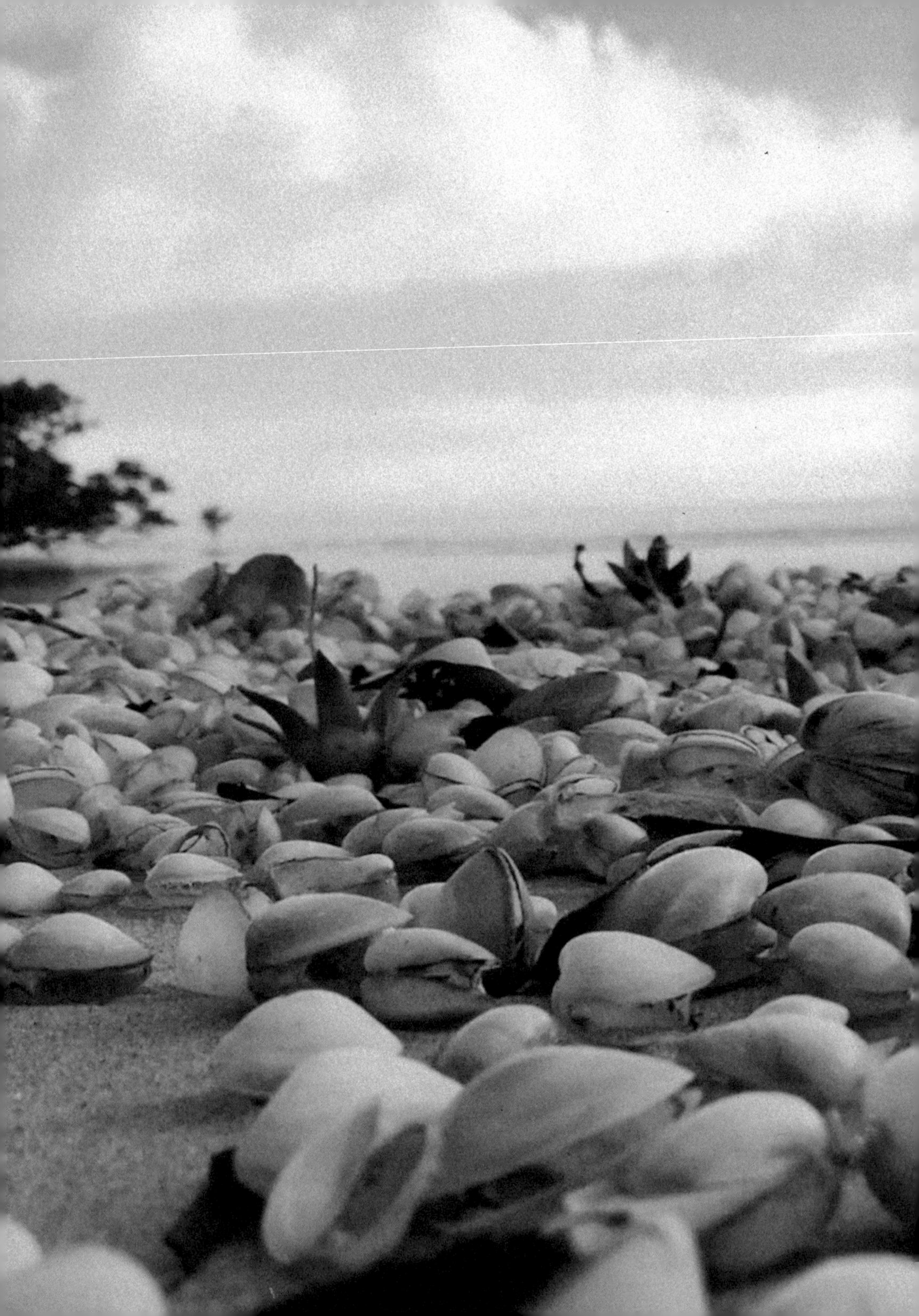

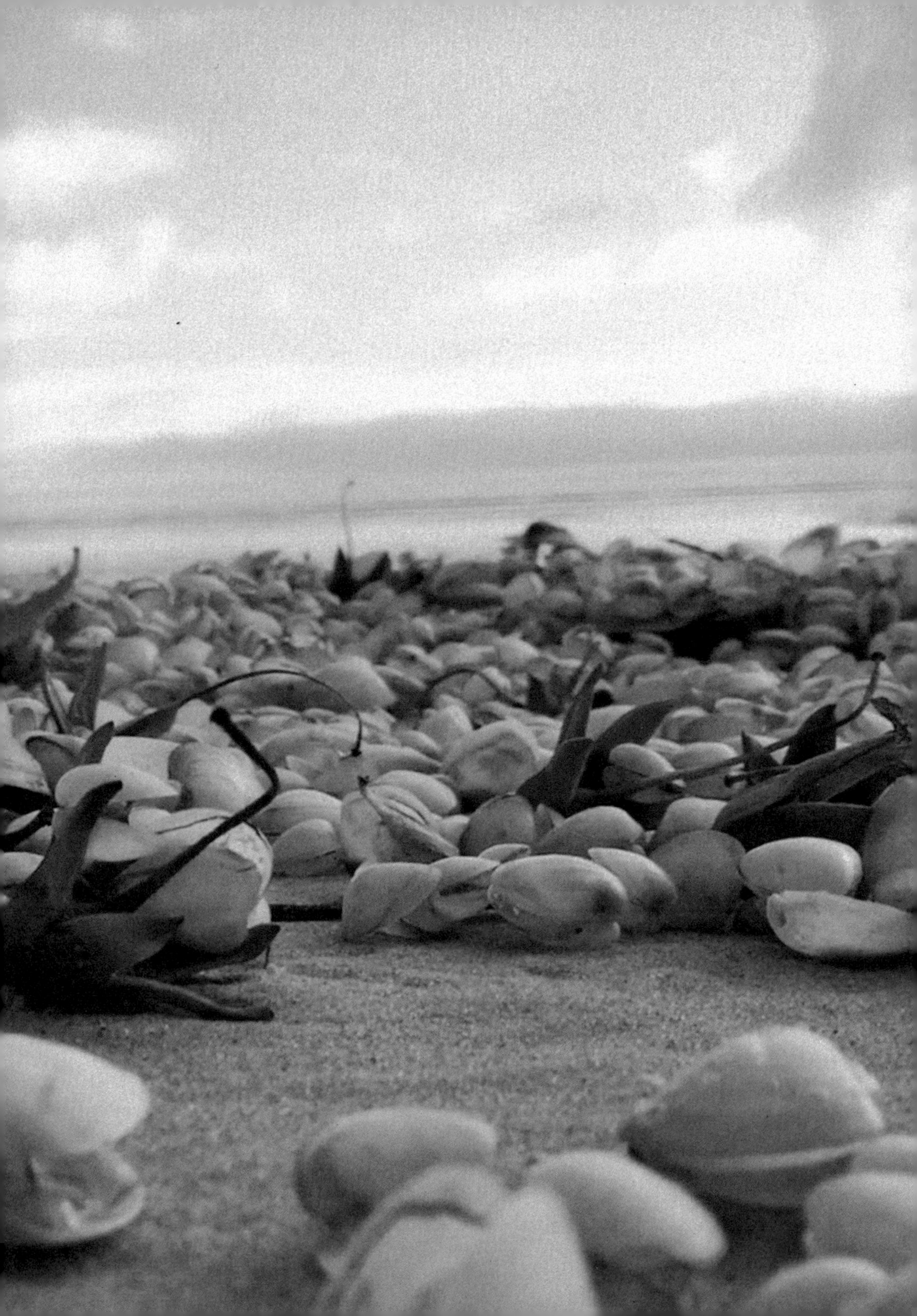

Foreword

Andrea Lissoni

‘Our films are neither fiction nor nonfiction. They come from and return to our ancestral lands. They emerge from and sink back into the lives we are actually living with our *durlg* (Dreamings).’

Haus der Kunst München is committed to bringing together and intertwining exhibitions, performances, music events, and engagement, through which we strive to generate multifaceted, participatory, and inspirational reflections on contemporary art practices, allowing for the establishment of new discourses and the exchange of knowledge. In keeping with this vision, we are honoured to present both the survey exhibition *Karrabing Film Collective. Wonderland,* as well as this Reader—a significant collection of writings. Based in Australia’s Northern Territory, Karrabing uses filmmaking and installation as a form of Indigenous grassroots resistance and self-organisation. In the Emmiyengal language, the word ‘karrabing’ describes the moment when the tide comes in, denoting both a coming together as well as a form of fluid collective practice, operating in tandem with, but also ancillary to, top-down government-imposed structures of clanship or land ownership. The approximately thirty members of Karrabing hail from different generations, and mostly live in the Belyuen community. The Collective’s films are often described as ‘improvisational realism’: a form of cinema that seeks to open up a space beyond binaries of the fictional and the documentary, or the past and the present.

With this in mind, we have chosen to respond to the inherently mutable nature of 'karrabing' by presenting a multi-format exhibition project that is characterised by moments of attuned watching, listening, and reading. Functioning both independently and in tandem, each of these elements allows for multiple entry points, thereby engendering a non-hierarchical, discursive temporary zone through which the public may engage with the group's multifarious practice. Karrabing's works critically interrogate notions of representation, belonging, and cultural memory, and replacing this with a form of dynamic interaction and creative exchange.

Underpinning the rationale for this approach is the question of what the unique filmic language developed by the Karrabing Film Collective can tell about the porosity and elasticity of contemporary society and of constructed realities. Although several of the narratives that drive the films are deeply rooted in the daily realities of Indigenous existence in Australia, the wider themes and issues—such as the relationship between human and non-human life forms, or the maintenance and care of the land and of the earth's varied ecosystems—resonate with all viewers, allowing for slow contemplation and open deliberation.

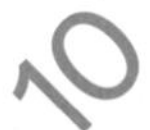

The comprehensive Karrabing Reader features a series of commissioned essays, alongside a selection of key texts and interviews spanning the decade since the Collective's first film *When the Dogs Talked* (2014). By concatenating interviews and scholarly writings, the Reader discursively introduces the myriad of cultural, political, and environmental threads that inform Karrabing's practice. The publication is sought to extend far beyond—and function independent of—the exhibition: working as a means through which readers gain a deeper understanding of the living environment of Karrabing's members.

The realisation of projects such as this requires the great commitment of many individuals who passionately and dedicatedly work together. Firstly, I want to express our deepest gratitude towards all members of Karrabing Film Collective, who significantly contributed to both the exhibition itself, as well as to this current publication. I would also like to extend my deepest gratitude to all contributors of the Reader: with the help of their texts, we were able to produce the first extensive publication on Karrabing. In addition, thanks also need to be extended to the publishing house Distanz Verlag in Berlin, and in particular Matthias Kliefoth and Rebecca Wilton. My gratitude also goes to the graphic designer Eva Schlotter from Distanz Verlag, as well as to the editor Olivia Parkes. I should also acknowledge the generous support of the Free State of Bavaria, Gesellschaft der Freunde Haus der Kunst München, and our main supporter, the Alexander-Tutsek-Stiftung.

As an institution, we take great pride in the dedicated commitment of our staff. The care each member of the team brings to the realisation of exhibitions and publications creates the conditions that make them a stimulating and collective experience. My special thanks go to the editor of this publication and curator of the exhibition, Damian Lentini, who has thoughtfully brought together a range of voices and perspectives that cover Karrabing's multifaceted practice. Thanks also to curatorial fellow Anne Pfautsch who worked with Lentini and key Karrabing member Elizabeth A. Povinelli to create an immersive and carefully considered show.

I would also like to thank the Exhibition Realisation department here at the museum, most notably Hanna Kriegleder, Martin Oster, and Markus Brandenburg, for their outstanding efforts in implementing the exhibition. Furthermore, my gratitude extends to Emma Enderby for her attention to research and curation, as well as to Wolfgang Orthmayr and Biljana Gligoric for their administrative support. Moreover, I wish to thank the communication department, most notably, Tina Anjou, Saskia Müller-Bastian, Claudia Illi, and Manuela Illera as well as Pia Linden and Camille Latreille from the Learning and Education department.

In close collaboration with the artists, Haus der Kunst München was able to realise a significative show and the current publication, both of which critically interrogate vital questions concerning Indigenous Australians. Karrabing's films function as a tool for Indigenous resilience, cultural continuity, and a conduit for new forms of cinematic storytelling. They put forward another worldview that can be experienced both in the exhibition and the book.

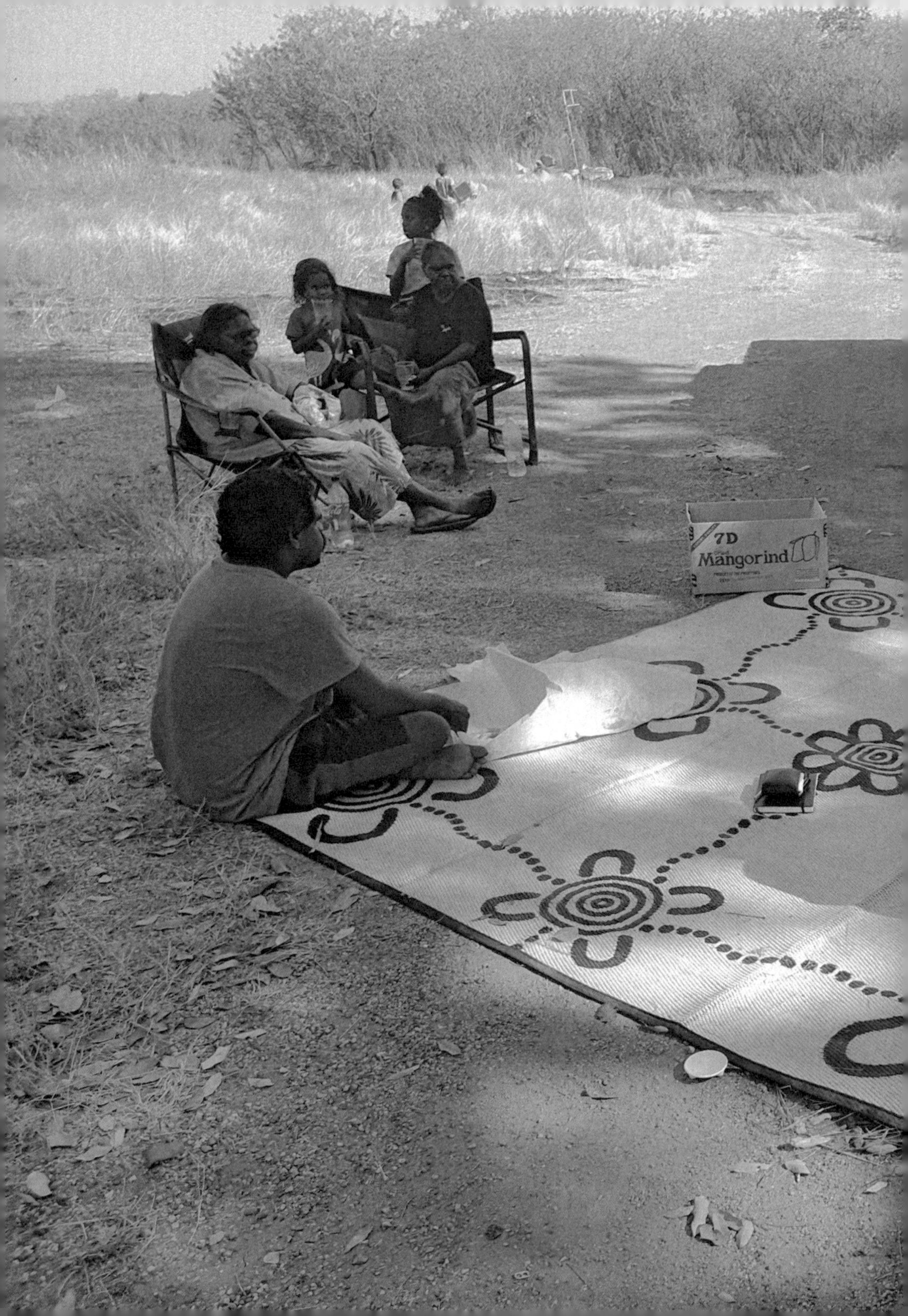
7D
Mangorind

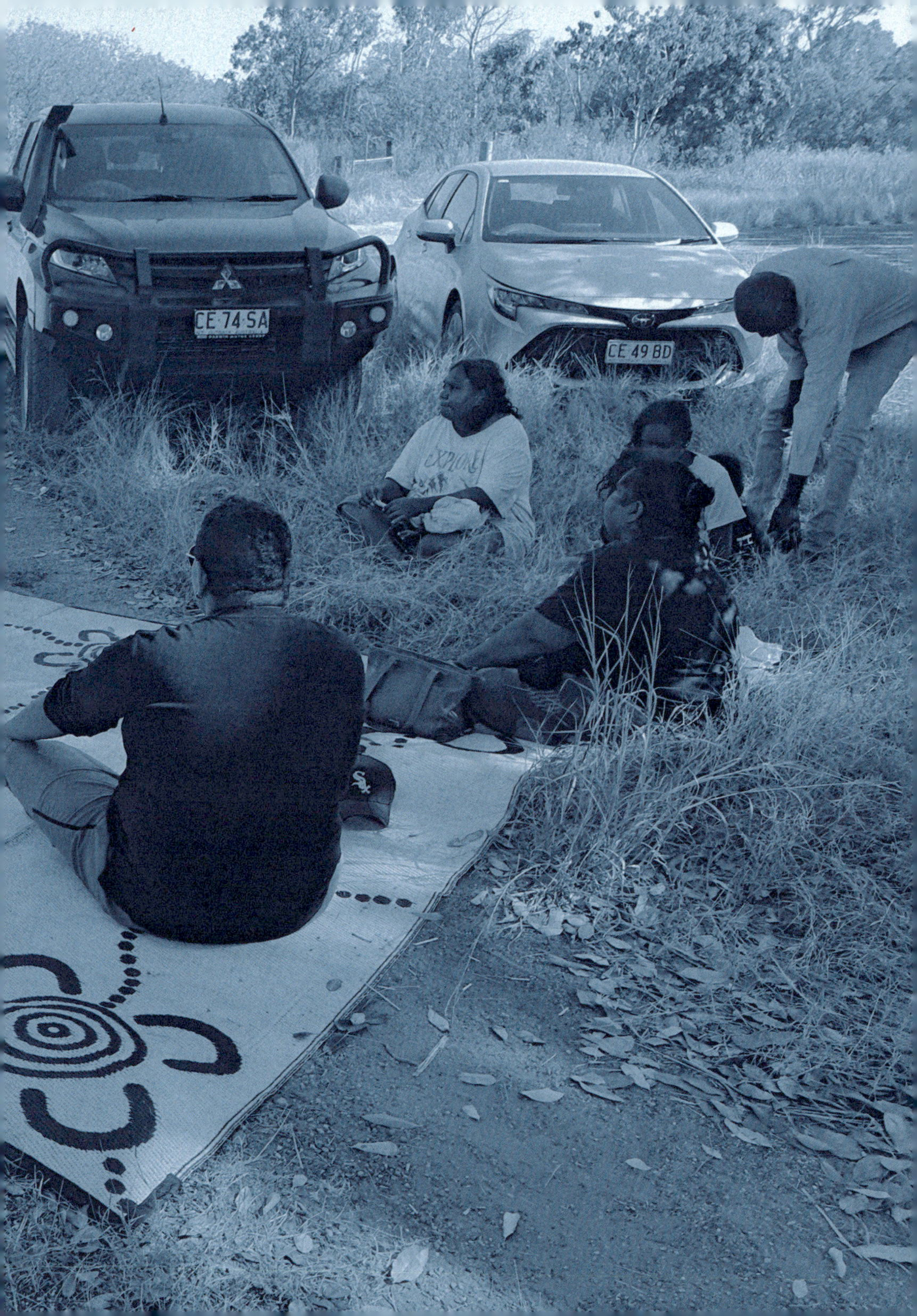
CE 74 SA
CE 49 BD

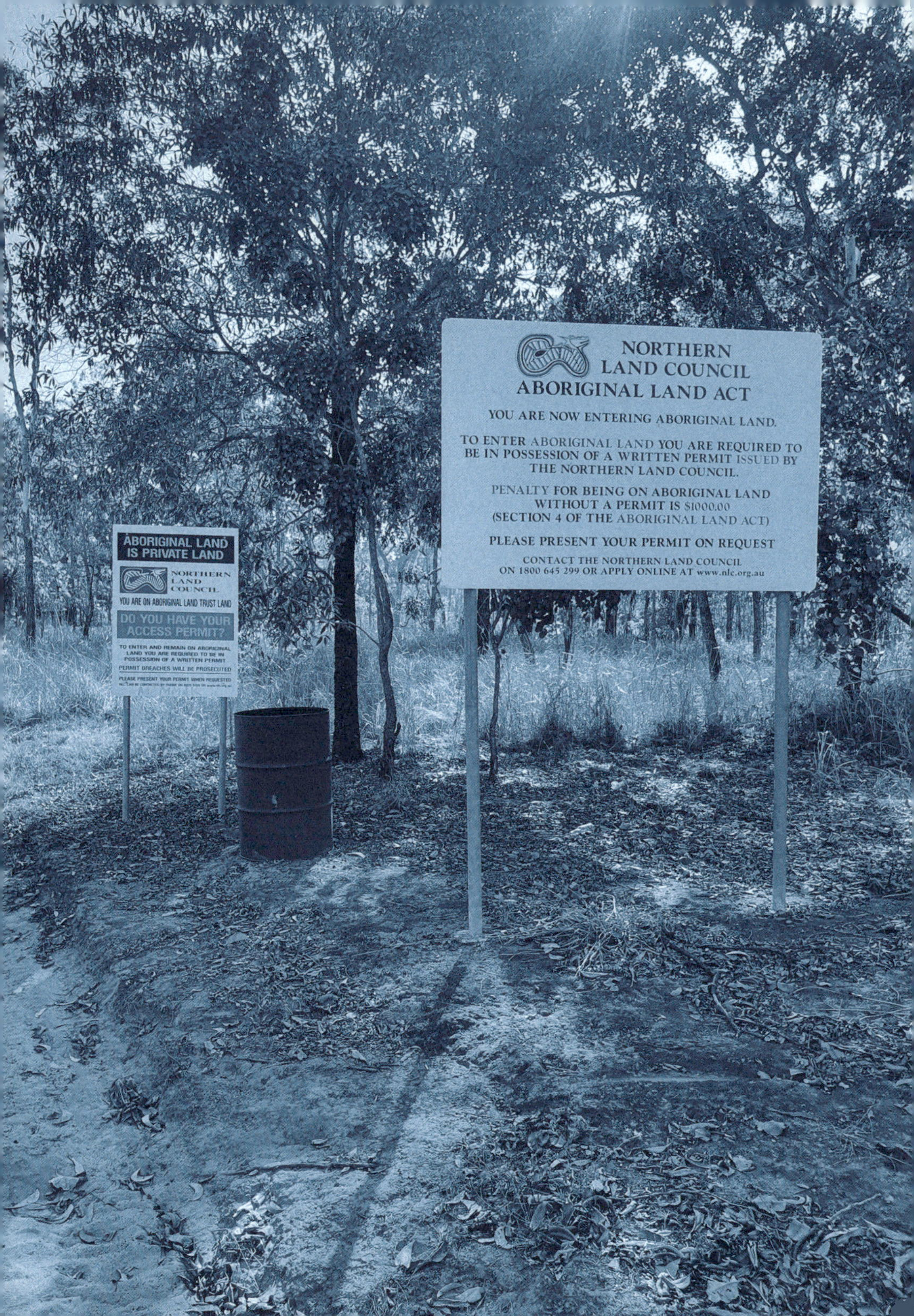
ABORIGINAL LAND
IS PRIVATE LAND
NORTHERN
LAND
COUNCIL
YOU ARE ON ABORIGINAL LAND TRUST LAND
DO YOU HAVE YOUR
ACCESS PERMIT?
TO ENTER AND REMAIN ON ABORIGINAL
LAND YOU ARE REQUIRED TO BE IN
POSSESSION OF A WRITTEN PERMIT
PERMIT BREACHES WILL BE PROSECUTED
PLEASE PRESENT YOUR PERMIT WHEN REQUESTED
NORTHERN
LAND COUNCIL
ABORIGINAL LAND ACT
YOU ARE NOW ENTERING ABORIGINAL LAND.
TO ENTER ABORIGINAL LAND YOU ARE REQUIRED TO
BE IN POSSESSION OF A WRITTEN PERMIT ISSUED BY
THE NORTHERN LAND COUNCIL.
PENALTY FOR BEING ON ABORIGINAL LAND
WITHOUT A PERMIT IS $1000.00
(SECTION 4 OF THE ABORIGINAL LAND ACT)
PLEASE PRESENT YOUR PERMIT ON REQUEST
CONTACT THE NORTHERN LAND COUNCIL
ON 1800 645 299 OR APPLY ONLINE AT www.nlc.org.au

Photographic Impressions of Karrabing's Wonderland

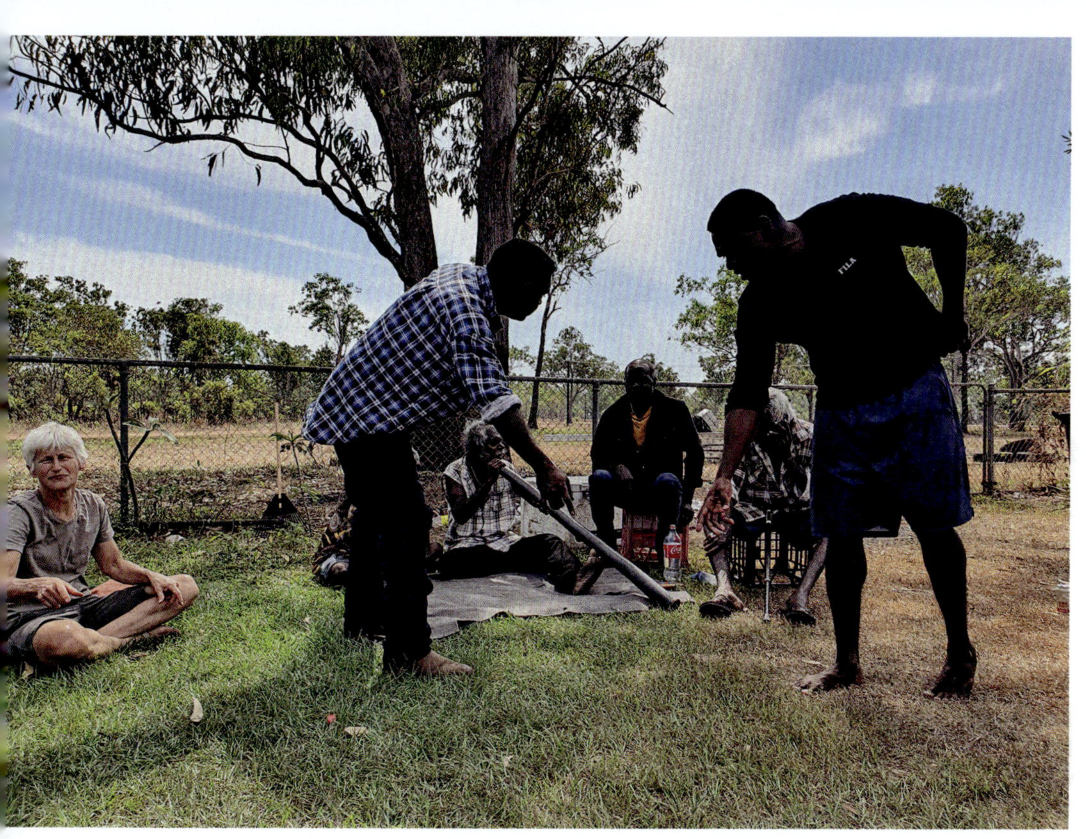

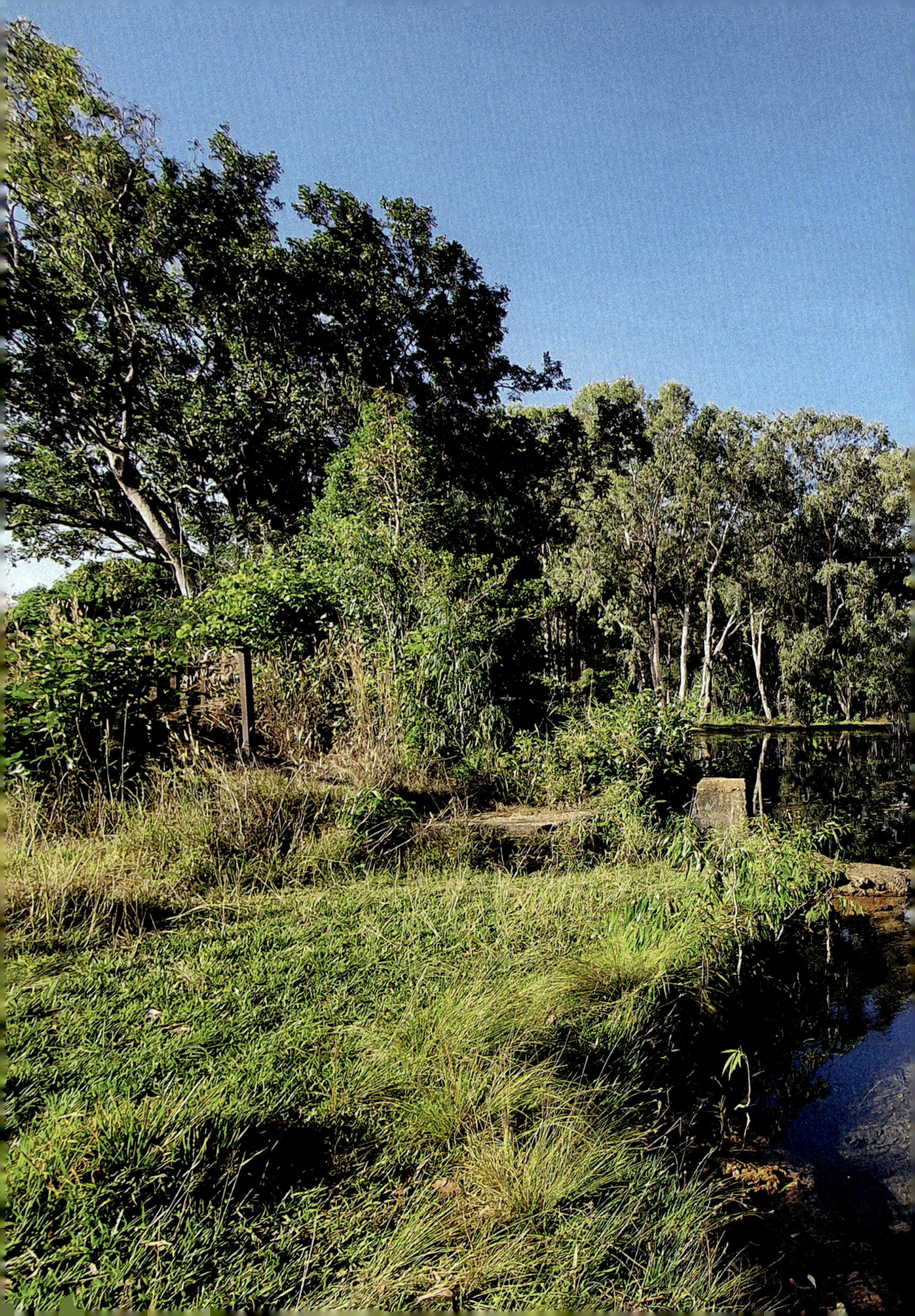

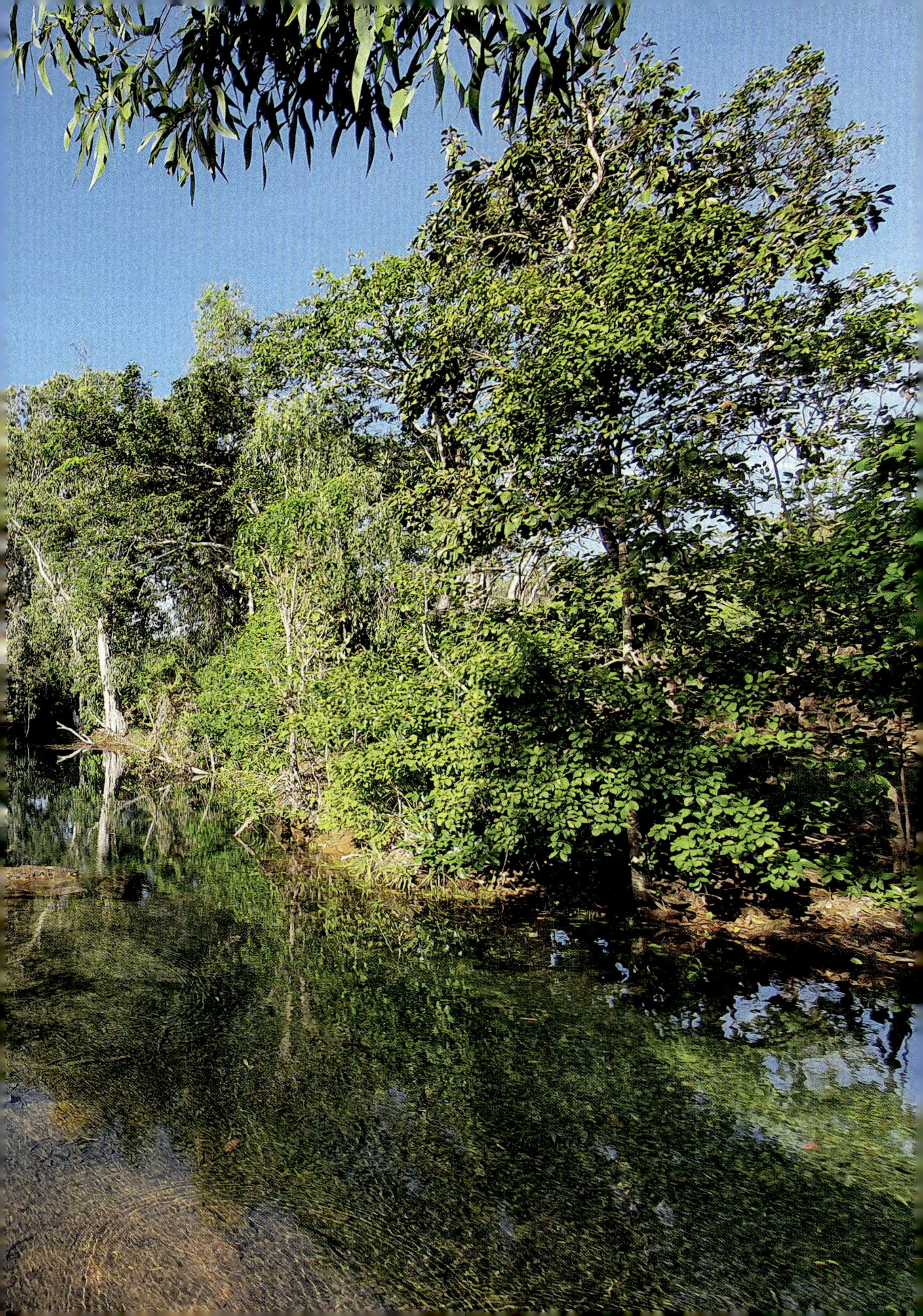

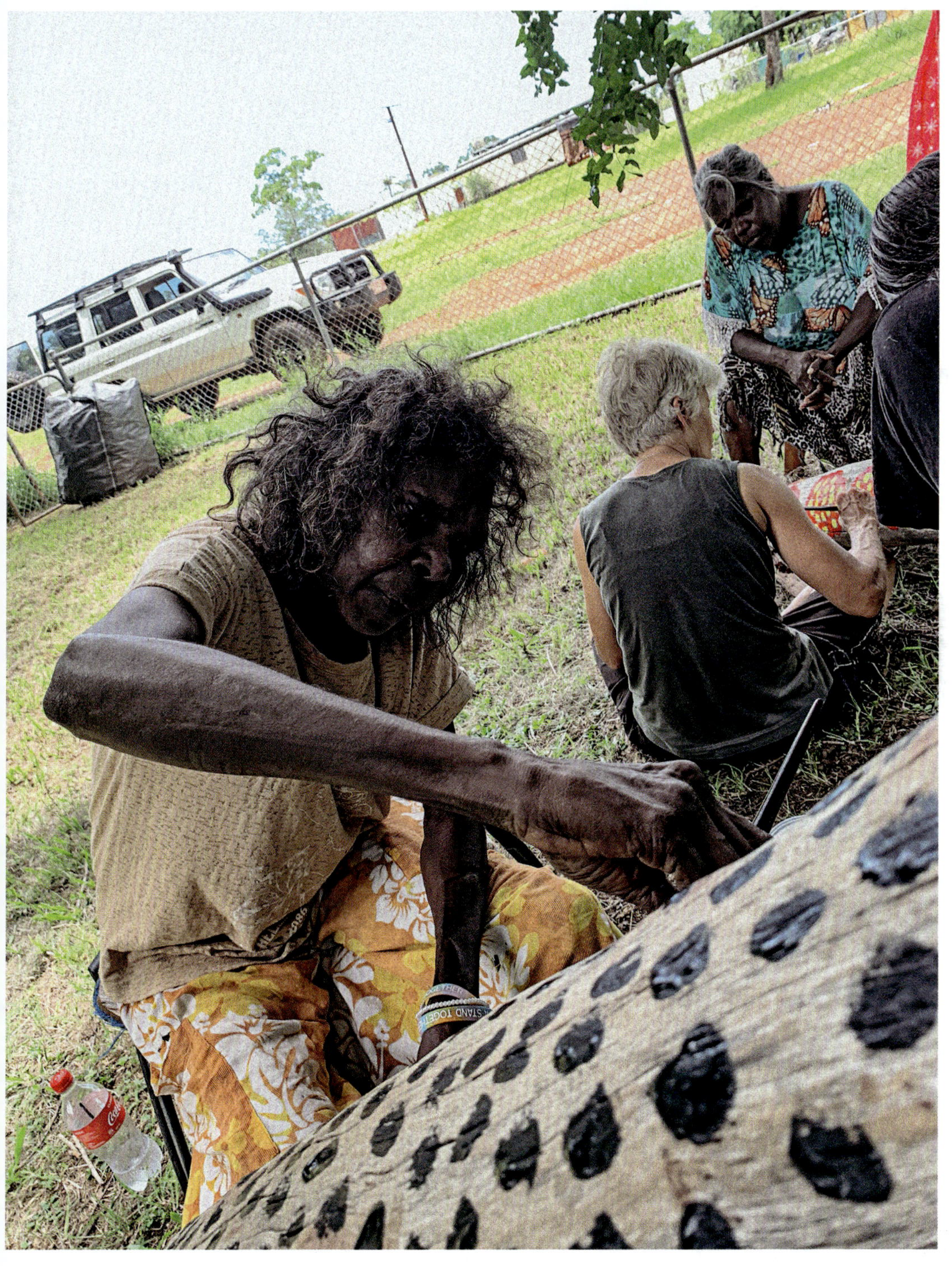

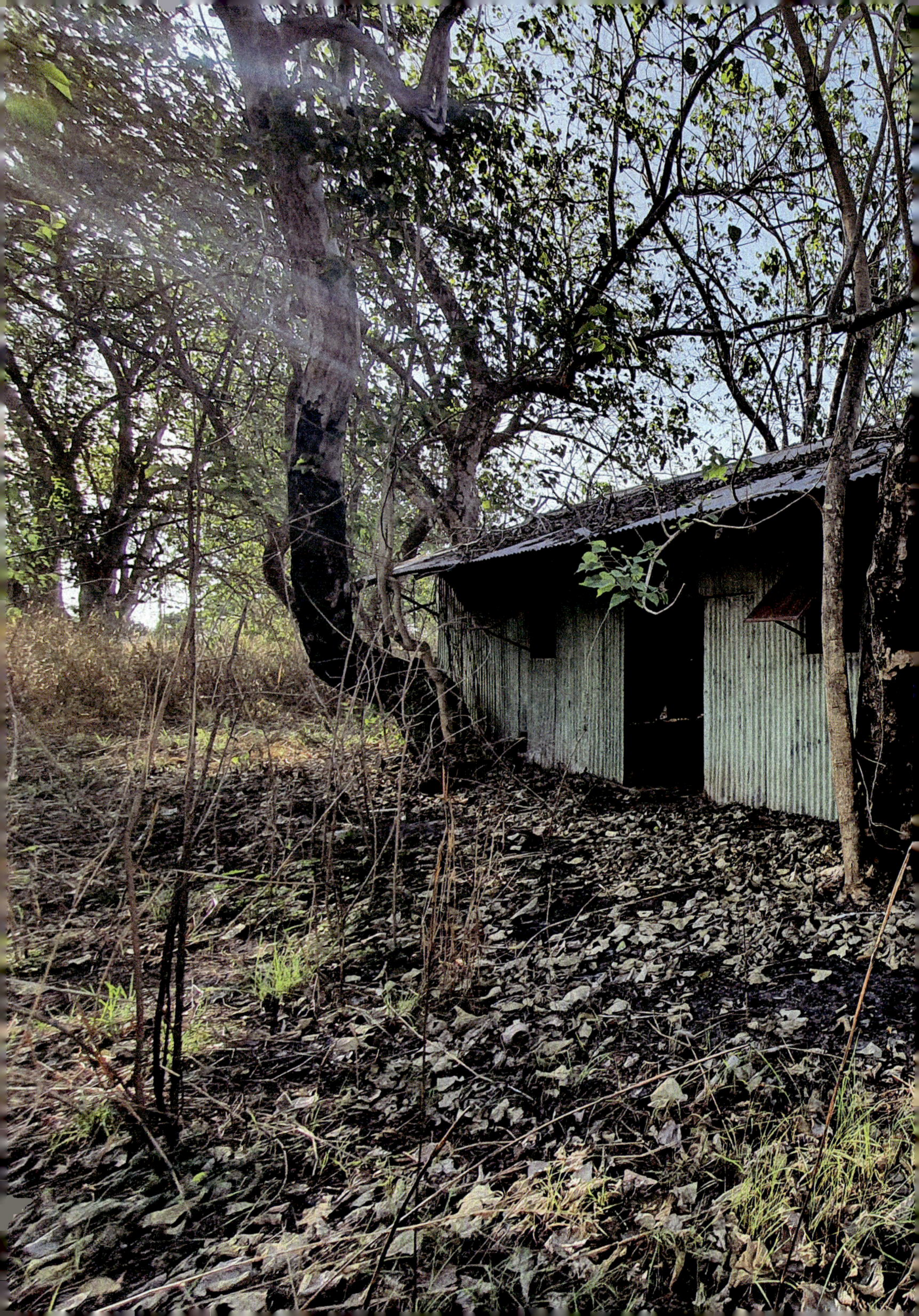

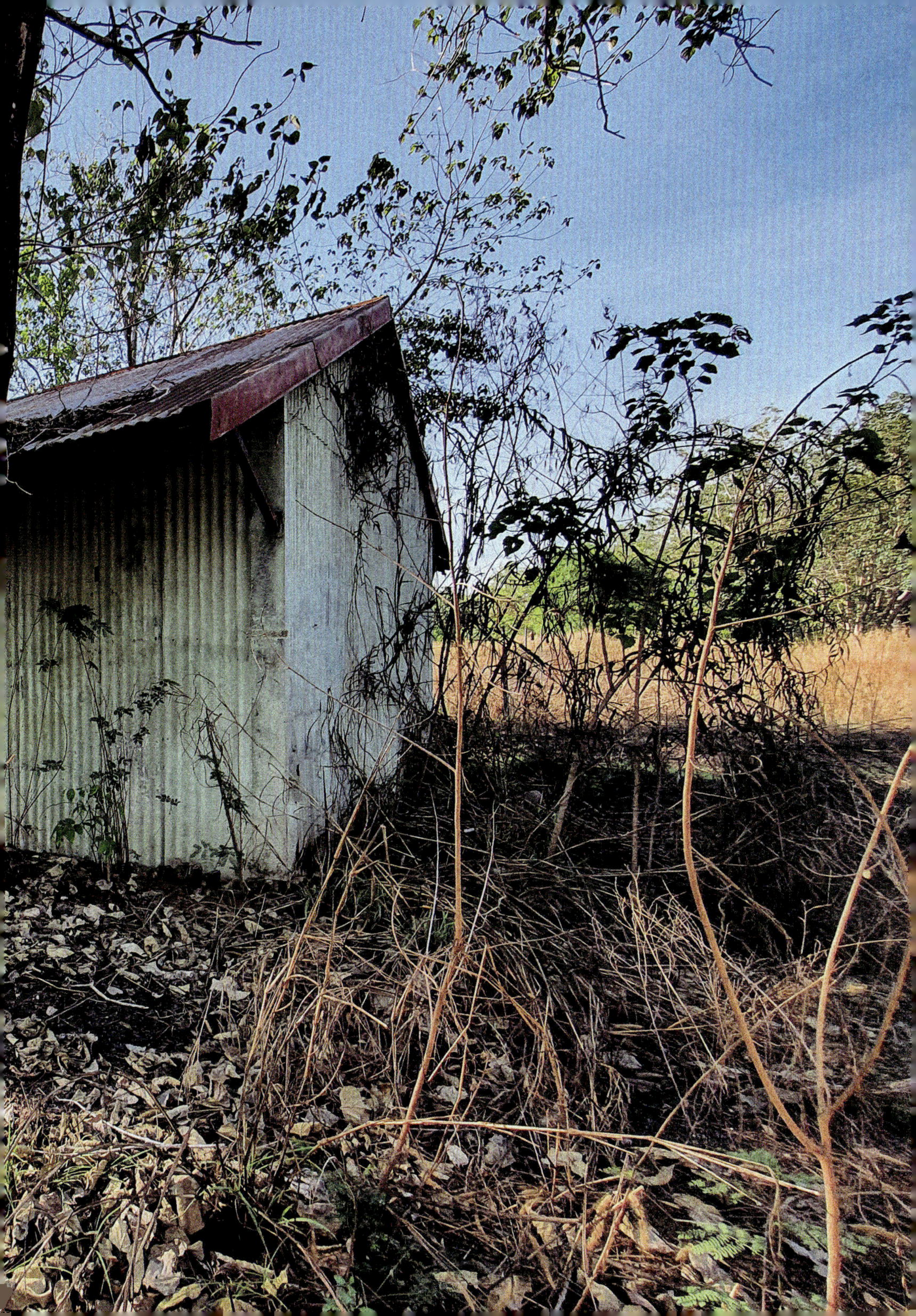

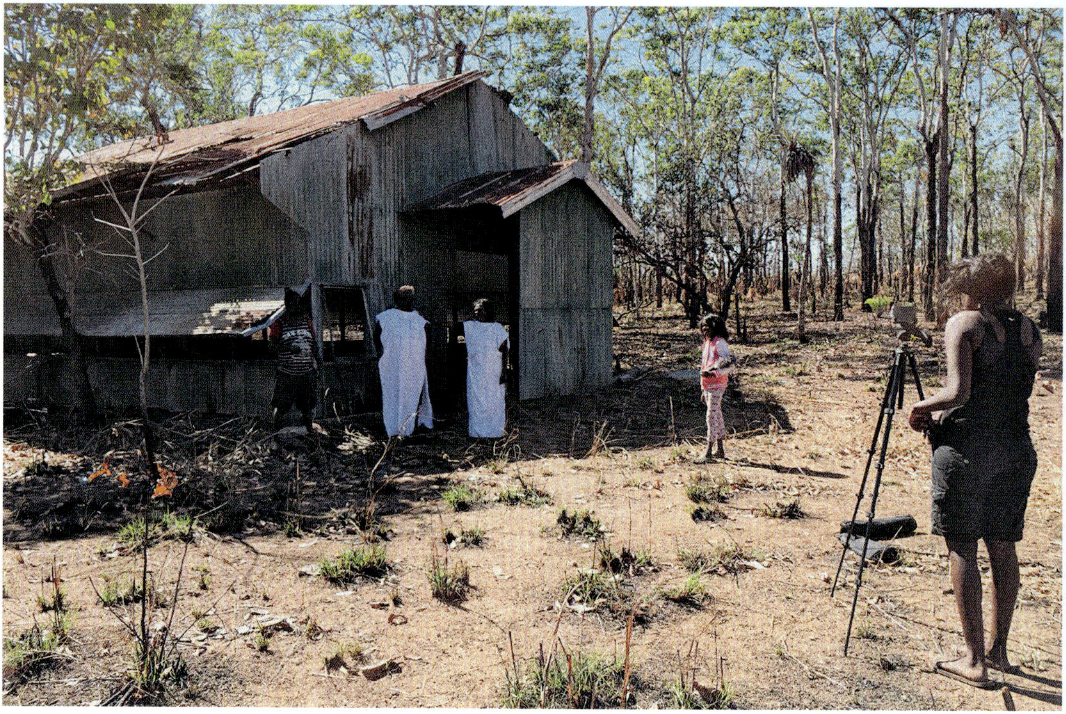

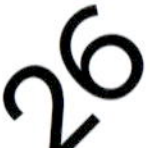

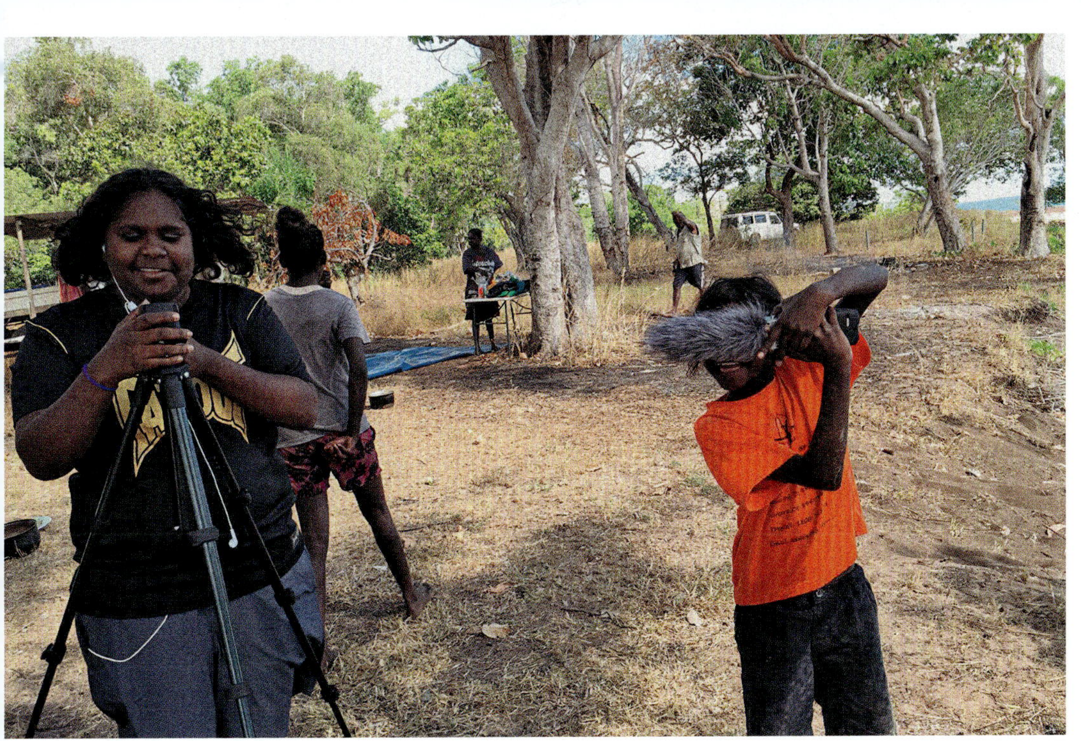

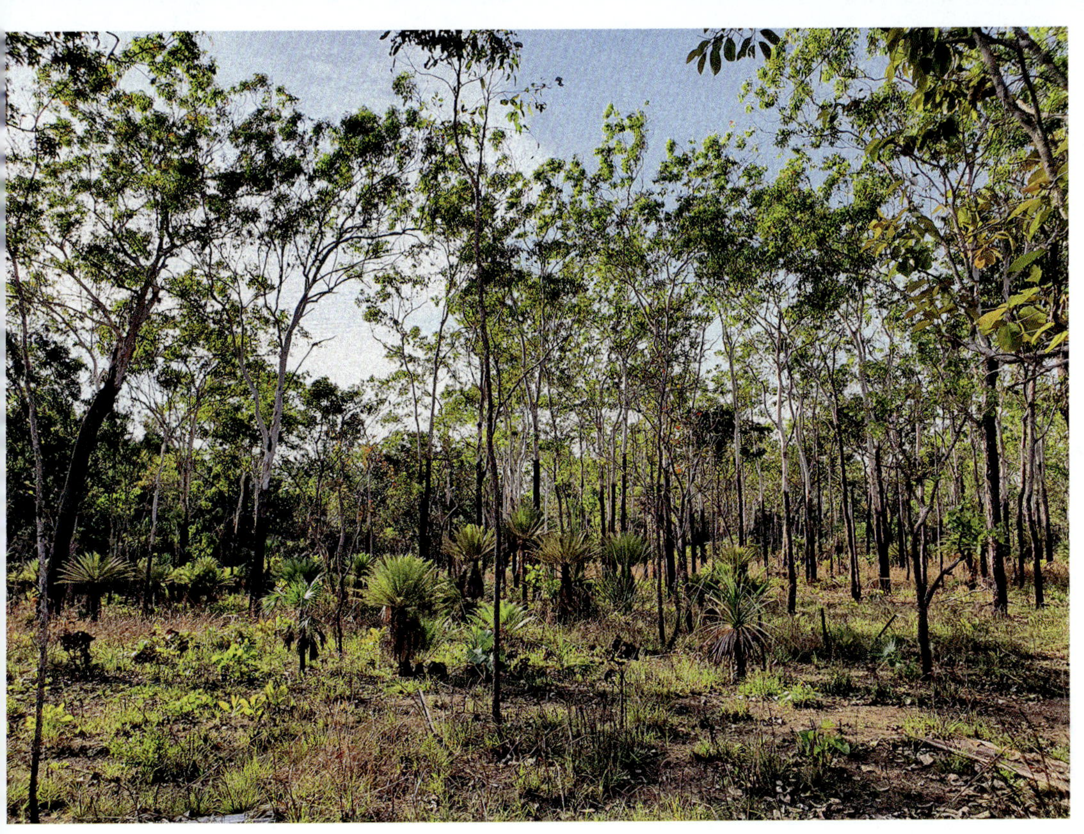

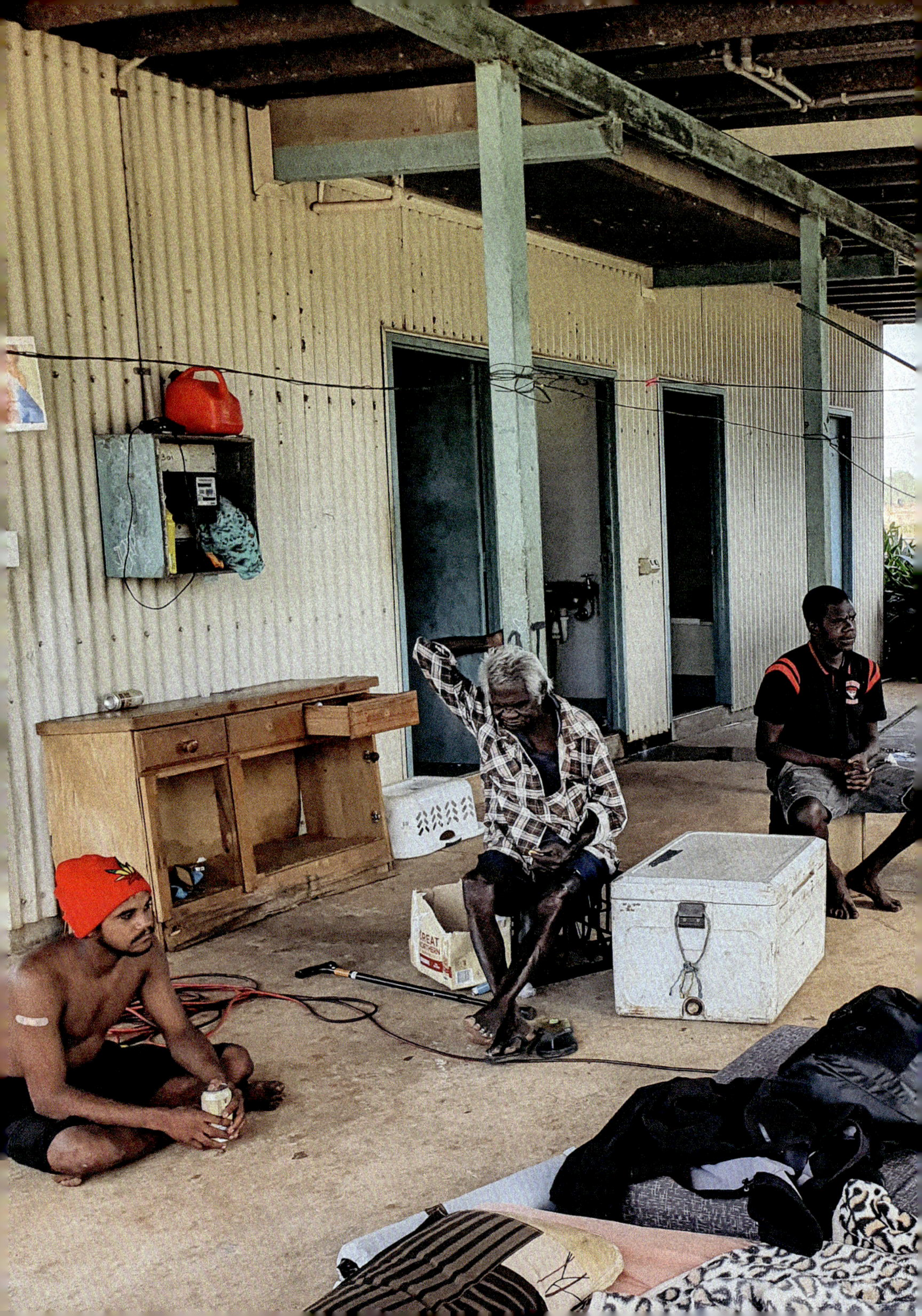

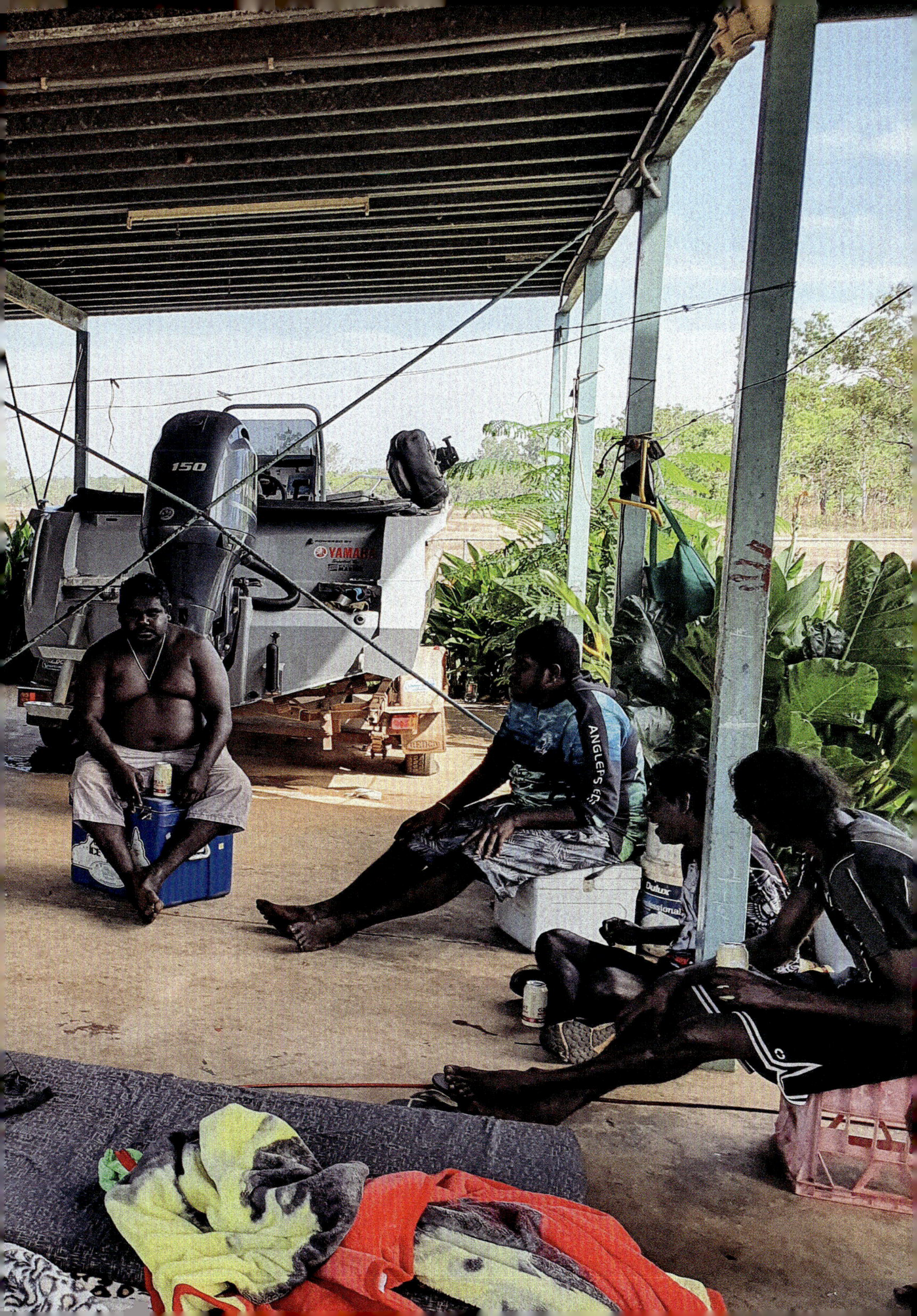
150
Dulux

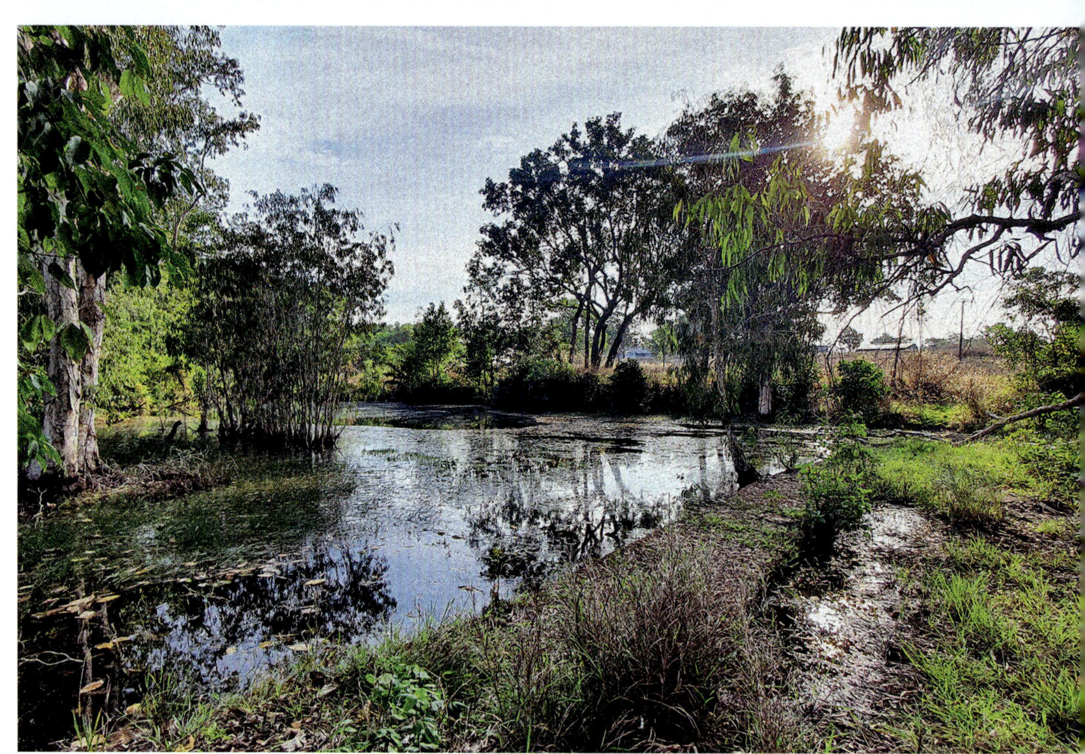

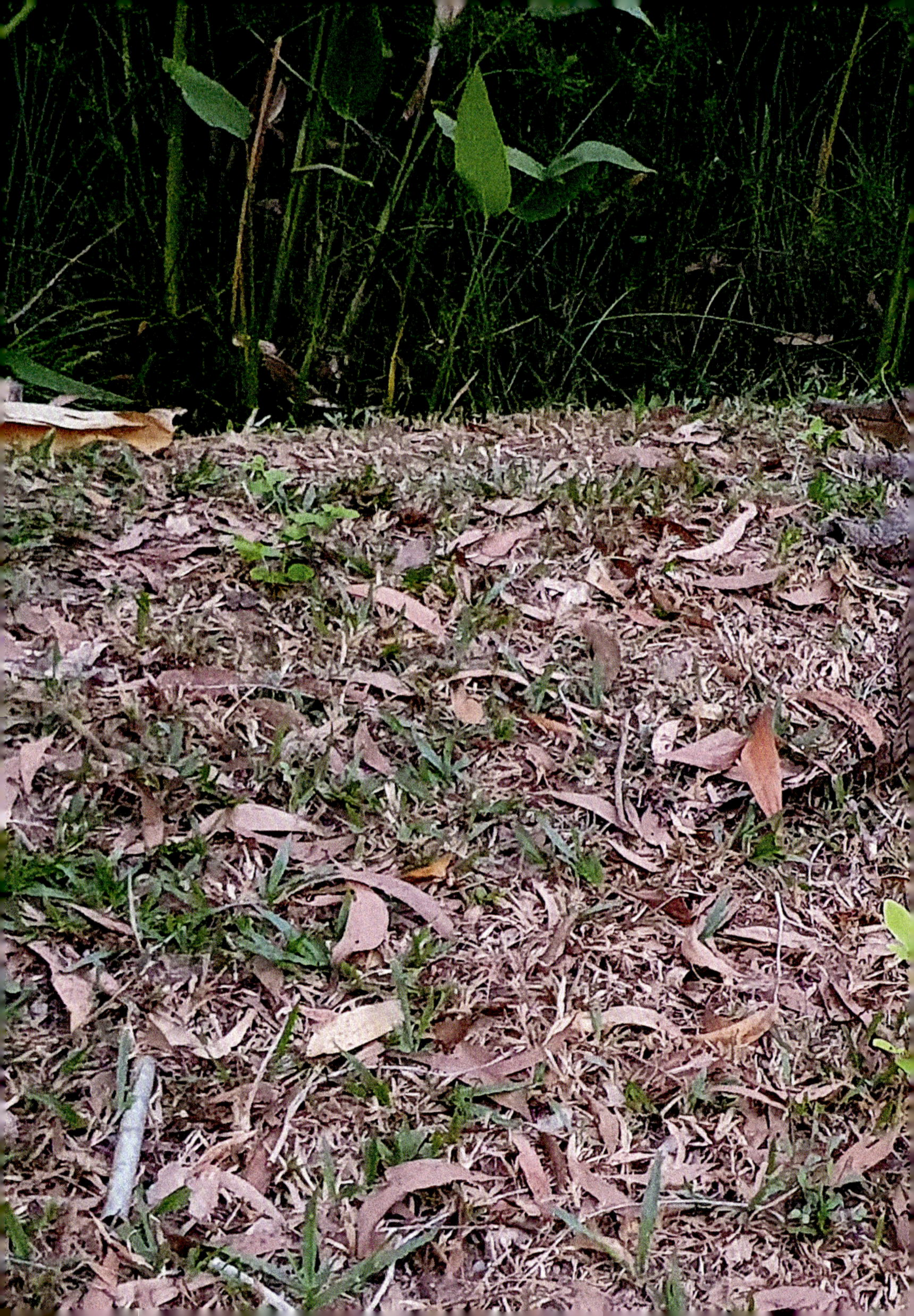

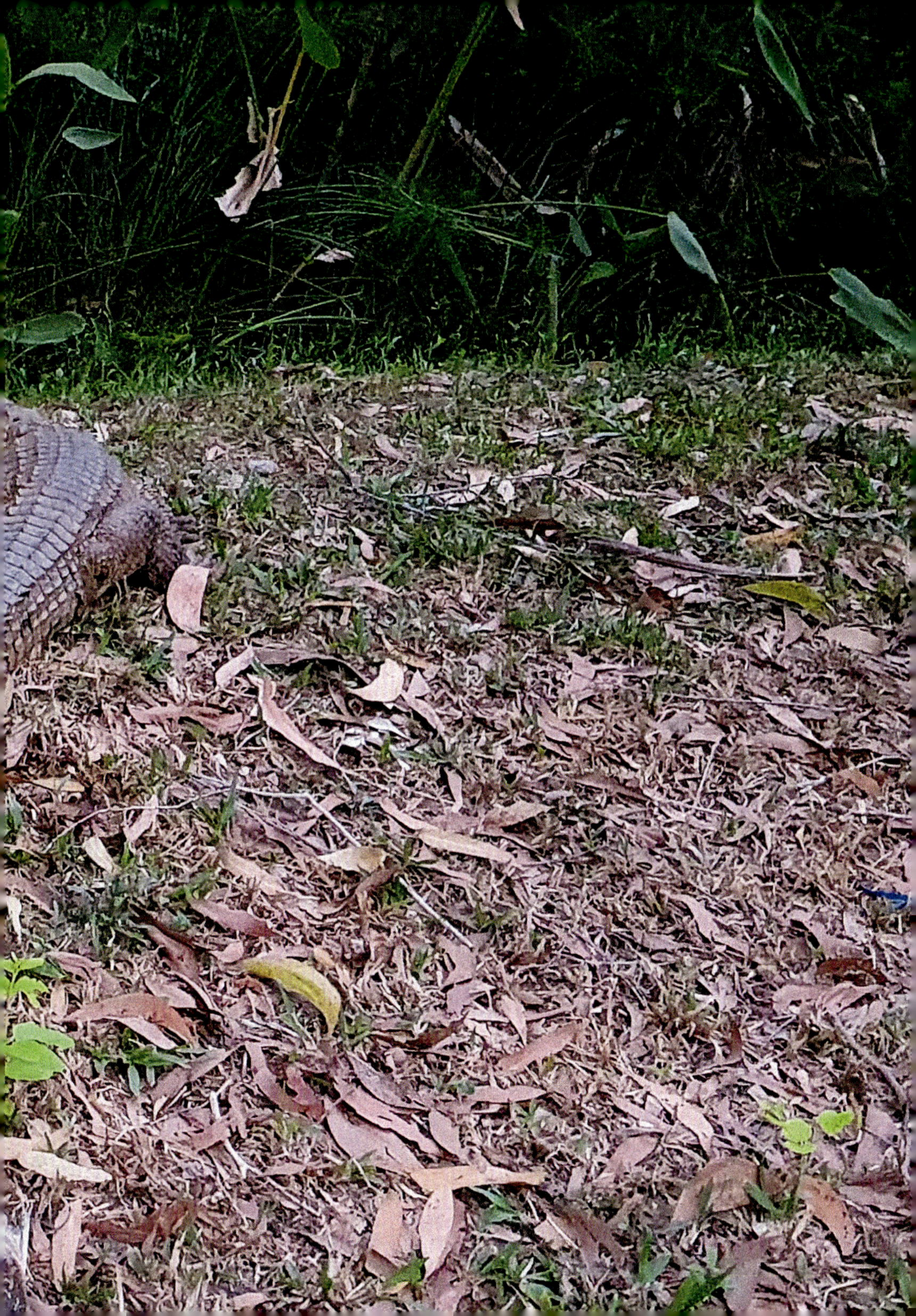

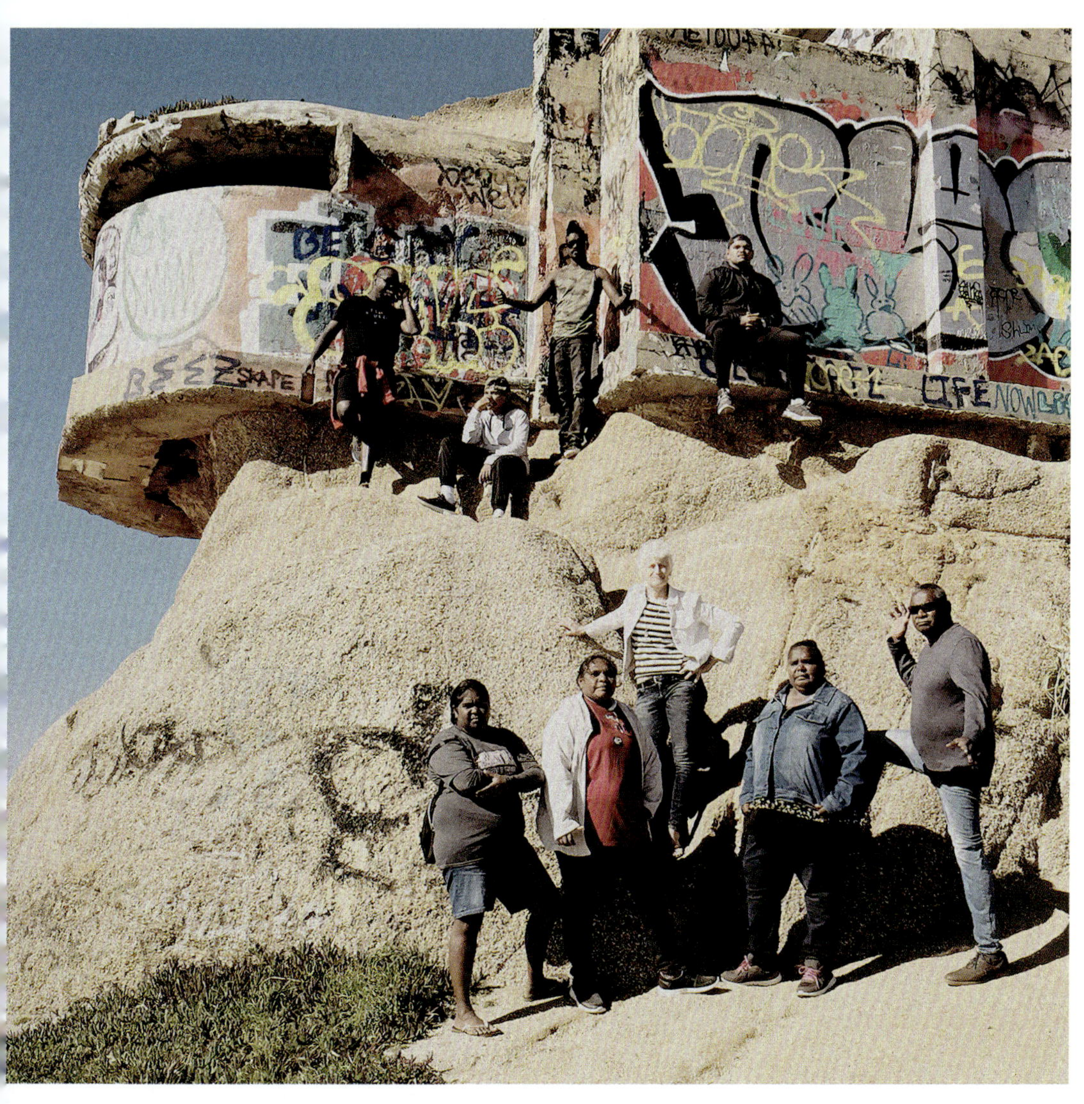

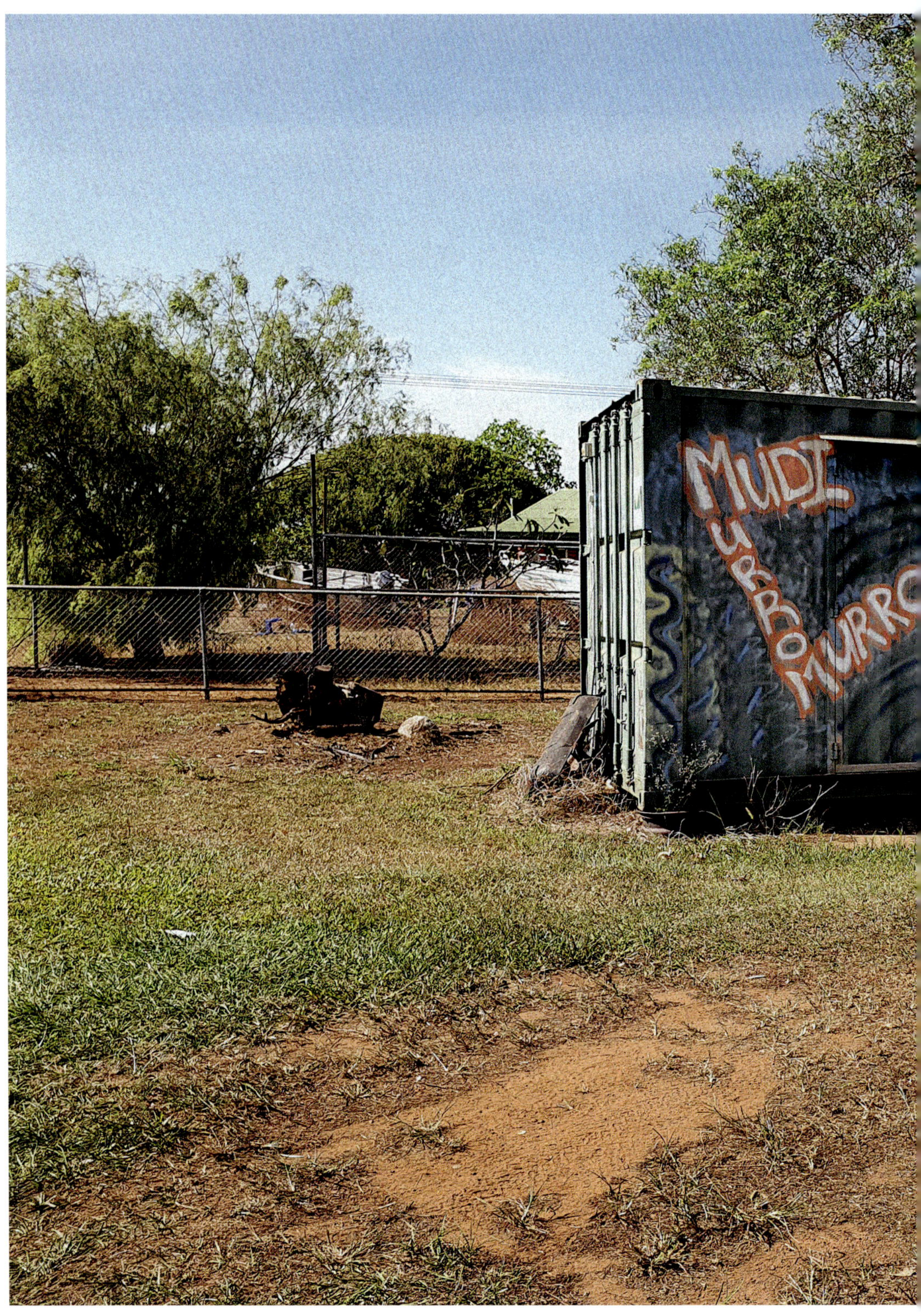
MUDI

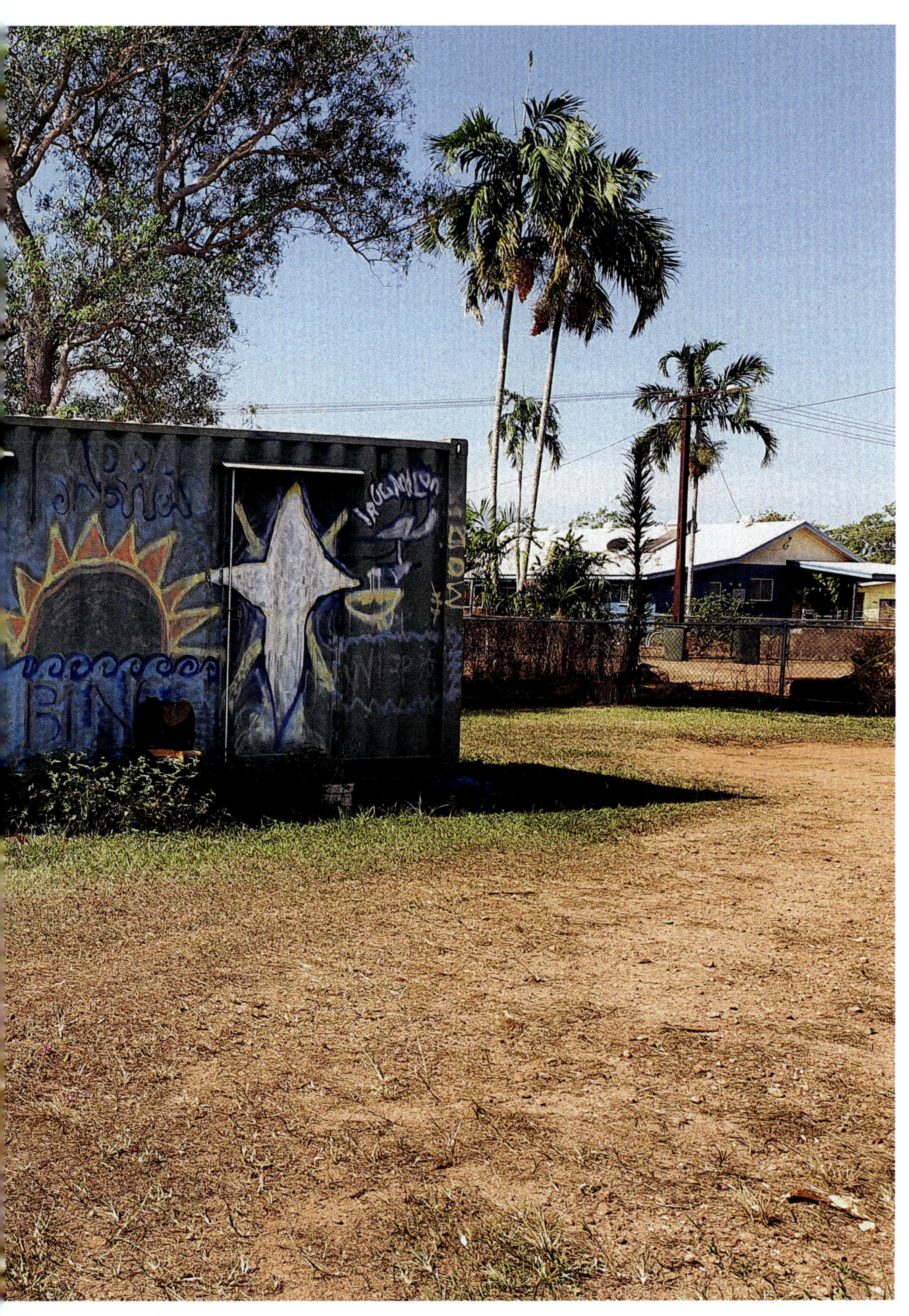

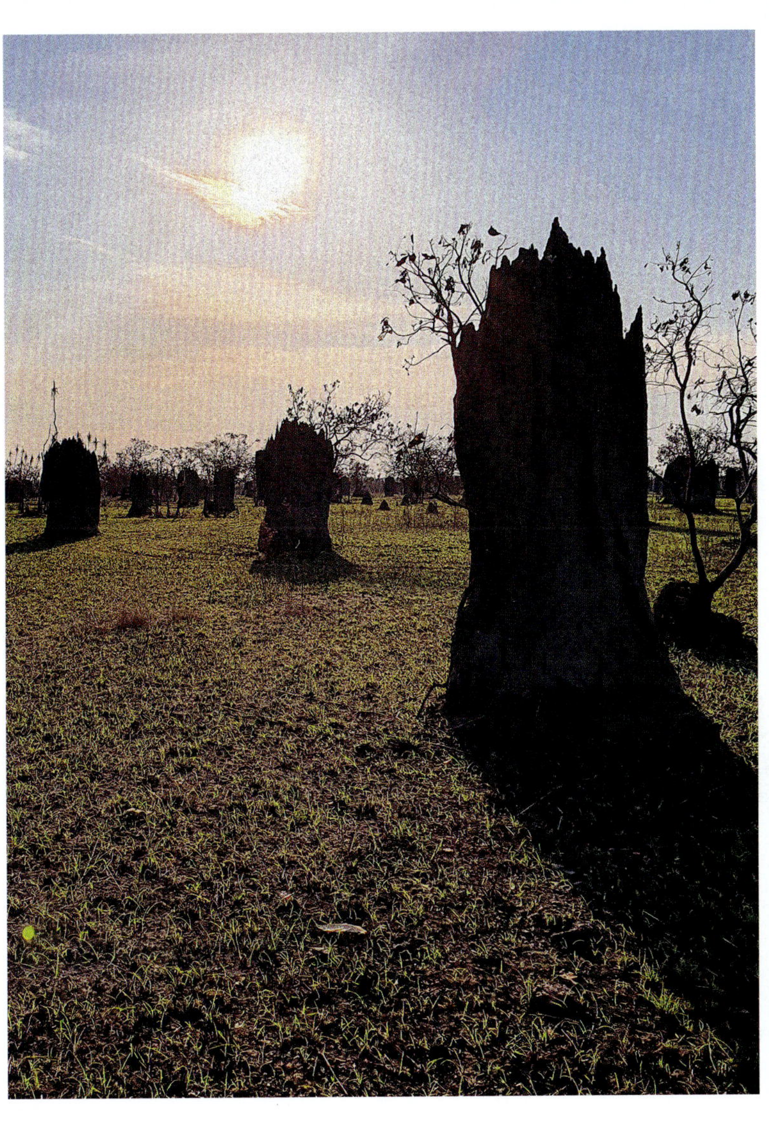

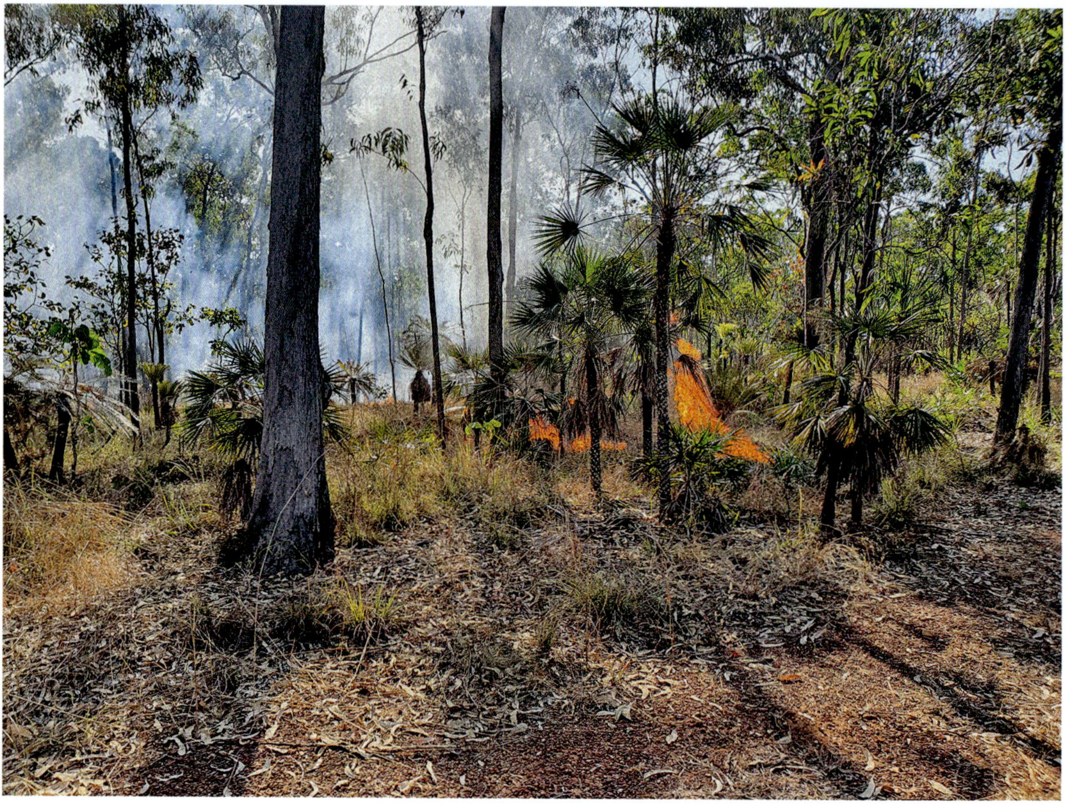

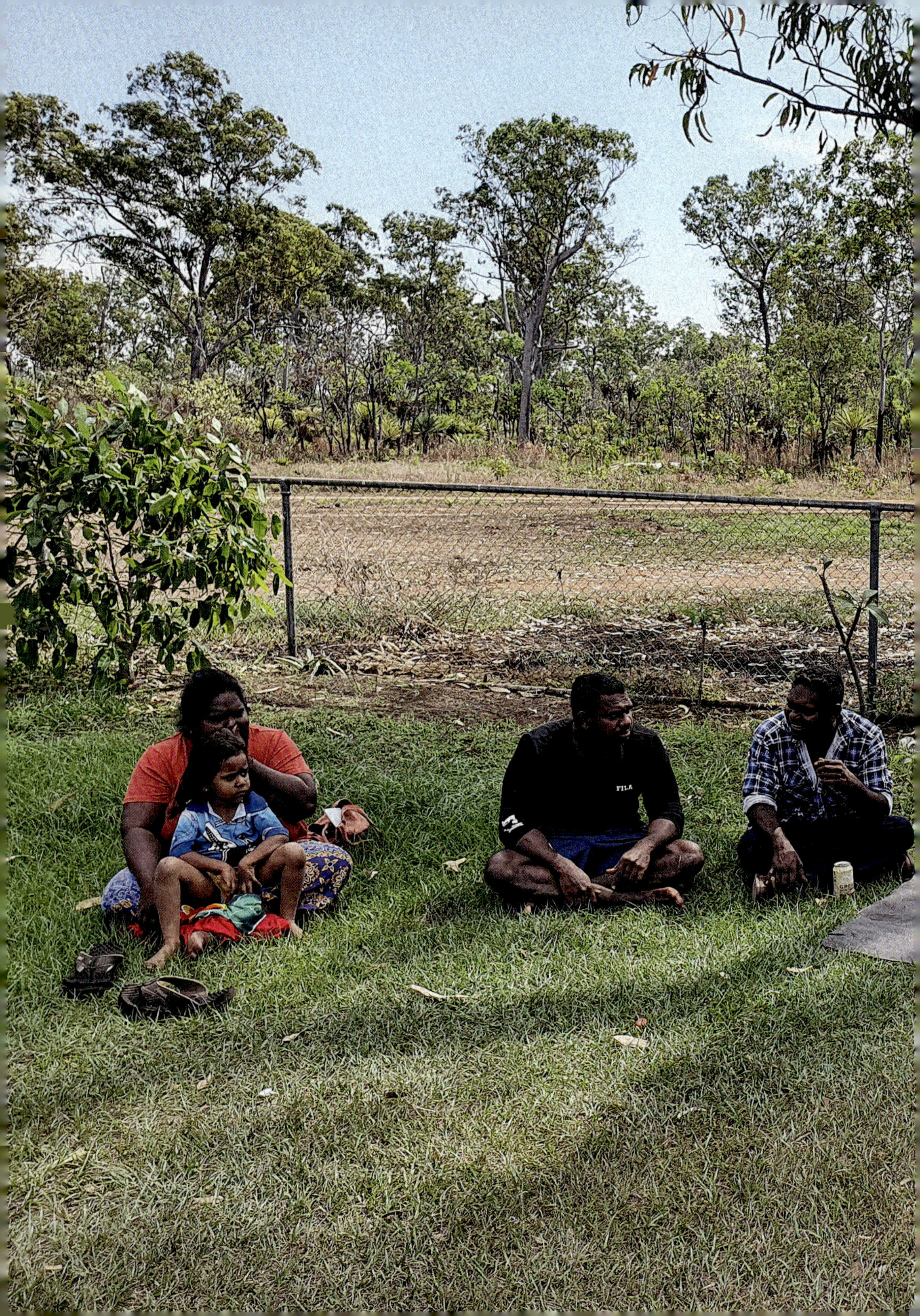
FILA

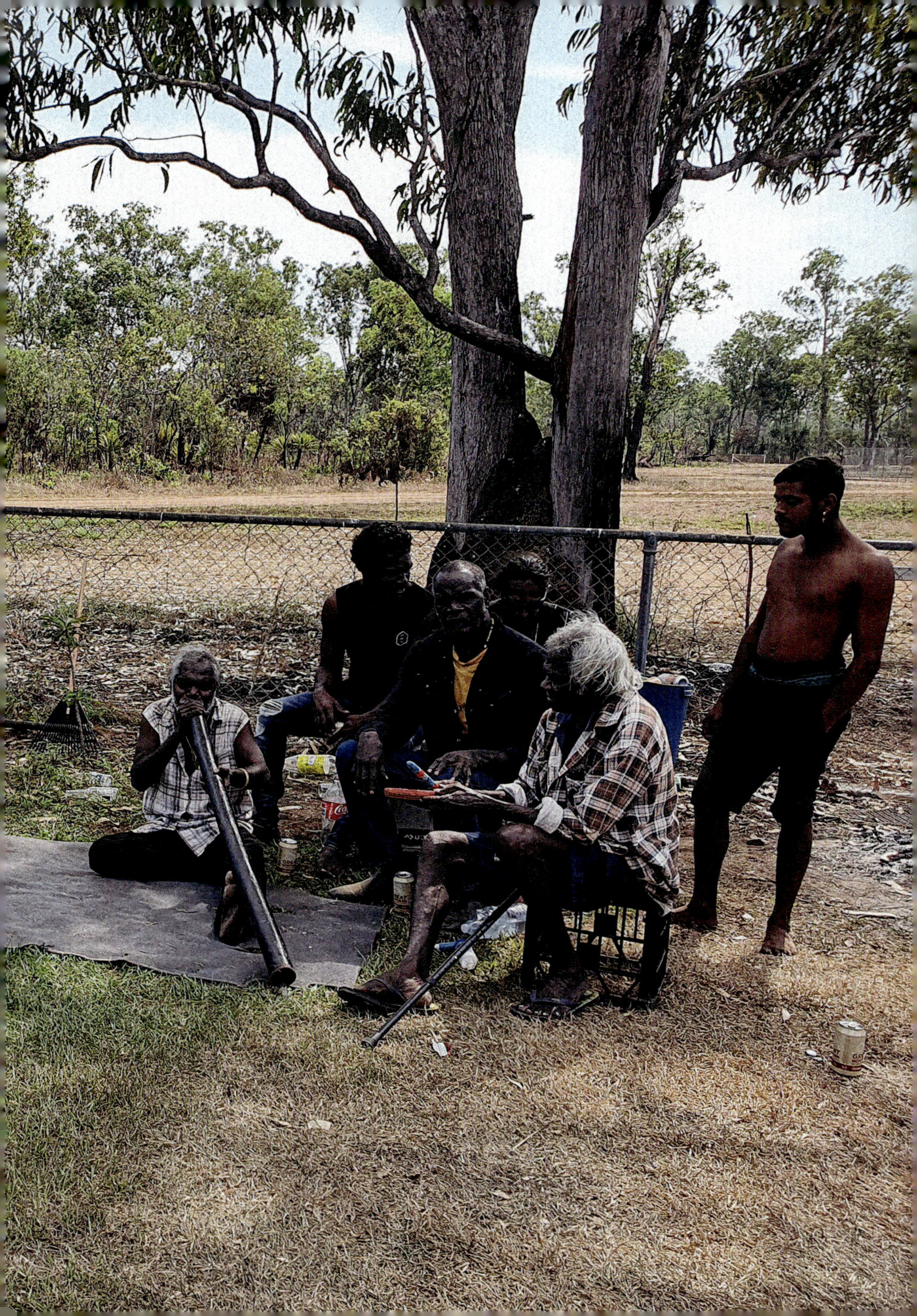

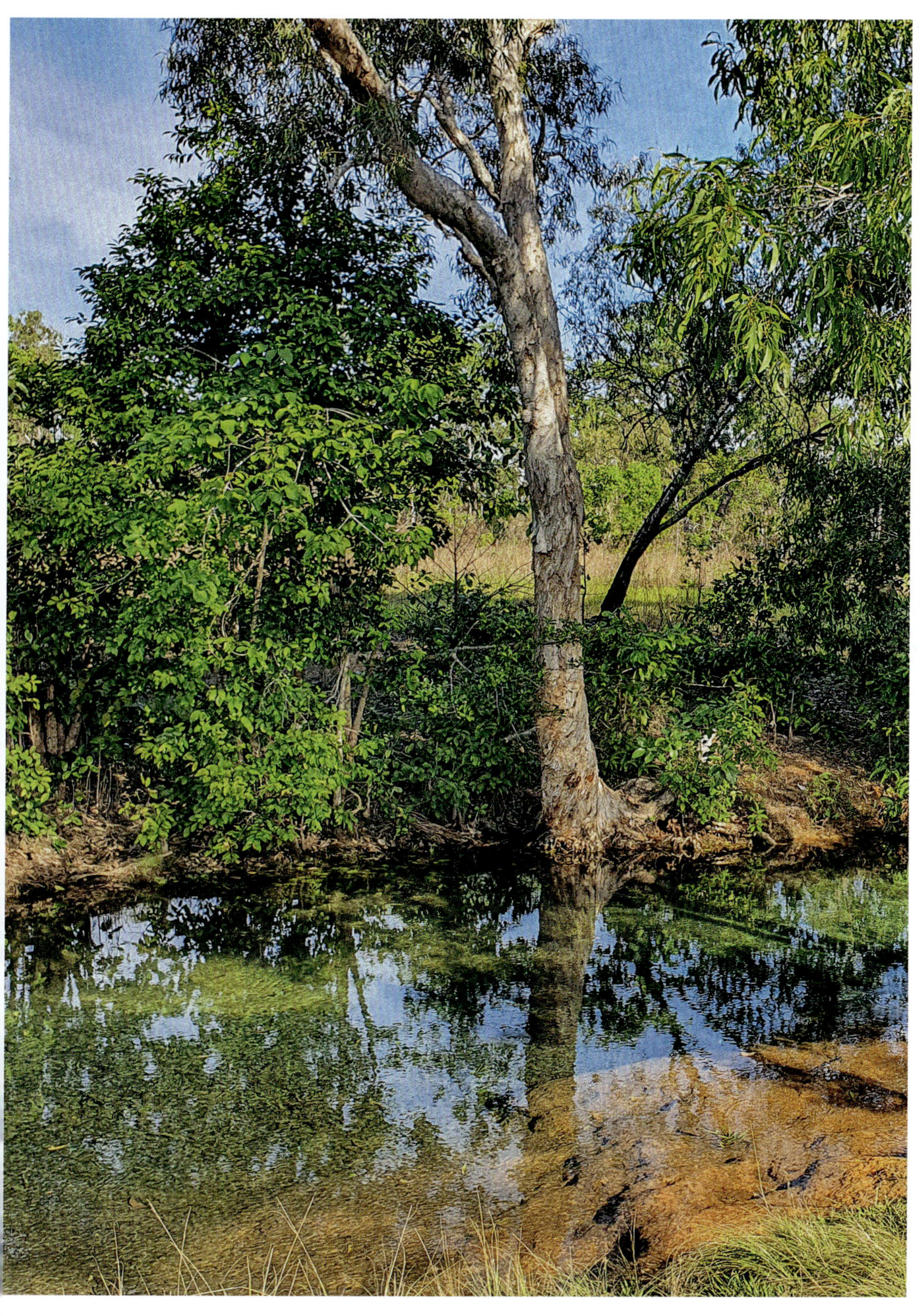

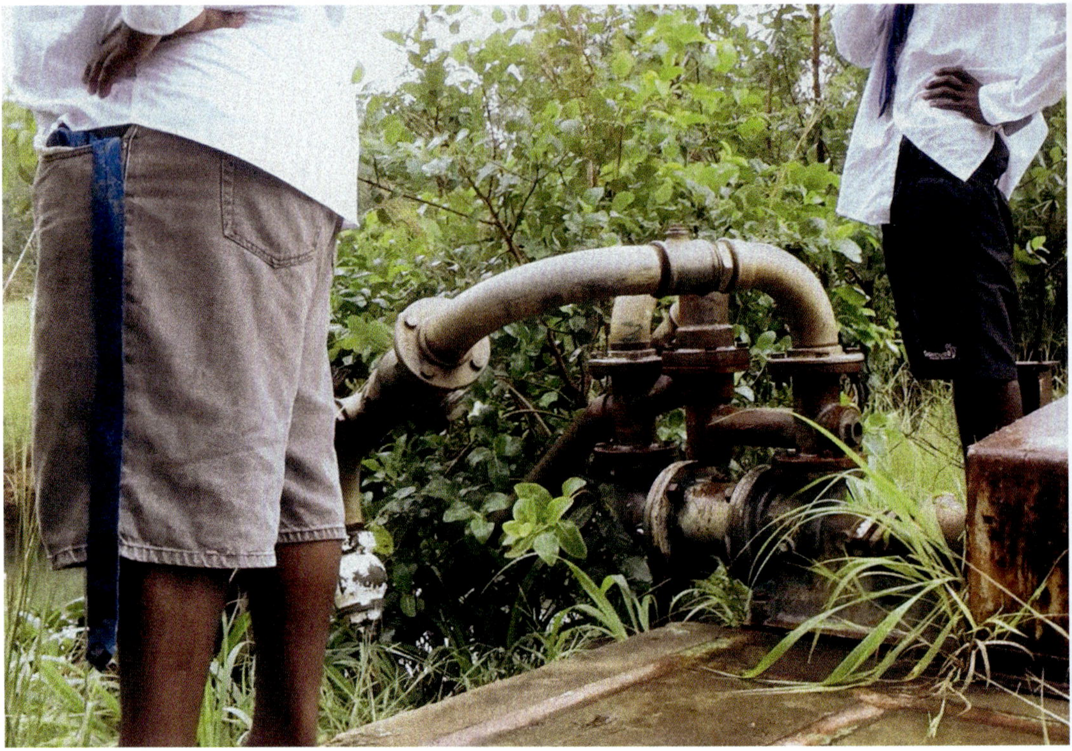

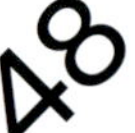

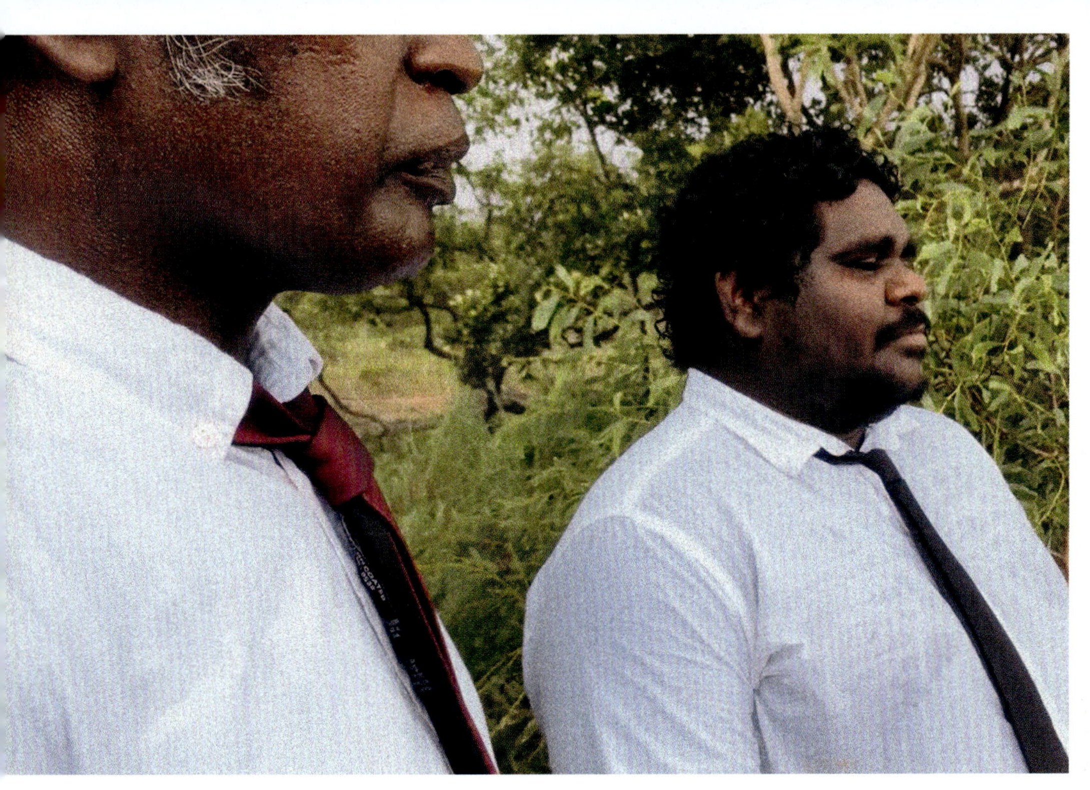

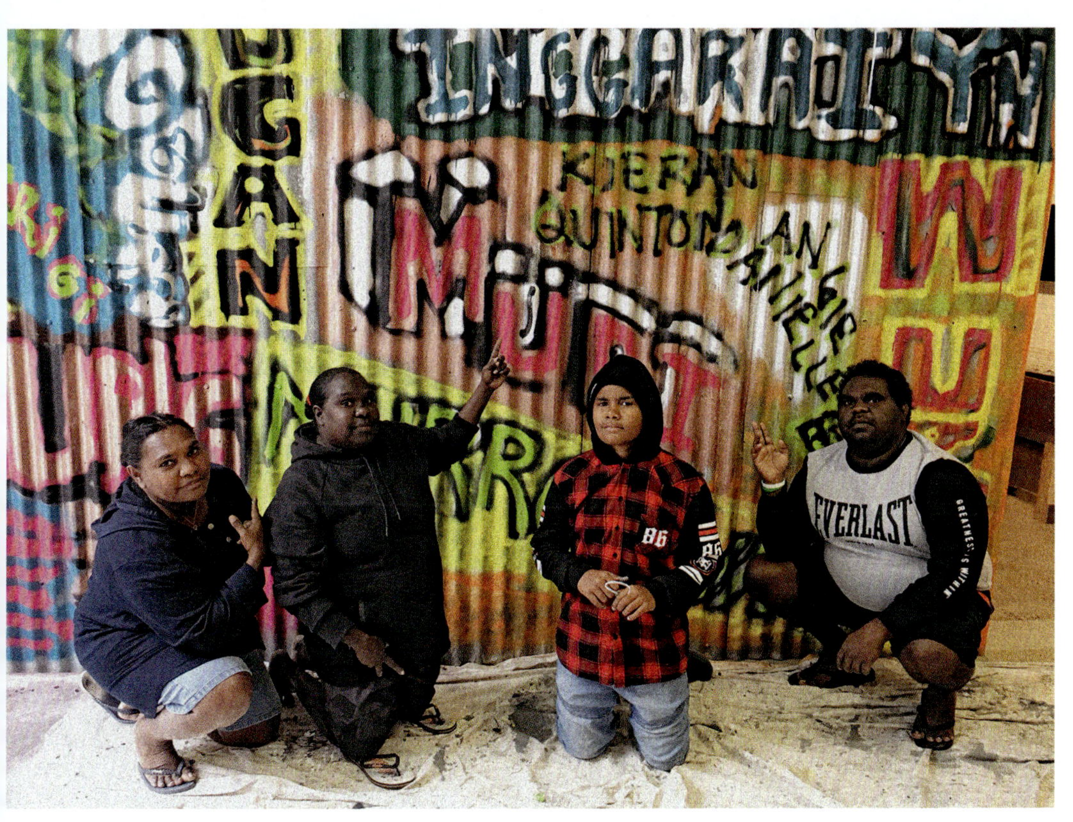
KIERAN
QUINTON
EVERLAST

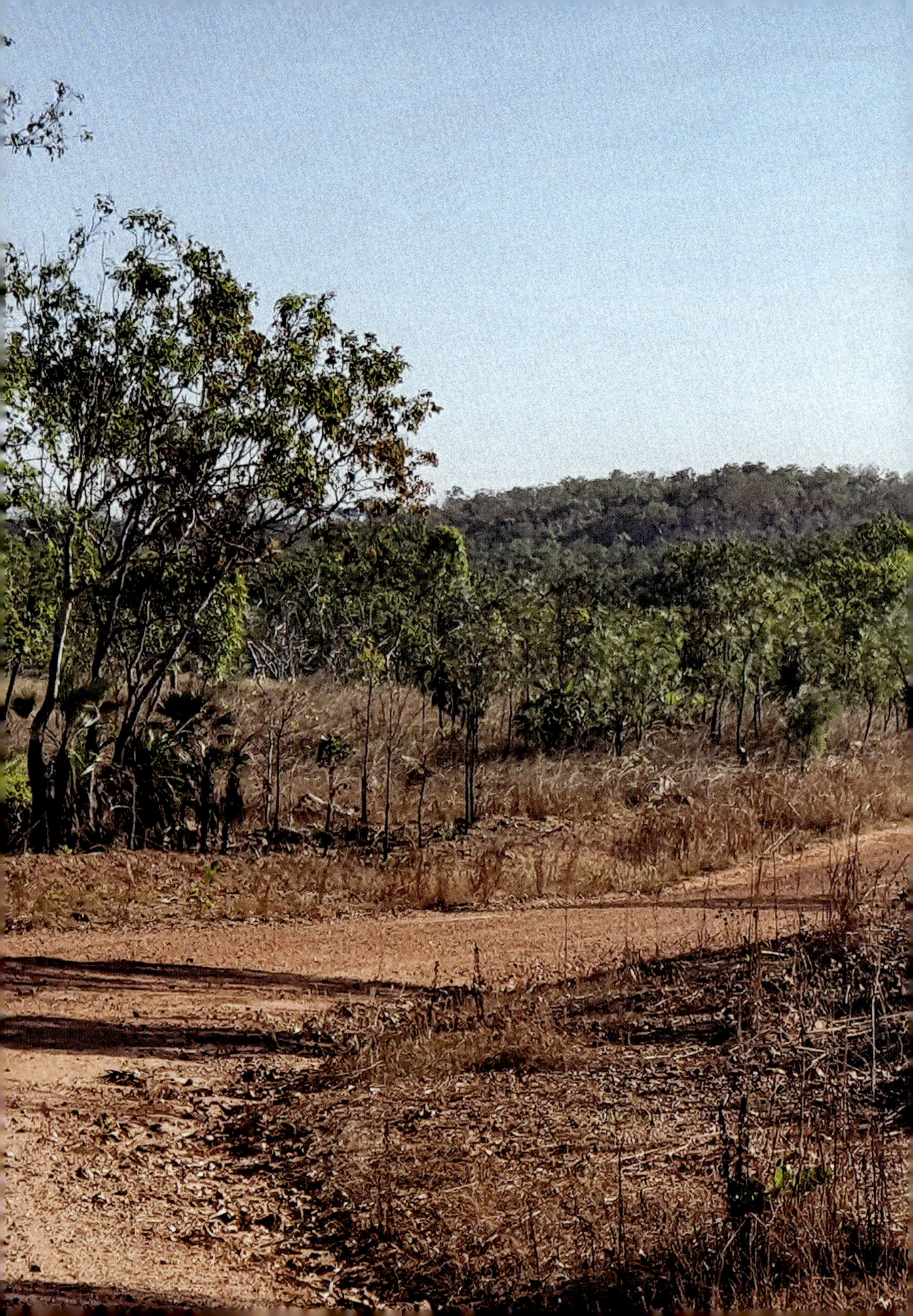

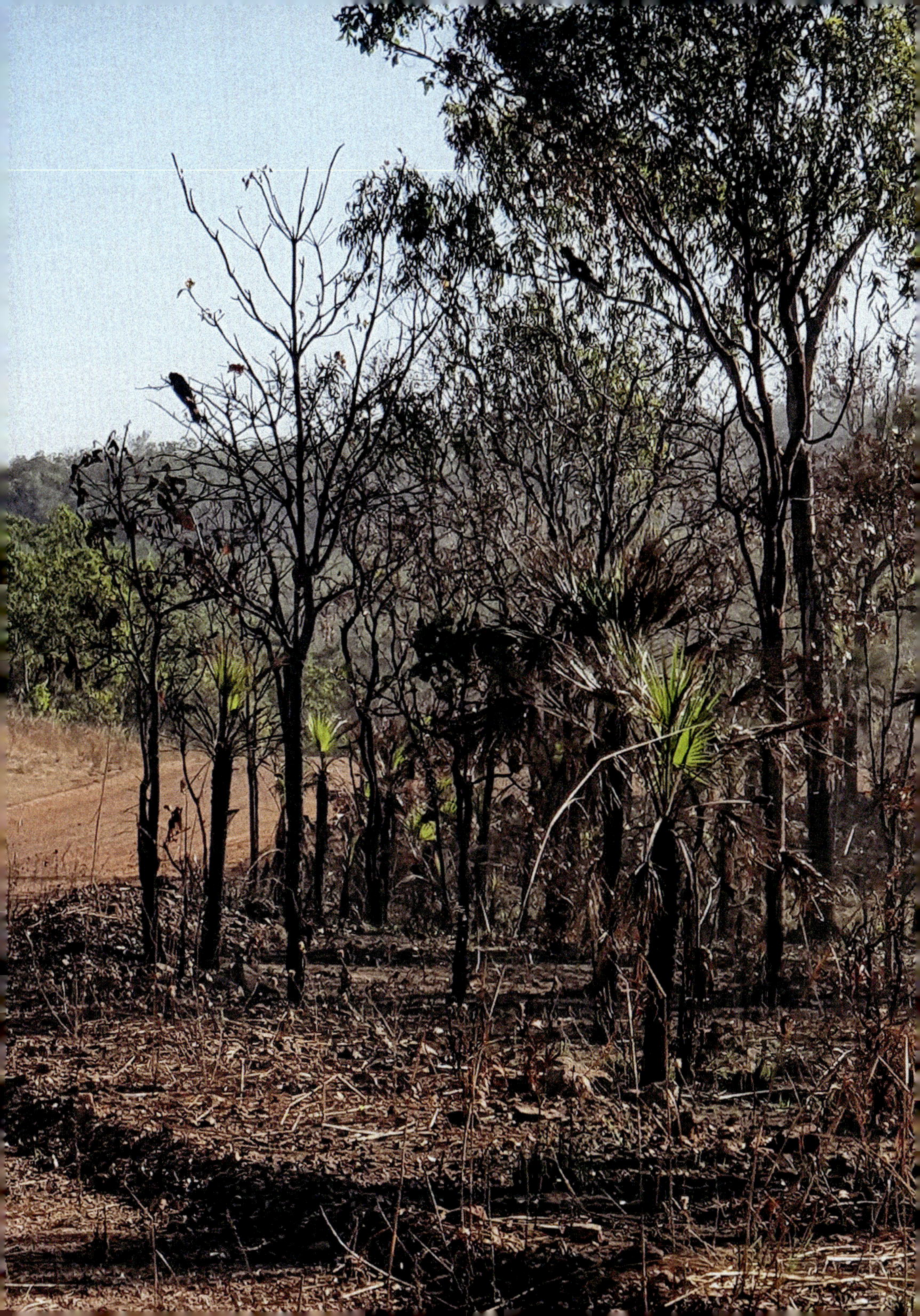

Artworks

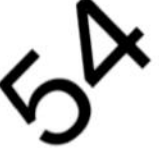

When the Dogs Talked (2014, 33:56)

As a group of Indigenous adults argue about whether to save their government housing or their sacred landscape, their children struggle to decide how the ancestral Dreaming makes sense to their contemporary lives. Listening to music on their iPods, walking though bush lands, and boating across seas, they follow their parents on a journey to reenact the travel of the Dog Dreaming. Along the way individuals run out of stamina, the car battery goes flat and the boat's fuel does not suffice for the trip. All the while, children press their parents and each other about why these stories matter and how they make sense in the context of Western understandings of evolution, the soundscapes of hip-hop, and the technologies of land development. *When the Dogs Talked* mixes documentary and fiction to produce a thoughtful yet humourous drama about the everyday obstacles of structural and racialised poverty and the dissonance of cultural narratives and social forms.

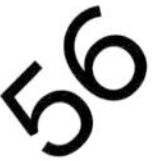

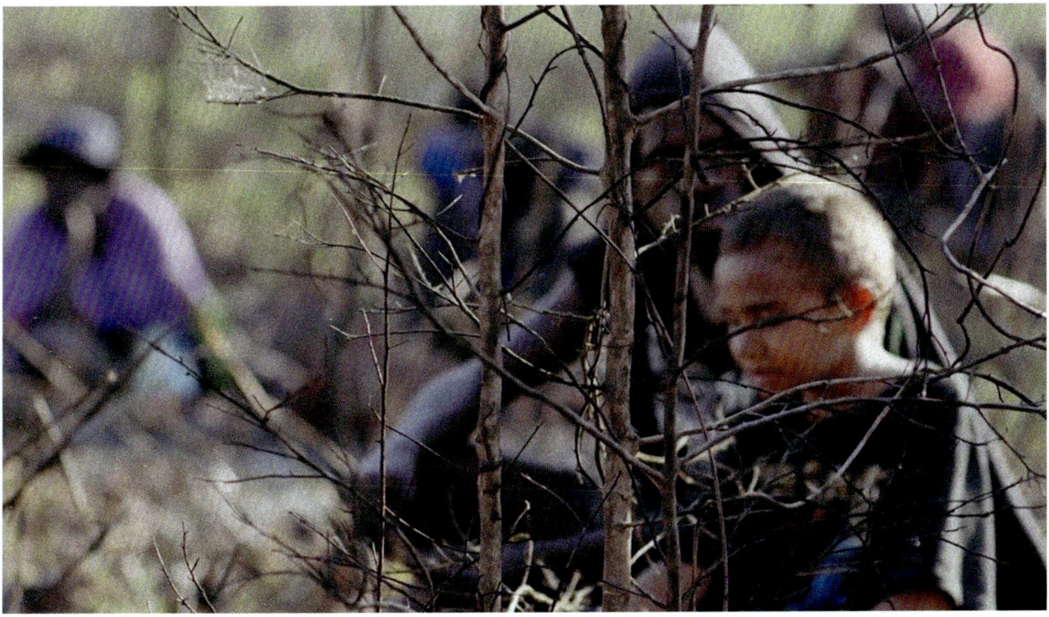

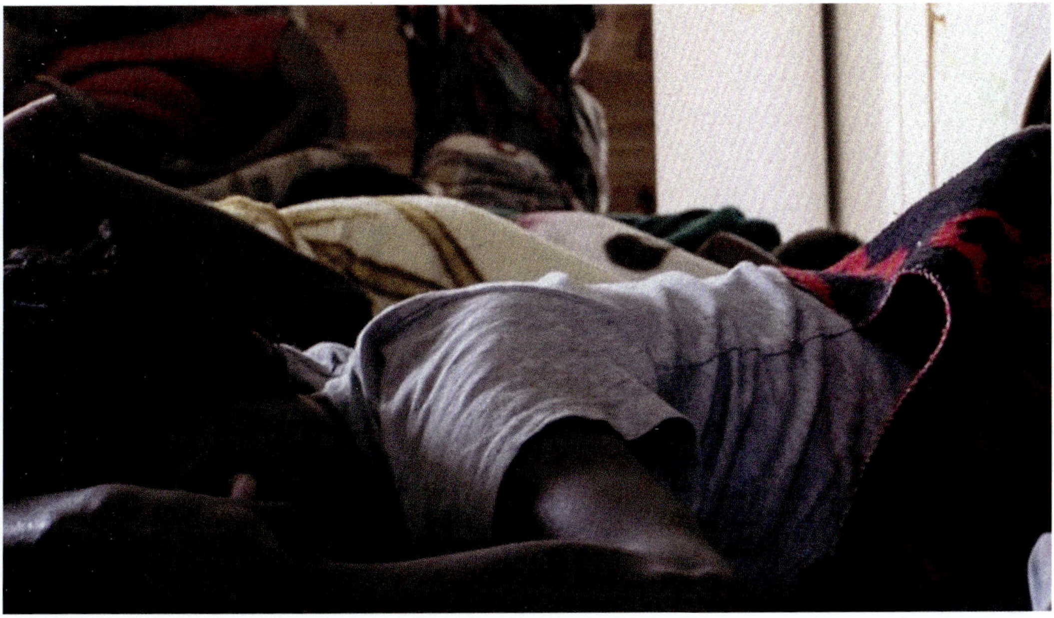

Windjarrameru, The Stealing C*nt$ (2015, 36:33)

Four young Indigenous men happen upon two cartons of beer, while another seems to be doing nothing more than kicking back nearby, listening to R&B on his phone. Then everything starts going wrong. Blending Indigenous storytelling with modern worries over environmental degradation and substance abuse, *Windjarrameru* tells a story about a group of young Indigenous men hiding in a chemically contaminated swamp after being falsely accused of stealing some beer, while all around them miners pollute their land. Blending Indigenous storytelling with modern worries over environmental degradation and substance abuse, *Windjarrameru* ask us to reflect upon the question of who really are the 'Stealing C*nt$': the children who allegedly took some beer, or the generations of white people who have been robbing and contaminating Indigenous land for over two centuries?

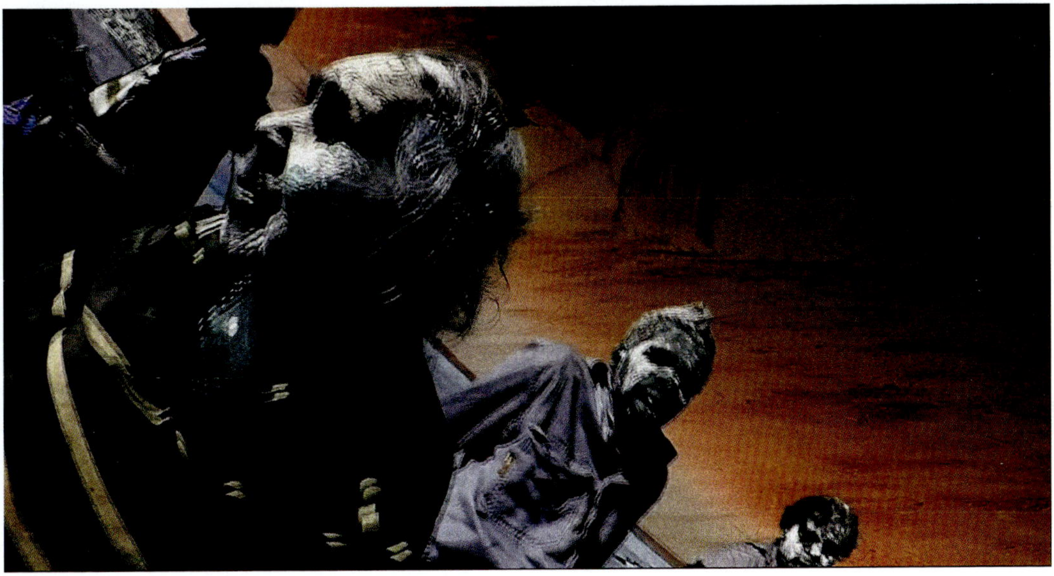

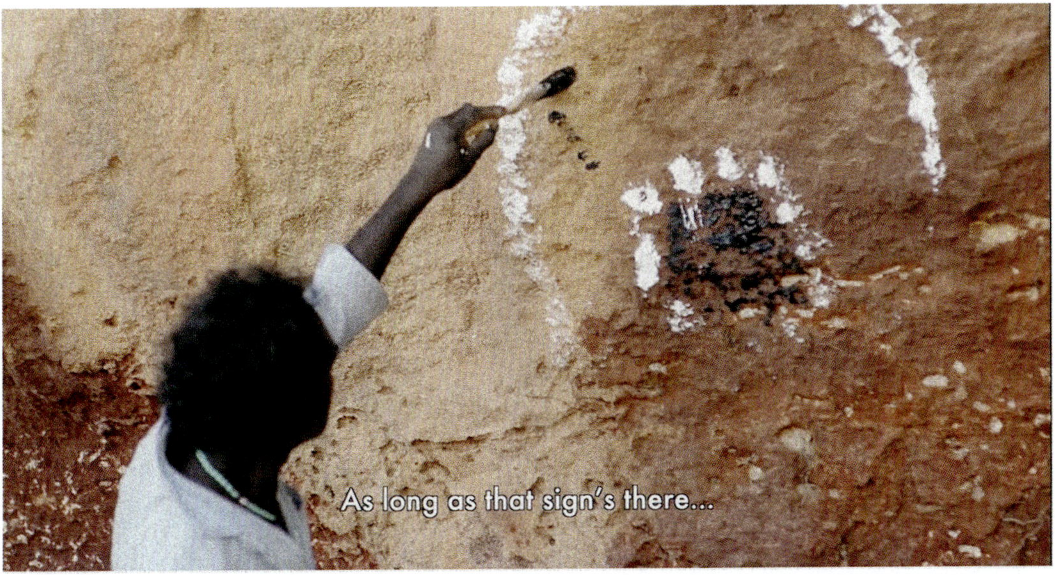

As long as that sign's there...

Wutharr, Saltwater Dreams (2016, 28:53)

Three wildly varying accounts are offered by members of an Indigenous Australian family for the cause of their boat's breakdown, leaving them stranded in the outback. Based upon a true story, settler bureaucracy, modern Christian faith, and displeased ancestral spirits are invoked via a series of flashbacks, each offering a new perspective on the dilemma. *Wutharr, Saltwater Dreams* explores the multiple demands and inescapable vortexes of contemporary Indigenous life, examining how the Collective experience the containments of missionary-Christian moral codes as well as settler-colonial rule-of-law, and how these layer, displace, but are ultimately absorbed into ancestral territorial arrangements secured by sweat and passed on through generational obligation.

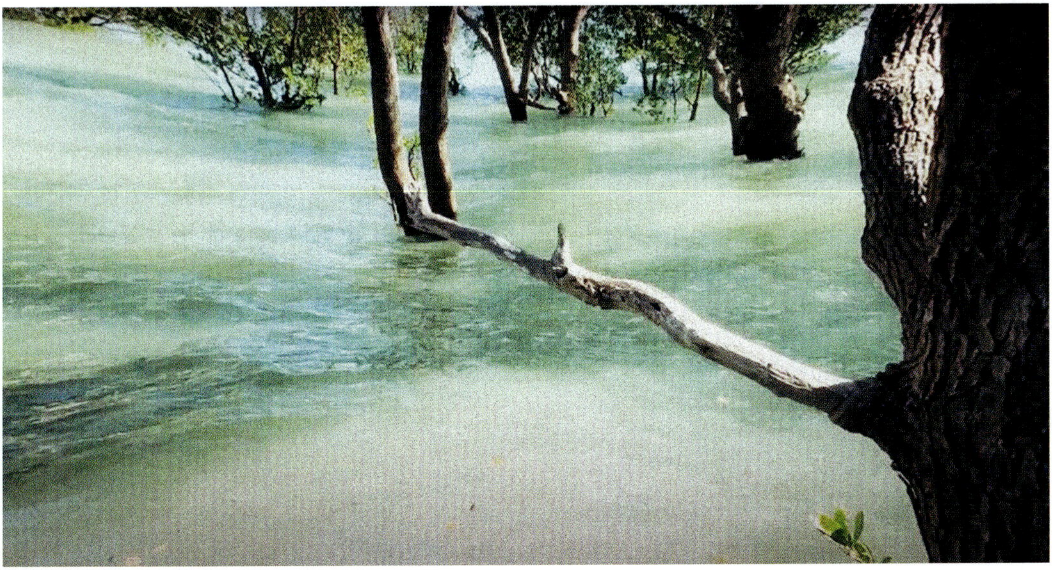

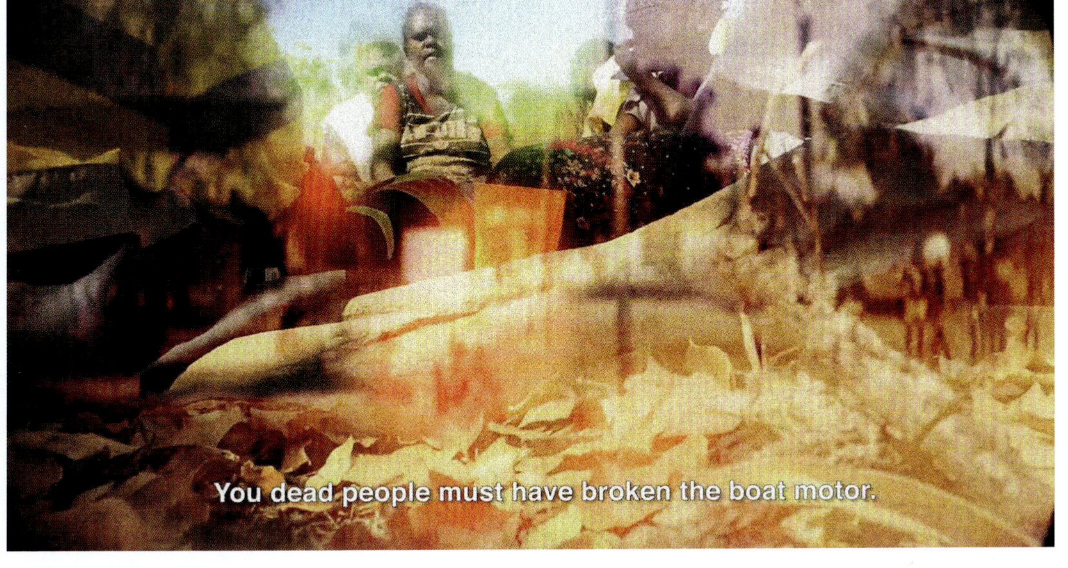
You dead people must have broken the boat motor.

The Jealous One (2017, 29:17)

As an Indigenous man weaves through bureaucratic red tape to get to a mortuary service on his traditional country, a fight breaks out as another man is consumed with jealousy over his wife. The two stories meet in a dramatic and explosive final encounter as tensions build up and revenge is sought on both sides. Hanging over all of this is the compliancy of colonial settler bureaucracy and its incommensurability to Indigenous life. In the words of the jealous-*durlg*: 'I am not the cause. This problem, this story has a long history in the country.' *The Jealous One* is therefore based on a traditional story that establishes a connection between the lands of the Karrabing, evoking questions about possession, tradition, resentment, and the settler state.

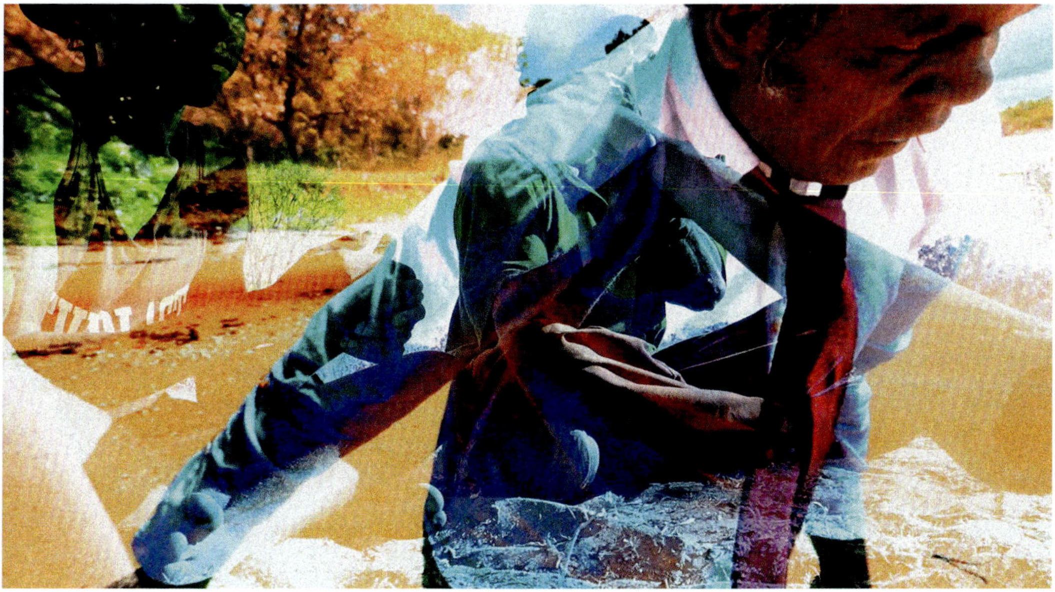

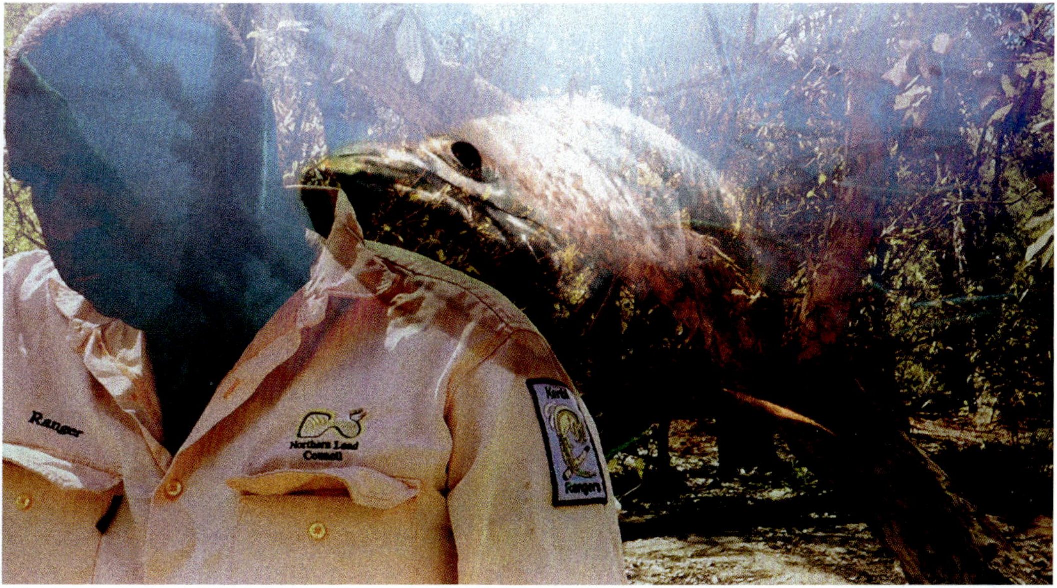
Ranger
Northern Land Council
Rangers

Night Time Go (2017, 31:10)

Night Time Go begins by telling the story of how, on 19 September 1943, a group of Karrabing ancestors escaped from a war internment camp and walked over three hundred kilometres back to their coastal homelands in Northern Australia. Hewing closely to the actual historical details of this ancestral journey, the film then slowly turns into an alternative history in which the group's escape inspires a general Indigenous insurrection that results in all settlers being driven out of Australia's Top End. Combining drama and humour, history, and satire, *Night Time Go* pushes subaltern history beyond the bounds of propriety, exploring the settler state's attempt to remove Indigenous people from their lands, as well as the refusal of the Karrabing ancestors to be detained.

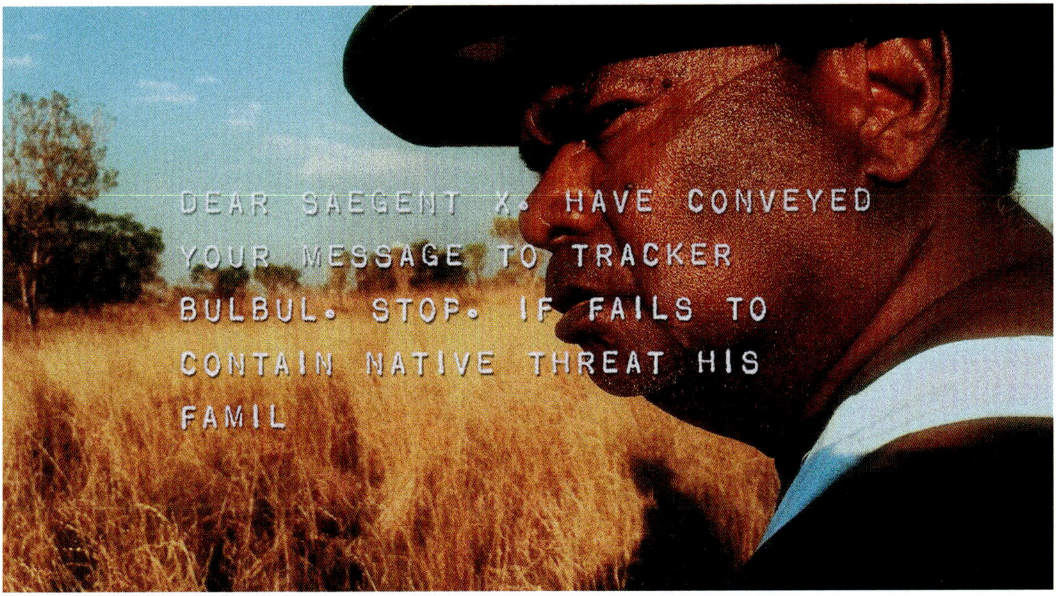

DEAR SAEGENT X. HAVE CONVEYED
YOUR MESSAGE TO TRACKER
BULBUL. STOP. IF FAILS TO
CONTAIN NATIVE THREAT HIS
FAMIL

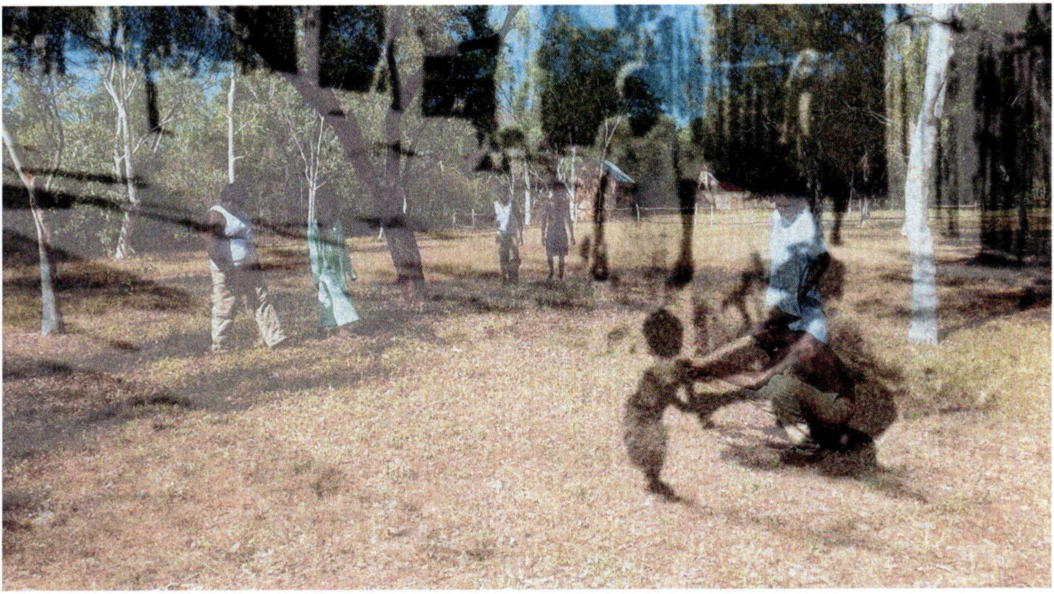

The Riot (2017, 21:39)

The Karrabing Film Collective emerged from the violence of contemporary settler colonialism, as evidenced by a riot that broke out in the Belyuen Community in 2007. This was sparked by two significant events: on the one hand, the settlement of the Kenbi land claim—the longest running Indigenous title claim in Australia's history—served to reiterate all the perversities of circular colonial logics: some families would receive recognition and a certain degree of enfranchisement, while others would remain in poverty. On the other hand, in 2007 the federal government used the spectre of child sexual abuse in order to implement the so-called 'Northern Territory Emergency Response'—more commonly referred to as 'The Intervention'—in so-called 'remote' or 'proscribed' communities, which for many people brought back the trauma of the Stolen Generation and over two centuries of colonial settler abuse. Composed as a series of short interviews taken in various hotel rooms, *The Riot* allows members of the Collective to reflect upon these calamitous events, as well as the wider meaning and purpose of their work.

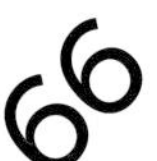

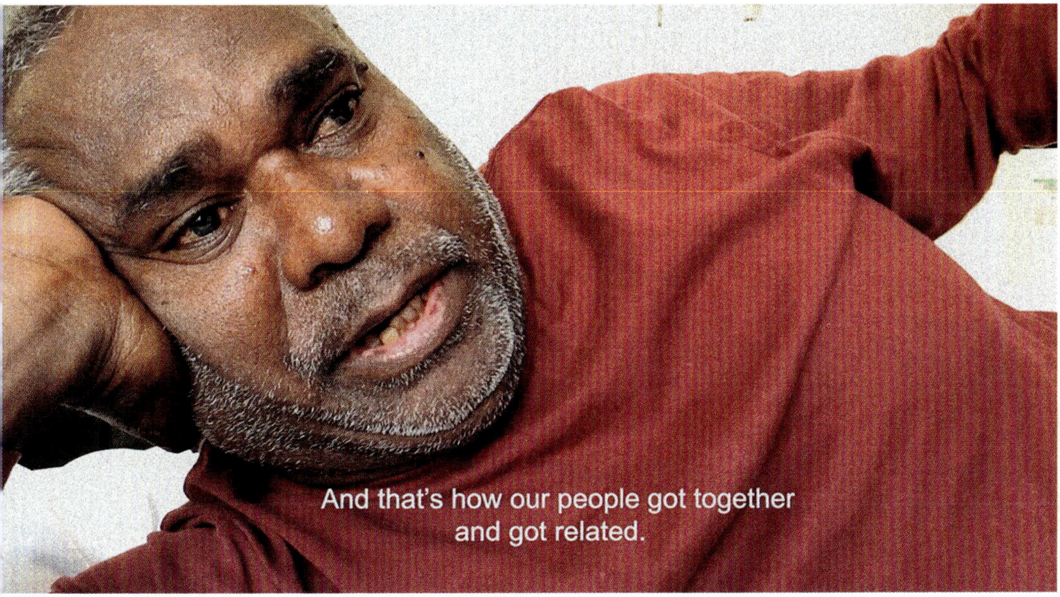

And that's how our people got together
and got related.

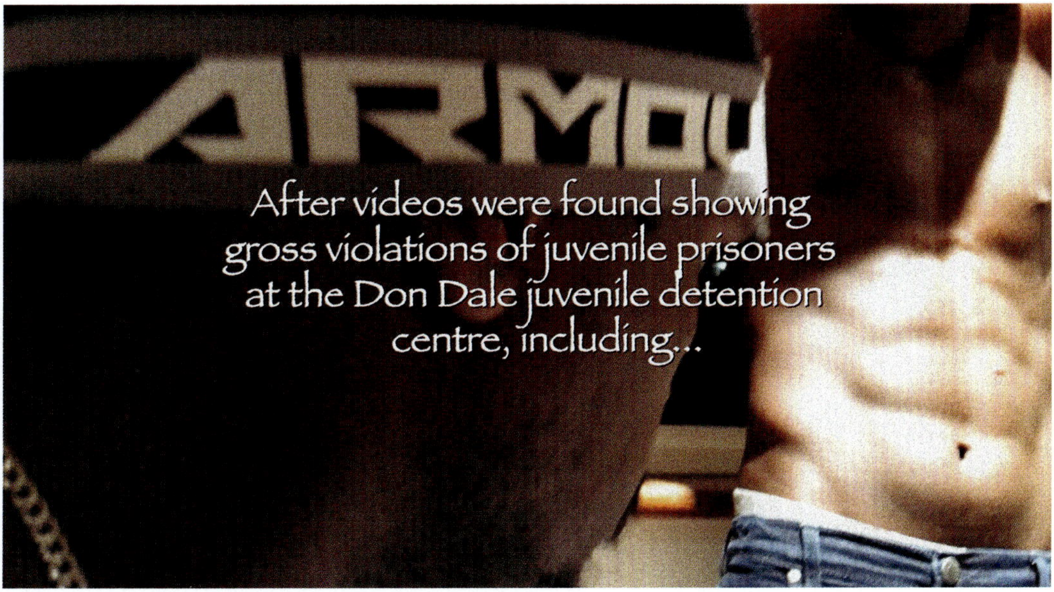

After videos were found showing
gross violations of juvenile prisoners
at the Don Dale juvenile detention
centre, including...

Mermaids, Mirror Worlds (2018, 34:50)

Mermaids, Mirror Worlds is the dual-screen reimagining of the film *The Mermaids, or Aiden in Wonderland* (2018), both of which shift between a fictional account of a toxic ravaged world and nonfictional promotional material from industrial giants such as Monsanto and the Dow Chemical Corporation. In the near present fictional world, Europeans can no longer survive for long periods outdoors in a land and seascape poisoned by capitalism, but Indigenous people seem able to. A young Indigenous man, Aiden, taken away when he was just a baby to be a part of a medical experiment to save the white race, is released into the world of his family. In the nonfictional world, wild claims are made about the healthy, safe, and protective practices of multinational capitalisation of nature. As viewers travel with Aiden and his father and brother across these landscapes they confront two possible futures and pasts.

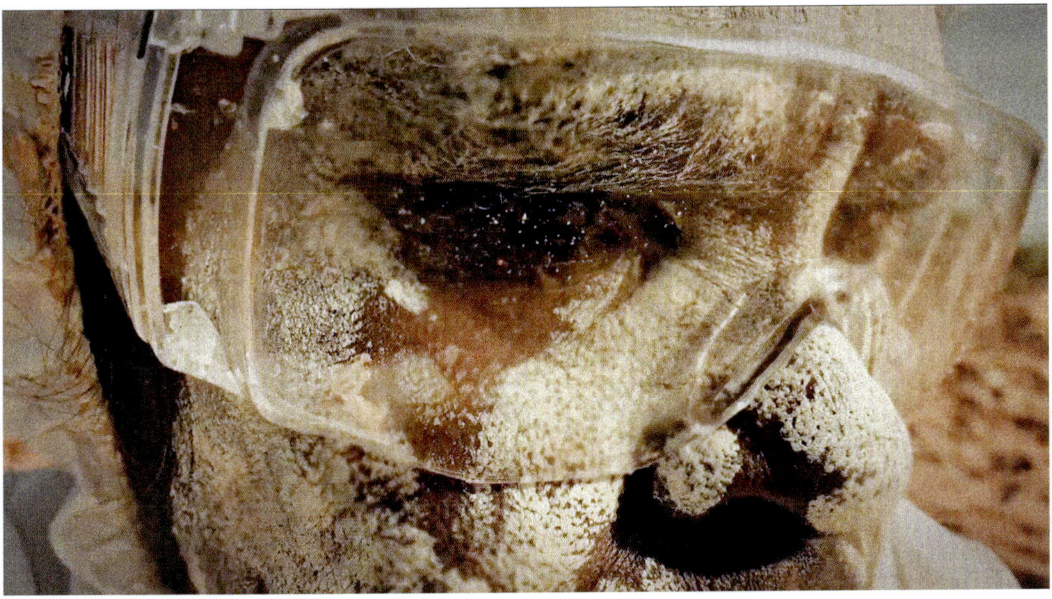

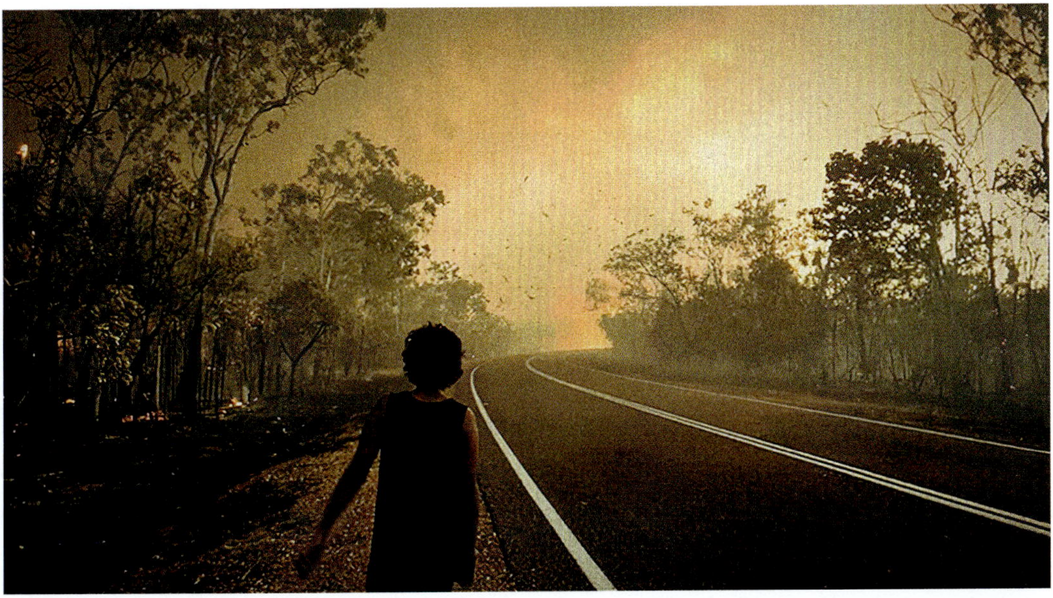

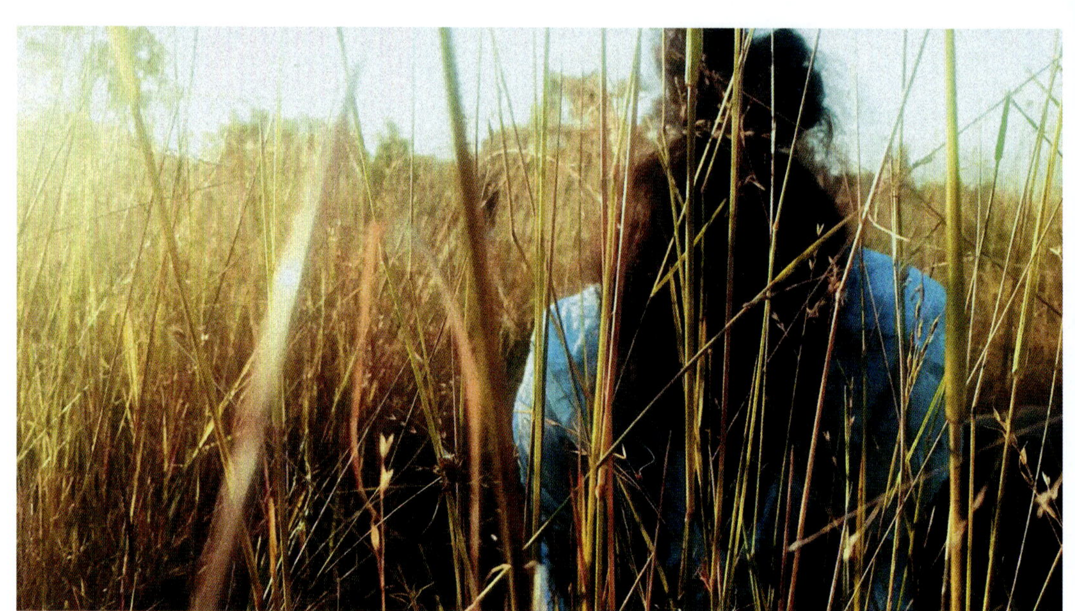

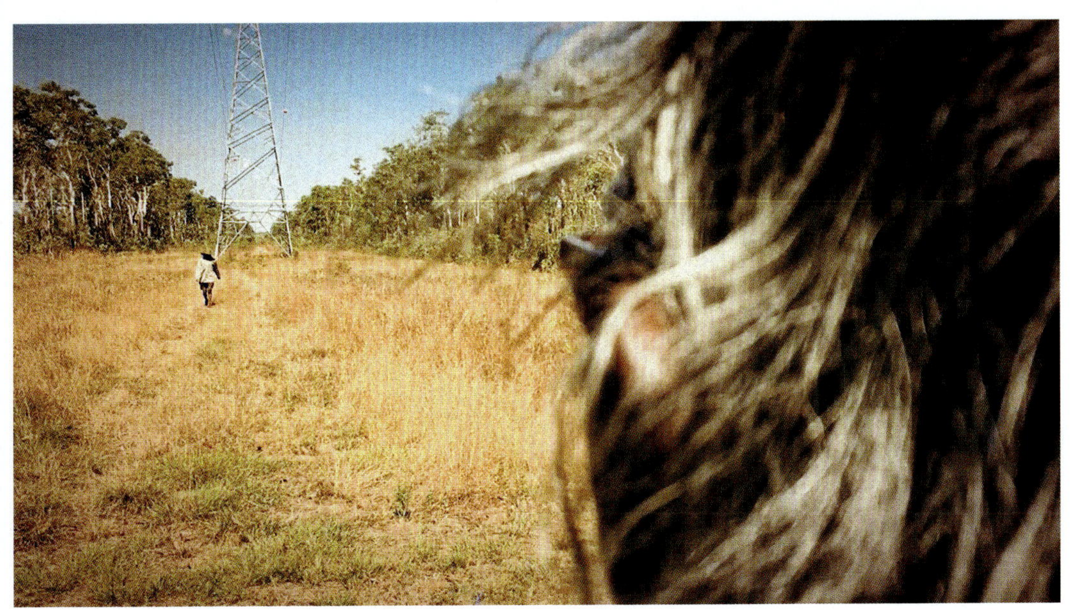

Day in the Life (2020, 32:37)

Day in the Life explores the ordinary obstacles Indigenous families face as they move through an ordinary day. Spread across five chapters—Breakfast, Playtime, Lunch Run, Cocktail Hour, and Dinner Time—the film combines snippets from radio and television shows with a soundtrack composed and directed by the Collective's youngest members. Throughout the course of a single day, the opinions of various 'experts' (ranging from politicians to members of the public to radio 'shock jocks') can be heard professing concern about the problems faced by Indigenous communities, along with 'solutions' that do not correspond to the reality experienced by Karrabing members every single day. *Day in the Life* therefore creates a visual and sonic landscape that dramatises and satirises forms of settler governance and extractive capitalism, as well as points to the cognitive dissonance that continues to shape and inform contemporary opinions in respect to Indigenous life.

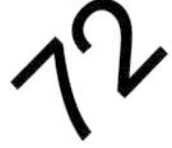

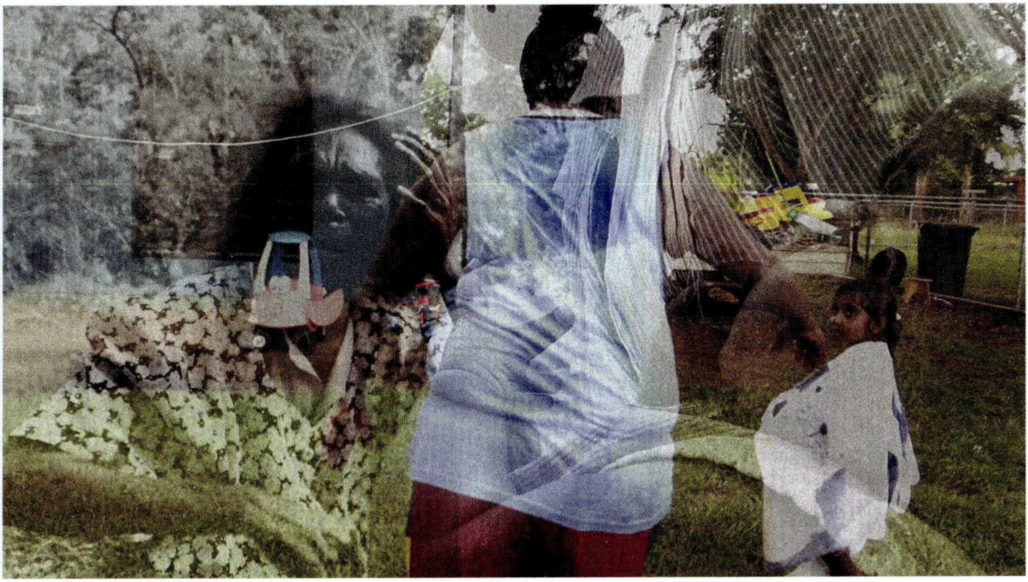

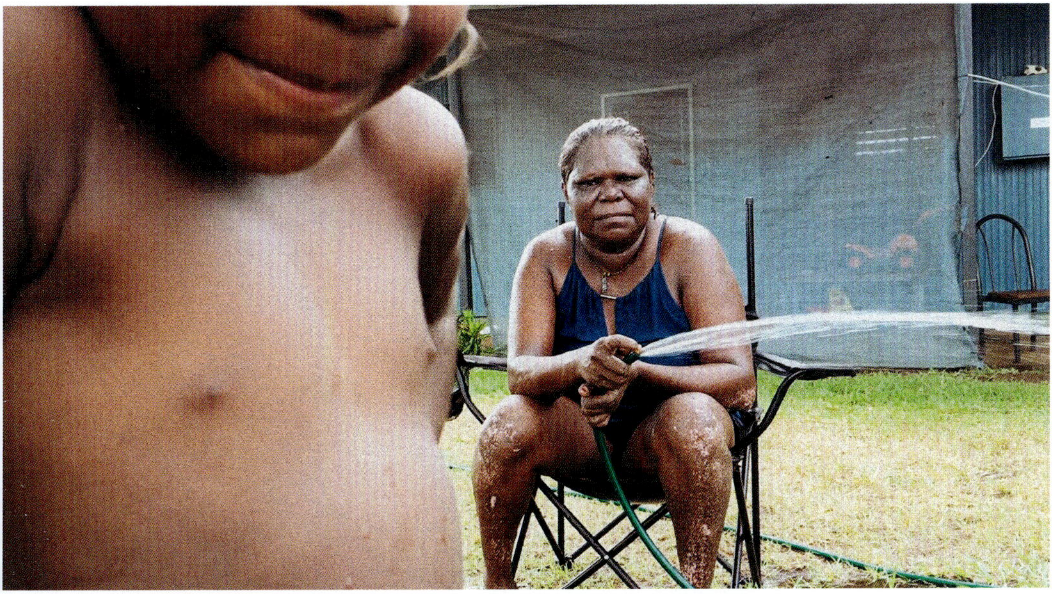

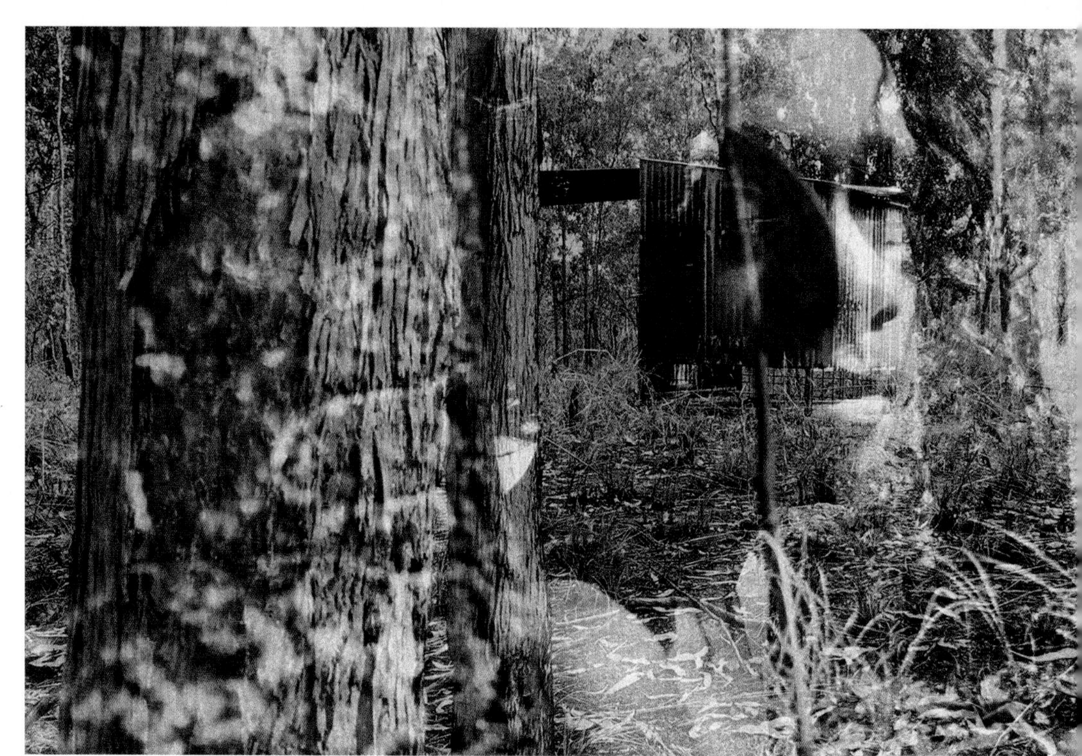

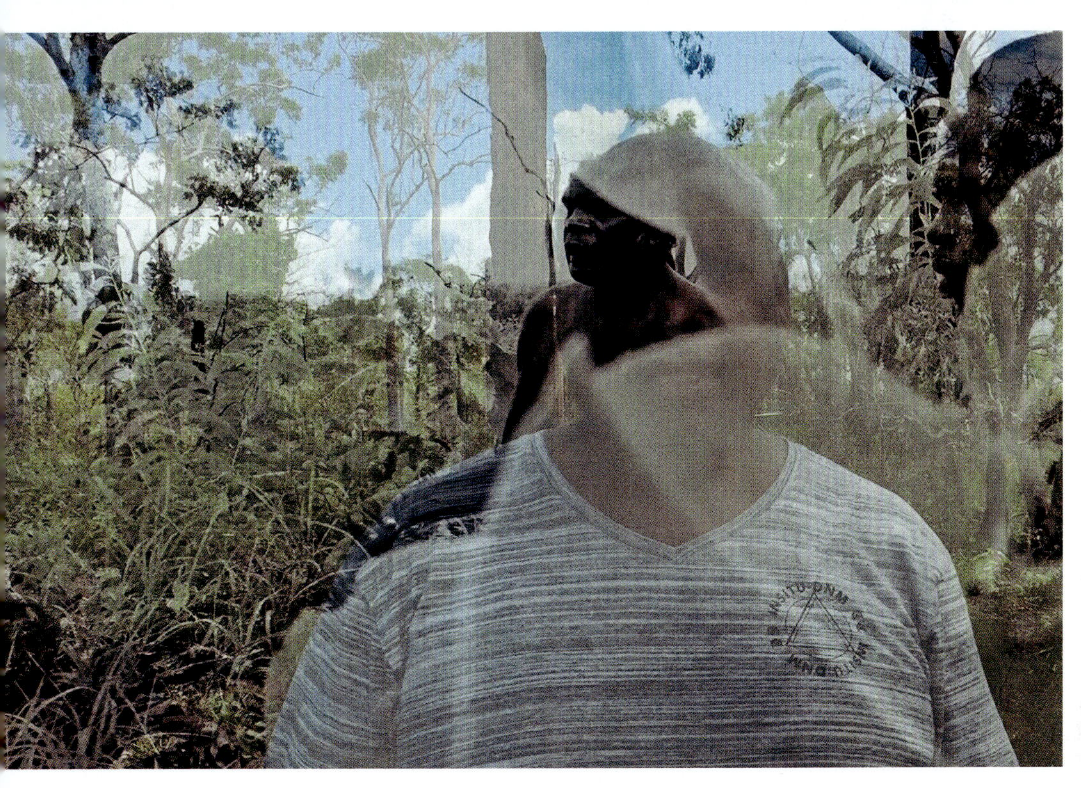

The Family (A Zombie Movie) (2021, 29:23)

The Family (A Zombie Movie) opens with future ancestors digging yams and their children playing happily around them. Without warning, a zombie emerges slowly from behind a log, its skin crusted with an oozing white substance, extending a clawed arm toward the children. However, when they notice this figure, they simply laugh, causing the figure to quickly recoil. The children then follow the creature to its lair of rusted cars, plastic debris, and tarnished woodland: the detritus of extractive capitalism. By the end of the film, the monster has been killed, but more zombies no doubt lie hiding in the shadows. What began as a fairly innocent scene has turned into a commentary on the toxic dangers of unbridled Western consumption. Subverting expectations of 'authentic' Indigenous life, *The Family (A Zombie Movie)* evokes the metaphor of zombie-as-*Berragut* (the group's term for white people) in order to point to the correlation between ecological breakdown, Indigenous destruction, and cultural erasure caused by settler colonialism elsewhere.

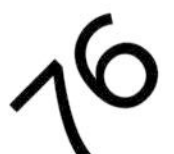

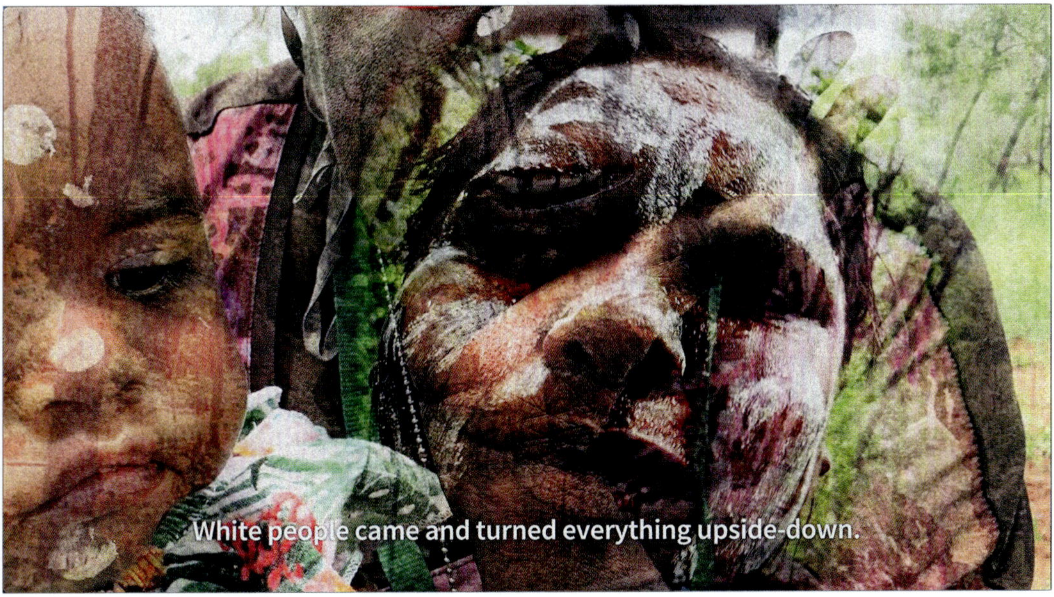

White people came and turned everything upside-down.

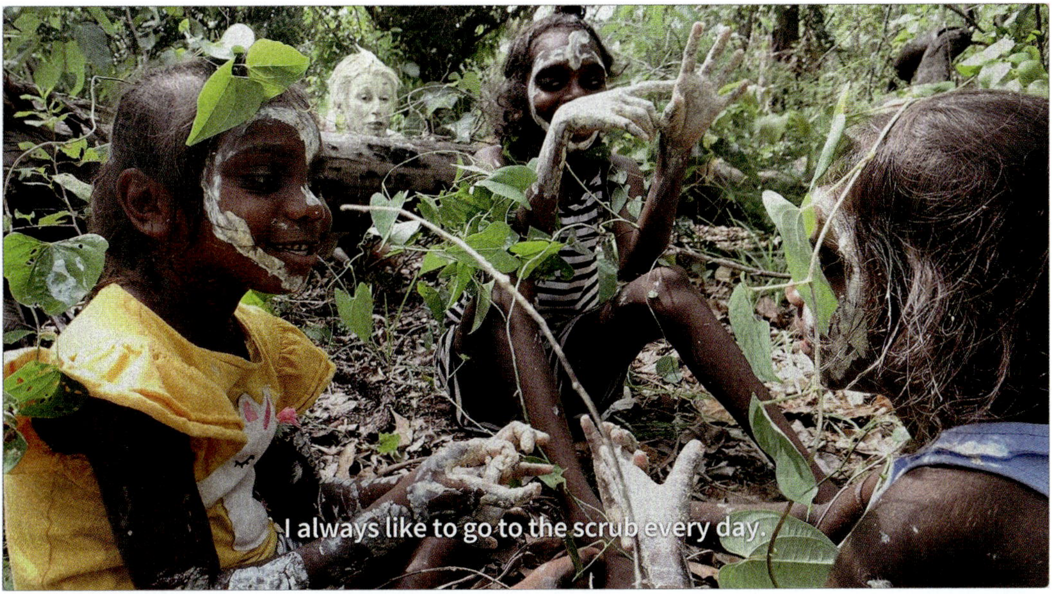

I always like to go to the scrub every day.

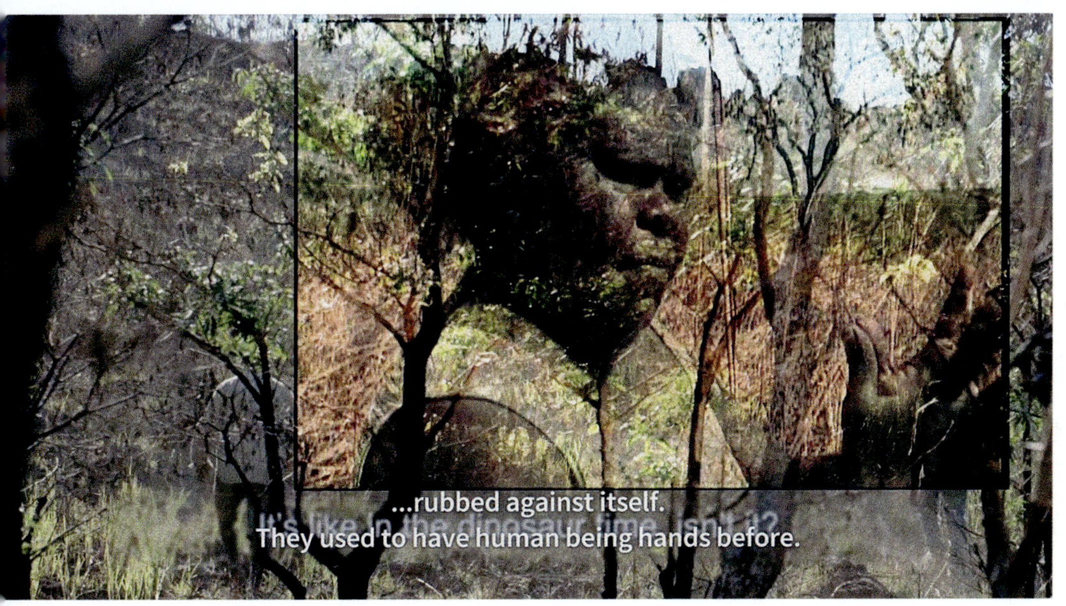
...rubbed against itself.
It's like in the dinosaur time, isn't it?
They used to have human being hands before.

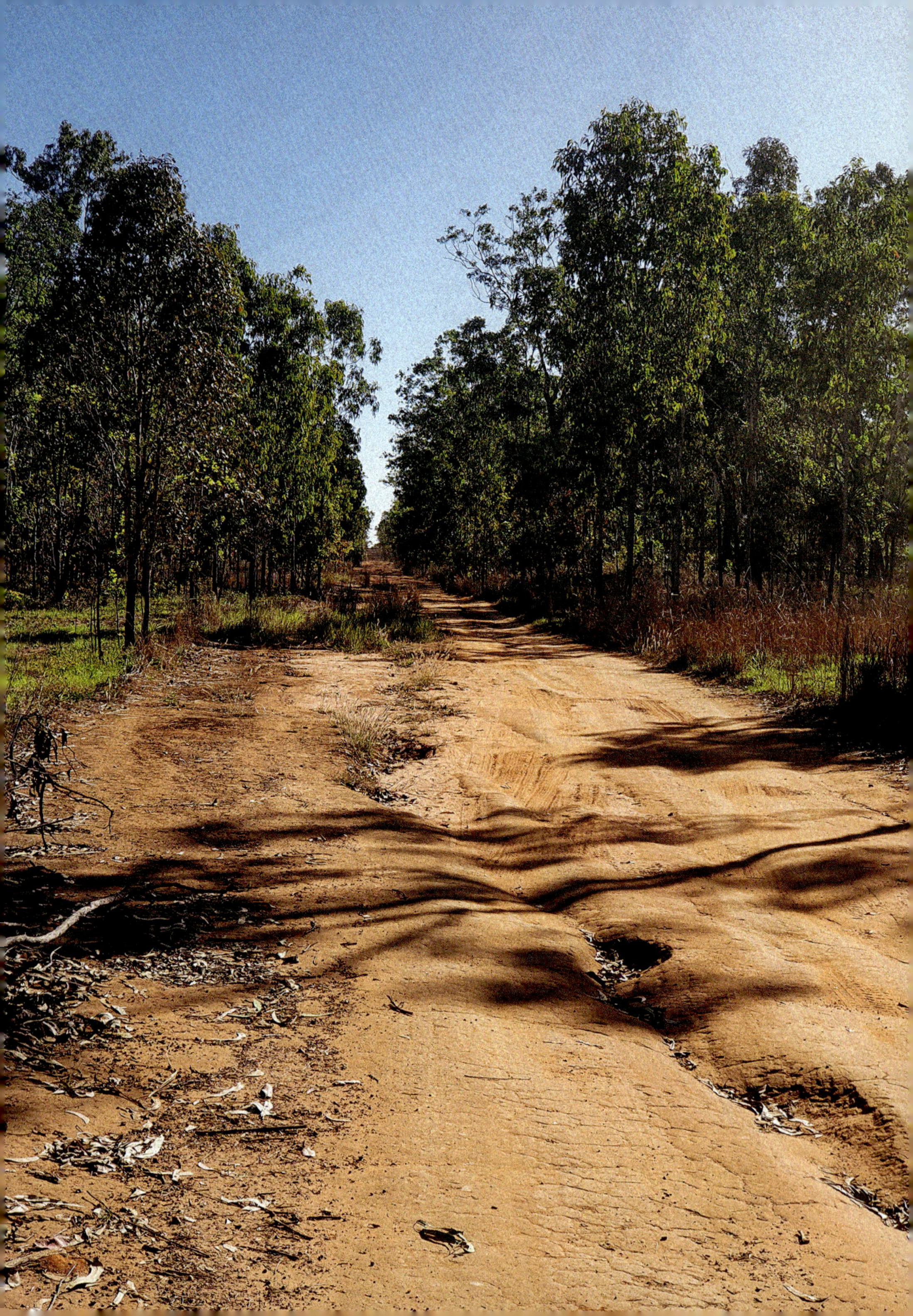

Karrabing Film Collective. Wonderland

A Reader

‘A Schoolhouse Made out of Film’: The Karrabing Film Collective

Damian Lentini

Two short scenes taken from recent works of the Karrabing Film Collective succinctly encapsulate the difficulties of positioning their practice within the established frameworks that conventionally demarcate contemporary filmic practices. In the first scene of the film *Wutharr, Saltwater Dreams* (2016), three explanations are given as to why a fishing boat motor is not starting. For Linda Yarrowin, it is a question of (Judeo-Christian) faith: 'If you put your faith in the Lord it will start,' she contends. Although also professing to having 'faith in my heart too for Lord Jesus,' Trevor Bianamu ascribes the problem to the interference of ancestors: 'When I was walking through the bush I found evidence of our ancestors everywhere,' he notes. Rex Edmunds, on the other hand, is not convinced: 'I don't know about the Lord, but I know about wiring,' he observes, arguing that saltwater had eaten through the wiring and damaged the spark plugs.

In the second film, *The Jealous One* (2017), a Kenbi Ranger from the Northern Land Council is on the phone with a faceless 'Hands of State' (we only ever see her hands typing on a keyboard) from the State Control Over Indigenous Lands department, trying to get access to part of his country, which has been blocked off by a locked gate. 'You have to have the paperwork filled out ... You have to have an anthropologist go over your claim ... look. It's the law,' the Hands recounts, before retorting, 'Well how am I supposed to know it's your country?!' when the Ranger points out the insanity of asking permission 'to go to my own country'. Later on, when it becomes apparent that several people have simply gone to their country anyway, the Hands chides a colleague: 'Well the anthropologist hasn't completed her report yet ... Too fucking bad, honestly! ... Well, what are they doing? ... We need to be there. They need our permission. They need authorisation ... Well go over there and explain it to them!'

Although it is the first series of patronising remarks—'We need to be there. They need our permission ... Well go over there and explain it to them!'— that stands out most emphatically in this exchange, I would argue that the previous comment—'Well how am I supposed to know it's your country?!'—proves most insightful when thinking about the sense of bewilderment that accompanies attempts to reconcile two evidentially incommensurate systems of knowledge. How indeed is this low-level public bureaucrat expected to know whether it is the Ranger's country, when two centuries of colonial-settler occupation has failed to answer the question as to when, if ever, 'ownership' was taken from—or ceded by—the Indigenous population, especially when there is still no mutual understanding as to the meaning of terms such as 'ownership', 'knowledge' and 'country'! Faced with such an impasse—and equipped only with the conviction that the form of settler governance she is trying to impose is irrefutable—the Hands is left with no other answer but to insist that the other party simply does not understand: 'Well go over there and explain it to them! (again).'

As with the legal-bureaucratic-complex, so too does the 'art history complex' end up tying itself in knots when attempting to contextualise practices such as Karrabing's. For example, the normal goal of an essay such as this—locating the works within a specific art historical continuum, demonstrating the various commonalities and interests between them and wider contemporary/historical sources—could very easily be construed as simply being a more academic way to 'go over there and explain it to them!' On the other hand, one also naturally has to be wary of falling into the trap of casting Karrabing's practice in terms of an 'exotic other', as if the collective and their work exist completely anterior to debates concerning contemporaneity. Indeed, both the contents of the films themselves—which are replete with references to contemporary pop culture, politics, economics, and debates concerning history—as well as the fact that the Belyuen community is located just across the harbour from the city of Darwin, speaks very much to a society absolutely attuned to—and continually affected by—contemporary debates and politics. Such a position of being both enmeshed within, yet also able to function independent of, contemporary colonial-settler society, was also perpetually reinforced during a recent trip of mine to Belyuen in June 2022. During this trip, conversation shifted seamlessly from discussions about the importance of Country and knowledge of specific totems to pop music (especially Bon Jovi) and—upon discovering that the author grew up in Melbourne—musings on Australian Rules football or exasperations of disbelief that anyone could 'actually live' in a climate as cold and wet as Australia's temperate south.

These sorts of conversations bring to mind the excerpt from *Wutharr* cited above, and offer an insight into how one can begin to conceptualise Karrabing's works. For rather than simply denying the existence of multiple and often contradictory conceptions of our collective life worlds, this passage instead chooses to shift and move through these different positions. Furthermore, it also acts in a self-reflective manner, proffering an insight into the discursive environment that characterises the creation of all of the Collective's work: one in which everyone is able to contribute to almost every aspect of a film's realisation. By working in this manner, Karrabing is able to foreground the lacunae and voids that exist within conventional Western historical and artistic thinking: one that outright denies the existence of anything that does not accord with one's specific world view. Far from being simply a facile artistic gesture, however, such an approach also constitutes an exercise in continuance, a perpetual act of defiance and making visible the unceasing attempts at erasure that have accompanied the entire history of relations between First Nations and colonial-settler Australians, a history that the following essay will briefly outline.

'Nobody's Land'

The very first example of this was enacted by Lieutenant James Cook on what is now called Possession Island (but also known as 'Bedanug', 'Thunadha', 'Bedhan Lag', or 'Tuidin' by the diverse clans that have inhabited the region for millennia) on 22 August 1770. There, in an almost unprecedented act of erasure, Cook planted the Union flag and claimed possession of the entire eastern coast of the Australian continent in the name of King George III. That such an act was in complete disregard of both the advice he had received from James Douglas (President of the Royal Society, which had sponsored the voyage) prior to his departure was seemingly a moot point. In fact, the British crown would then formalise and significantly extend this act on 26 January 1788, when Governor Arthur Phillip landed with a fleet of ships in Port Jackson and, on 7 February, established the British penal colony of New South Wales—which obscenely now included more than half of mainland Australia.

Although the term *terra nullius* (literally 'nobody's land') was not formally used in the eighteenth century, it was subsequently applied to the British claim for the subsequent colonisation of the continent. Widely understood within European colonial policy, the term implied that a nation or state could claim territory as part of the crown, provided said territory was not already inhabited by peoples who possessed permanent settlements, agriculture, property rights, or political organisation as recognised by European states.[1] As was evident to both Cook and Phillip, this was plainly not the case with Australia, which at the time had been home to hundreds of complex hunter-gather societies spread out across the entire continent.[2] Indeed, at the time of Phillip's landing in 1788, the stretch of land that would become Sydney was populated by up to 8,000 peoples, all of whom occupied lands that were demarcated by traditional boundaries.[3] But rather than recognise this, British settlers instead sought to eradicate the pre-colonial landscape that had been shaped and nurtured by First Nations'

1 Merete Borch, 'Rethinking the Origins of Terra Nullius', *Australian Historical Studies* 32, (117), 2001, pp. 223–24.

2 Elizabeth Williams, 'Complex hunter-gatherers: a view from Australia,' *Antiquity*, Cambridge University Press, 61 (232), 2015, pp. 310–321.

3 Josephine Flood, *The Original Australians*, Sydney: Allen and Unwin, 2019, p. 217.

peoples for 50,000 years, 'convert[ing] what they saw as an unhomely environment into a replica of that other place on the other side of the world which they continued to think of as their home.'[4] This ancillary, ecological form of colonisation would prove just as traumatic to the continent's Indigenous peoples as the settlements themselves, as it involved an irreversible and physical transformation of the land and its flora and fauna, in addition to the devastating introduction of foodstuffs such as tobacco and alcohol. As is well documented in the paintings of colonial artists such as John Glover, such actions transformed the landscape into what WTJ Mitchell called 'a place of amnesia and erasure, a strategic burying of the past'.[5] Although principally intended to alleviate the 'ontological shock' of occupying Indigenous lands,[6] this wholesale erasure of Indigenous Country could only be justified by evoking *terra nullius*; the notion that this was indeed 'nobody's land', alleviating any aspect of guilt on the part of the settlers.

This idea that colonial-settler Australians were living on 'nobody's land' would continue right up until the High Court's decision in the case of Mabo v Queensland (No 2) in 1992; in which they finally declared the doctrine of *terra nullius* to indeed be both a factual and legal fiction. However, rather than initiate the process of healing, this decision simply begat a fresh wave of intellectual and physical erasure on the part of a significant segment of the nation's colonial-settler population. This would be most famously exemplified in the policies of the conservative federal government of John Howard (1996–2007), alongside the so-called 'history wars' which sought to either downplay or straight out deny the two hundred years of dispossession, genocide, and conquest that had proceeded the colonisation of the continent.[7] As the term 'history wars' indicates, these debates predominantly centred on the notion that the erasure of Indigenous voices and histories was something confined to the past, rather than an ongoing process that had merely commenced in 1788. In other words, many of these texts worked on the supposition that these debates were occurring within a post-colonial space—as if the colonial project had long-since ceased—whereas for a large number of Indigenous Australians, colonialism continues to be an ongoing, contemporary struggle.

Contributing to the notion that Australia existed in a postcolonial space was the fragmented nature of colonisation that took place across the country. At the beginning, this was mainly confined to the temperate third of the continent, encompassing what are now the states of New South Wales, Victoria, Tasmania, and the southern parts of South Australia. These areas were gradually taken over by first the British penal complex and then British, Irish, and eventually German settlers

4 Sheila Collingwood-Wittick, 'Ways of Seeing "Country": Colonial, Postcolonial, and Indigenous Perceptions of the Australian Landscape', *LiNQ (Literature in North Queensland)*, vol. 35, 2008, p. 60.

5 W.J.T. Mitchell (ed.), *Landscape and Power*, Chicago: University of Chicago Press, 2002, p. 262.

6 As David Bunn writes: 'Colonial space is a site of regular ontological shock. It is filled with competing indigenous meaning.' (David Bunn, '"Our Wattled Cot": Mercantile and Domestic Space in Thomas Pringle's African Landscapes' in W.J.T. Mitchell (ed.), *Landscape and Power*, Chicago: University of Chicago Press, 2002, p. 129.

7 Richard Broome, *Aboriginal Australians, A History Since 1788*, Sydney: Allen and Unwin, 2019, pp. 55–56.

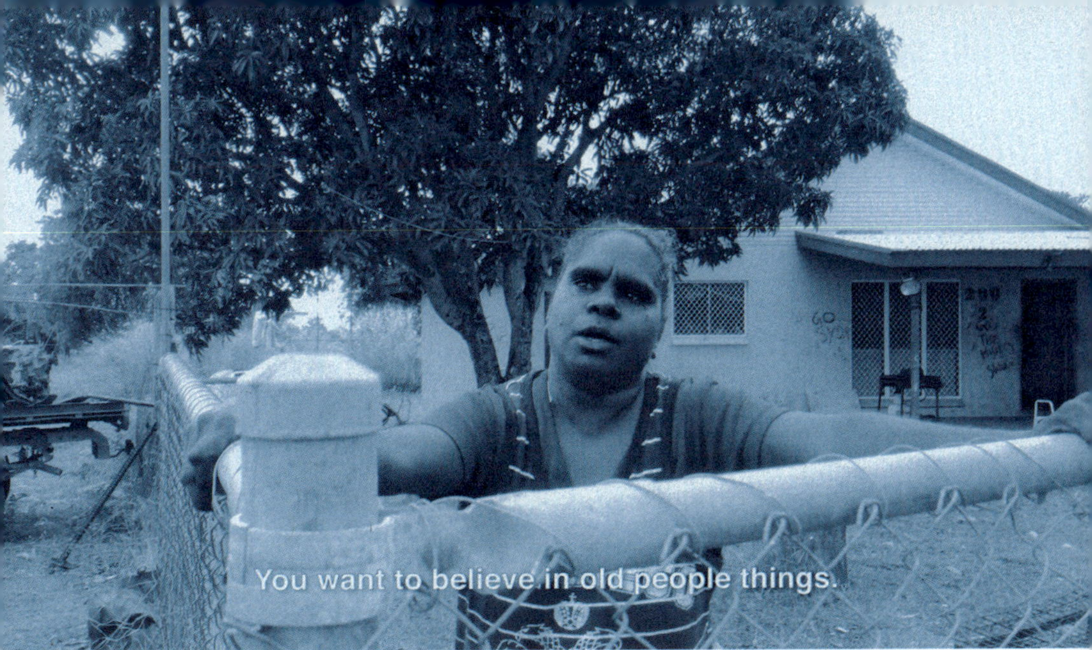

during the first seventy years since Phillip's landing. This meant that by the middle of the century, the cities that would exercise the overwhelming majority of political, financial, and intellectual influence with respect to European understandings of Australian colonialism for the next century—Sydney, Melbourne, Hobart, and Adelaide—were also all located on a relatively isolated corner of the continent. Furthermore, up until this point, colonial policy was still being formulated in Britain, where it was administered locally via the Colonial Office. This point is important as, in spite of the horrendous crimes that were being perpetrated by many colonialists against First Peoples in these parts of the continent—which included murder, rape, dispossession, and enslavement—Indigenous Australians were nonetheless still regarded as British subjects by official imperial law. This meant that they were, in theory, protected under common law, which included the provision within pastoral leases that allowed them to remain on their traditional lands and have access to water, game, and other sacred sites (a fact upheld by the Wik decision in 1996).

The second phase of colonialisation within Australia—that is, into the much larger regions deemed by Europeans to be less conducive to establishing settlements—that occurred during the second half of the nineteenth and well into the twentieth century, was undertaken under significantly different circumstances. During this period—which extended well past the federation of the country in 1901—colonial governments, as opposed to the Colonial Office, were ultimately responsible for administering policy with respect to First Nations. Therefore, although they were still technically beholden to imperial law, the colonial governments that oversaw the expansion of the colony and the establishment of Queensland, Western Australia and, importantly, the Northern Territory, essentially ignored this. As a result, the push into the north and west of the continent was significantly more murderous and traumatic for Australia's Indigenous populations than even the earlier period of colonisation;[8] a factor that was exacerbated by the official policy of removing mixed race children from their parents in regions such as the Northern Territory from 1910 until the 1970s (the so-called 'Stolen Generations').[9]

The Great Forgetting

As mentioned above, a facilitating factor within this later phase of the Australian colonial project was the fact that it occurred well away from the major centres of power in the southeast of the continent. As a result, the vast majority of white Australians knew little to nothing about the contemporary crimes being perpetrated against Indigenous peoples, let alone anything about their histories and relationship to Country (understood as both a noun and a proper noun). During this 'Great Forgetting'—which is said to cover approximately the first sixty years of the twentieth century, but extends in many respects much closer to the present day[10]—Australia's Indigenous peoples were essentially written out of both history books as well as current affairs media; except during times in which they were discussed with respect to the 'problems' surrounding vagrancy and crime rates. Thus almost every major publication on 'Australian history' written during this period would commence with the 'founding' of the continent in the years 1770–1788 and progress through a series of events which both constituted the national myth, but also implied that the colonisation of the country was in fact such a benign, past act that it barely rated a mention.[11]

Concomitant to this act of literary erasure, an image of Indigenous peoples was also being instrumentalised back in Europe in the service of the colonial aesthetics that were deployed in the spaces of

8 Henry Reynolds, *Truth-Telling: History, Sovereignty and the Uluru Statement*, Sydney: NewSouth Publishing, 2021, pp. 173–75.

9 Richard Broome 2019, pp. 96–99; 136–37; 198–200.

10 The below description of 'Australian History' is very much aligned with the author's experiences of undertaking primary and secondary education at four different schools in Melbourne during the 1980s and 1990s. Even then, one could quite easily progress through an entire school curriculum with barely a mention of Indigenous history, save for the odd mention during a retelling of the Burke and Wills expedition, or a reading of the myth of the Rainbow Serpent.

11 Henry Reynolds 2021, pp. 163–67.

the 'exhibitionary complex', including of course its ancillary, the nascent movie house/cinema.[12] Displayed alongside the tools of industry and science (which signified the technological sophistication of the host empire), Indigenous objects and bodies were displayed at 'World Exhibitions' in order to signify a museified and ethnologised 'other', reduced to pure images and deprived of any form of mediating function. As Matthias De Groof contends, such 'aesthetic displays' were in fact 'fundamental to the operations of colonialism, and constitute a primary signifier defining coloniality',[13] a binary which in turn extended to these displays within cinema. Noting that Georges Méliès cited a visit to the 1900 Exposition Universelle in Paris as formative within the creation of his iconic 1902 film *Trip to the Moon* (which serves as *the* emblematic example of the European encounter with the 'other'), De Groof observes that both the World Exhibition and the cinema combine:

> [I]deas of progress as manifest in cinematic devices, apparatuses, and the machine itself, with dehumanizing aesthetics and portrayals [resulting in the world becoming] visible, viewable, accessible, and ripe for domination. Evidently, this desire to own and commodify through media was not limited to space and the human, but was also directed towards the non-human/more-than-human and nature.[14]

This 'aestheticized display' of both the operations of colonialism and technological/sovereign progress were similarly evident in the opening of the First Parliament of the Commonwealth of Australia 9 May 1901. Interestingly, this ceremony took place at the Royal Exhibition Building in Melbourne, rather than at the Parliament House just down the road. As the name implies, the Royal Exhibition Building was originally the site of two major 'World Exhibitions': the Melbourne International Exhibition of 1880–81, as well as the Centennial International Exhibition of 1888–89. However, in contrast to the World Exhibitions held in Europe, Indigenous peoples and their cultures were conspicuous in their absence. Instead, these displays focused solely on 'modernity and [were] coupled with a generally widely held belief that the Victorian Aboriginal community was either confined to missions and reserves where they were expected to die out or had been absorbed into the wider society'.[15]

This absence of Indigenous objects and bodies within the discursive spaces of modernity was also evident in the writing and teaching of 'Australian art history', which was, up until recently, almost com-

12 The term 'exhibitionary complex' is taken from Tony Bennett's expanded reading of Foucault in order to explain 'the transfer of *objects and bodies* from the enclosed and private domains in which they had previously been displayed (but to a restricted public) into progressively more open and public arenas where, through the representations to which they were subjected, they formed vehicles for inscribing and broadcasting the messages of power (but of a different type) throughout society' (Tony Bennett, 'The Exhibitionary Complex', *New Formations*, no. 4, Spring 1988, p. 74, emphasis mine).

13 Matthias De Groof, 'Anticolonial Aesthetics: Towards Eco-Cinema', *Interventions*, vol. 24, no. 7, 2022, p. 1145.

14 Matthias De Groof 2022, p. 1146; See also Jennifer Fay, *Inhospitable World: Cinema in the Time of the Anthropocene*, New York: Oxford University Press, 2018.

15 Lynette Russell, '"An Unpicturesque Vagrant": Aboriginal Victorians at the Melbourne International Exhibition 1880–1881', *The La Trobe Journal*, no. 93/94, 2014, pp. 77–78. Although Indigenous peoples were not to be seen inside these exhibitions of 'modernity', several reporters nonetheless observed Indigenous groups begging in front of the building (Lynette Russell, 2014, pp. 78–80).

pletely devoid of the art of Australia's diverse Indigenous peoples. Indeed, upon surveying the work of art historians working in the country in 1983, Terry Smith concluded that:

> They make it clear that European, not Australian, art has been the main interest of historians working here, and that only quite recently have undergraduates had the opportunity to take courses in Australian art. Most courses centre on Europe, including England and sometimes the United States, with very few looking at Asian art and none at Aboriginal art.[16]

Indeed, Smith himself was a key figure is positioning Indigenous artists within the discourses of modern and contemporary art when he penned a chapter on 'Aboriginal Painting 1970–1990' in the 1991 edition of Bernhard Smith's (no relation) seminal book *Australian Painting 1788–1990*.[17] As the title for this chapter indicates, Smith's analysis centred on the formation of the Papunya Tula artist collective in the Western Desert region of the Northern Territory in 1972, and therefore chiefly concerned what has popularly been referred to as 'dot painting'. Importantly however, Smith's chapter was the first major text to propose a substantial theoretical framework for Aboriginal art to be understood as 'contemporary art'; for it to engage with contemporary art historical discourse.[18] This definition is crucial, as up until this point the designation of 'contemporary Indigenous art—which had come to replace 'primitive art'[19]—was used as a way to set such work apart from dominant discourses pertaining to 'modern' or 'postmodern' (i.e. Euro-American) art. Thus Smith's text was part of a wider effort to counter ethnocentric practices with respect to contemporary art, both nationally (the installation of Djon Mundine and the Bandjalung people's *The Aboriginal Memorial* in 1988 at the National Gallery of Australia or the exhibition *Balance 1990: Views, Visions, Influences* at the Queensland Art Gallery in 1990), but also internationally (Jean-Hubert Martin's *Magiciens de la Terre* at the Centre Georges Pompidou and the Grande halle de la Villette in Paris in 1989).

The Trauma of Intervention

As paradigmatic as all of these moments were, it also needs to be pointed out that they all took place in cities which had been founded during the 'first wave' of colonisation: Terry Smith was at that time living in Sydney, Bernhard Smith in Melbourne, while the National Gal-

16 Terry Smith, 'Writing the History of Australian Art: Its Past, Present and Possible Future', *Australian Journal of Art*, vol. 3, 1983, p. 12.

17 Terry Smith, 'From the Desert: Aboriginal Painting 1970–1990' in Bernhard Smith, *Australian Painting 1788–1990*, Melbourne: Oxford University Press, 1991, pp. 495–517.

18 Marie Geissler, *The Making of Indigenous Australian Contemporary Art: Arnhem Land Bark Painting, 1970–1990*, Newcastle-Upon-Tyne: Cambridge Scholars Publishing, 2020.

19 The first exhibition of Indigenous work within the context of an art museum was held in 1943 at the National Gallery of Victoria in Melbourne and was indeed titled 'Primitive Art' (see Jaynie Anderson, 'The Creation of Indigenous Collections in Melbourne: How Kenneth Clark, Charles Mountford, and Leonhard Adam Interrogated Australian Indigeneity', *Les actes de colloques du musée du quai Branly Jacques Chirac*, vol. 1, 2009, p. 4.

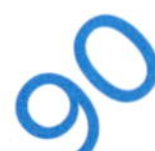

lery of Australia and Queensland Art Gallery are located in Canberra and Brisbane respectively. Just as it was at the beginning of the century, 'history' was being written almost exclusively from cities located along the southeastern/eastern coast of the country, far removed from the 'frontier' regions in the far north and west that were still experiencing the worst effects of colonisation. Increasingly referred to as the 'Indigenous Estate', this region encompasses approximately 1.5 million square kilometres (20 per cent of the Australian mainland) of environmentally intact desert and tropical savannahs, upon which 26 per cent of the Indigenous population (or 120,000 individuals) resided.[20] From the 1970s onwards—that is, precisely during the period in which 'contemporary Indigenous art' was coming into being—many Indigenous peoples moved away from the government and mission settlements and back to traditional lands. This so-called 'homeland movement' was driven by many factors, but was primarily driven by a deep connection to Country, as well as a desire to protect sacred sites from the increasing mineral prospecting that was taking place in Arnhem Land and other parts of the Northern Territory.[21] As the Australian economy became increasingly reliant upon mineral extraction and mining during the 1990s and into the new millennium, so too did the push back from government and bureaucratic bodies against Indigenous attempts to halt such extractive practices amplify 'with a ferocity that belies national celebrations of Indigenous creativity within the liberal settler community'.[22] Framed within the context of neoliberalism, these voices increasingly pointed to the unlikelihood or impossibility of a market economy being developed in these remote areas, thereby arguing that Indigenous peoples should relocate to urban areas on account of the 'greater economic opportunities' afforded there.[23] The timing of such a call coincided with the implementation of the Northern Territory Emergency Response—more commonly referred to as 'The Intervention'—in 2007, in which the conservative federal government instrumentalised the spectre of child sexual abuse in order to legitimate a series of new national policy restrictions on Indigenous peoples. Occurring almost exclusively in so-called 'remote' or 'proscribed' communities,[24] these measures included heavy regulations with respect to land tenure, local governance, household spending, school attendance, and health compliance, while at the same time reorganising or scrapping educational access, development programmes, and cultural considerations from criminal proceedings. In addition to single-handedly eradicating over three decades of bilingual and bicultural education in these communities, the Intervention also bestowed new, invasive powers on the federal police and

20 Jon Charles Altman, 'Alleviating poverty in remote Indigenous Australia: The role of the hybrid economy', *Addressing Poverty: Alternative Economic Approaches, Development Studies Bulletin*, no. 72, March 2007, pp. 47–51.

21 Wilfrid James Gray, 'Decentralisation Trends in Arnhem Land', in Ronald Murray Berndt (ed.), *Aborigines and Change: Australia in the '70s* (AIAS, Canberra, 1977), pp. 114–123.

22 Jennifer L. Biddle and Tess Lea, 'Hyperrealism and Other Indigenous Forms of "Faking It with the Truth"', *Visual Anthropology* Review, vol. 34, no. 1, Spring 2018, p. 9.

23 See Benedict Scambary, *My Country, Mine Country: Indigenous People, Mining and Development Contestation in Remote Australia*, Centre for Aboriginal Economic Policy Research, no. 33, Canberra: The Australian National University, 2013, pp. 1–23; and Helen Hughes and Jenness Warin, 'A New Deal for Aborigines and Torres Strait Islanders in Remote Communities', *CIS Issue Analysis*, no. 54, Sydney: The Centre for Independent Studies, 2005, pp. 1–20.

24 See Jon Altman and Melinda Hinkson, 'Very Risky Business: The Quest to Normalise Remote-Living Aboriginal People', in Greg Marston, John Moss, and John Quiggin (eds.), *Risk, Welfare and Work*, Melbourne: Melbourne University Press, 2010, pp. 185–211; Tess Lea, 'When Looking for Anarchy, Look to the State: Fantasies of Regulation in Forcing Disorder within the Australian Indigenous Estate', *Critique of Anthropology*, no. 32, 2012, pp. 109–24.

local rangers to patrol, intervene in, and discipline Indigenous communities throughout the Territory, which for many brought back the horrors of the Stolen Generation and over two centuries of colonial settler abuse. Indeed, the repercussions of the Intervention were a chief contributing factor to a large riot which broke out in the Belyuen community in 2007—an event which would in turn lead to the formation of the Karrabing Film Collective.

Such a policy of attempting to remove Indigenous communities from their homeland was soon extended to other states and reached its apotheosis in 2015, when the federal government threatened to close over half of the communities in Western Australia—another state whose financial prosperity was based upon mining and mineral extraction—by forcibly shifting people into larger regional towns. At the time, the far-right Prime Minister Tony Abbott justified such a move by noting that taxpayers should not be expected to finance Indigenous peoples' 'lifestyle choices';[25] equating Indigenous 'productivity' with their ability to generate profit within the framework of a market economy.

However, as multiple scholars have long argued, the value of 'Indigenous productivity' is in fact realised through multiple activities: including quantifiable pursuits such as hunting and gathering, or the production of art;[26] as well as activities such as development and maintenance of outstations, engagement in family or kin relations, conduct of ceremony, or by engaging with a sentient landscape in the production, reproduction, and reinterpretation of cultural identity, by 'just being there'.[27] An important voice within these debates is the American-born anthropologist Elizabeth A. Povinelli, who has been working within—and is a member of—the Belyuen community since the 1980s and was one of the founding members of the Karrabing Film Collective. When writing about Indigenous productivity in the 1990s, Povinelli contended that it:

> is a form of production in the fullest cultural and economic sense of this term, generating a range of sociocultural meanings and political-economic problems and rewards. Hunting and gathering grounds Belyuen Aborigines' relationship to the Cox Peninsula and, vis-à-vis other ethnic groups in the region, defines their Aboriginality.[28]

For all of the members of Karrabing, 'Indigenous productivity' is therefore a form of cultural continuity and *visibility*, both of which serve as an integral mechanism for the production of cultural identity. In the absence of media, literary, and other forms of historical archive,

25 Jennifer L. Biddle and Tess Lea 2018, p. 9.

26 Jon Altman, 'Development options on Aboriginal land: Sustainable Indigenous hybrid economies in the twenty-first century', in Luke Taylor, Graeme K. Ward, Graham Henderso, Richard Davis, and Lynley A. Wallis (eds.), *The Power of Knowledge, The Resonance of Tradition*, Canberra: Aboriginal Studies Press, 2005, pp. 34–48.

27 Benedict Scambary 2013, pp. 22–23.

28 Elizabeth A. Povinelli, *Labor's Lot: The Power, History, and Culture of Aboriginal Action*, Chicago: The University of Chicago Press, 1993, pp. 26–27.

the work of Karrabing provides primary witness to—and is indexical of—the sorts of contradictions that constitute the Collective's contemporary life worlds.[29] Importantly, Karrabing's works undertake an active, pedagogical operation, functioning, in the words of the Collective, as 'a schoolhouse made out of film'.[30] A primary goal of the Collective is thus to counter the aforementioned erasure of multilingual and bicultural education brought about by the Intervention. Indeed, the word 'karrabing' itself—which denotes the point at which the vast saltwater tides have reached their lowest point and are set to return to shore—was chosen to signify the manner in which the collective itself is comprised of four distinct family groups, rather than alluding to any form of homogeneity.

Schoolhouse as Method

However, as the two extracts cited at the beginning of this paper attest, Karrabing's films also serve as a manner through which they can reveal to both themselves and to viewers the fissures and frustrations of existing within contemporary settler-colonialism and the concomitant and ongoing ecological crisis that it entails. As Jennifer Biddle and Tess Lea have noted: 'the primacy of film-making was initially accidental, but is a key way for striving together playfully and staying as one, an act not of cultural preservation but of insistence: *we are still here, this is who we are, this is you, our country needs and heeds us.*'[31] By taking charge over the very technologies that had hitherto served to signify the opposite of the Indigenous bodies and objects displayed during the World Exhibitions, Karrabing enact what Faye Ginsburg notes as 'an extension of collective self-production in ways that enhance Indigenous regimes of value'.[32] In other words, by borrowing from the language of cinema for Indigenous-specific purposes—the indexical capacities of which have, historically, provided the very vehicle for enabling colonial-settler cultural perspectives to reaffirm their aesthetic/technological hegemony—Karrabing is able to speak directly to their audiences in a language with which they are familiar (the moving image, the use of subtitles, et cetera), but still maintaining their own voices. Through their films and their commitment to the notion of a 'schoolhouse', the Collective are literally 'explaining it to them!' and, 'too fucking bad, honestly!' if they are still unable to understand it. The impetus is now on viewers to comprehend the lived reality of Karrabing's contemporary situation, including all of the imposed inconsistencies and contradictory statements

29 Jennifer L. Biddle and Lisa Stefanoff, 'What Is Same but Different and Why Does It Matter?' *Cultural Studies Review*, vol. 21, no. 1, 2015, pp. 97-120.

30 Lorraine Lane, Cecilia Lewis, Elizabeth Povinelli, Linda Yarrowin and Sandra Yarrowin, 'A Conversation with the Karrabing Film Collective', *Commoning Ethnography*, vol. 2, no. 1, 2019, p. 174.

31 Jennifer L. Biddle and Tess Lea 2018, p. 10, (emphasis original).

32 Faye Ginsburg, 'Indigenous Media from U-Matic to YouTube: Media Sovereignty in the Digital Age', *Sociologia & Antropologia*, vol. 6, no. 3, 2016, p. 590.

that result in many of the dystopian scenarios proffered by these films. Ranging from toxic worlds (*Windjarrameru, The Stealing C*nt$*, 2015 and *Mermaids, Mirror Worlds*, 2018), zombie invasions (*The Family*, 2021) to a revolutionary Indigenous population (*Night Time Go*, 2017), these scenarios serve to highlight the fact that 'imperialism and ongoing (settler) colonialisms have been ending worlds for as long as they have been in existence'.[33] However, rather than merely offering up a series of 'end of days' scenarios—or simply reenacting revenge fantasies—what makes these works so remarkable is their ability to incorporate a multitude of voices and perspectives into every aspect of their creation. Ranging from their conception and storyboarding, through to their editing and presentation, all of Karrabing's works constitute a celebration of multiplicity and discrepancy in place of the singular voice of the auteur. Similarly, as a collection of commissioned and republished articles and interviews, this Reader similarly attempts to present a cacophony of positions and statements with respect to Karrabing's practice over the years. Drawing inspiration from The Collective's notion of the schoolhouse, it brings together a range of voices that, rather than presuming any form of comprehensiveness, instead introduces audiences to a variety of provisional entry points and propositions with respect to both the reception of Indigenous contemporary art in general, as well as to specific works and practices of Karrabing. Furthermore, in keeping with the discursive nature of the schoolhouse, the Reader contains commissioned essays by writers chosen specifically by Karrabing themselves, as well as a selection of older texts written over the few decades. In so doing, the publication hopes to act as a defiant affirmation of sovereignty in the face of the ongoing gestures of erasure that continue to impact "Indigenous productivity" throughout the world.

33 Kathryn Yusoff, *A Billion Black Anthropocenes or None*, Minneapolis: University of Minnesota Press, 2018, p. xiii.

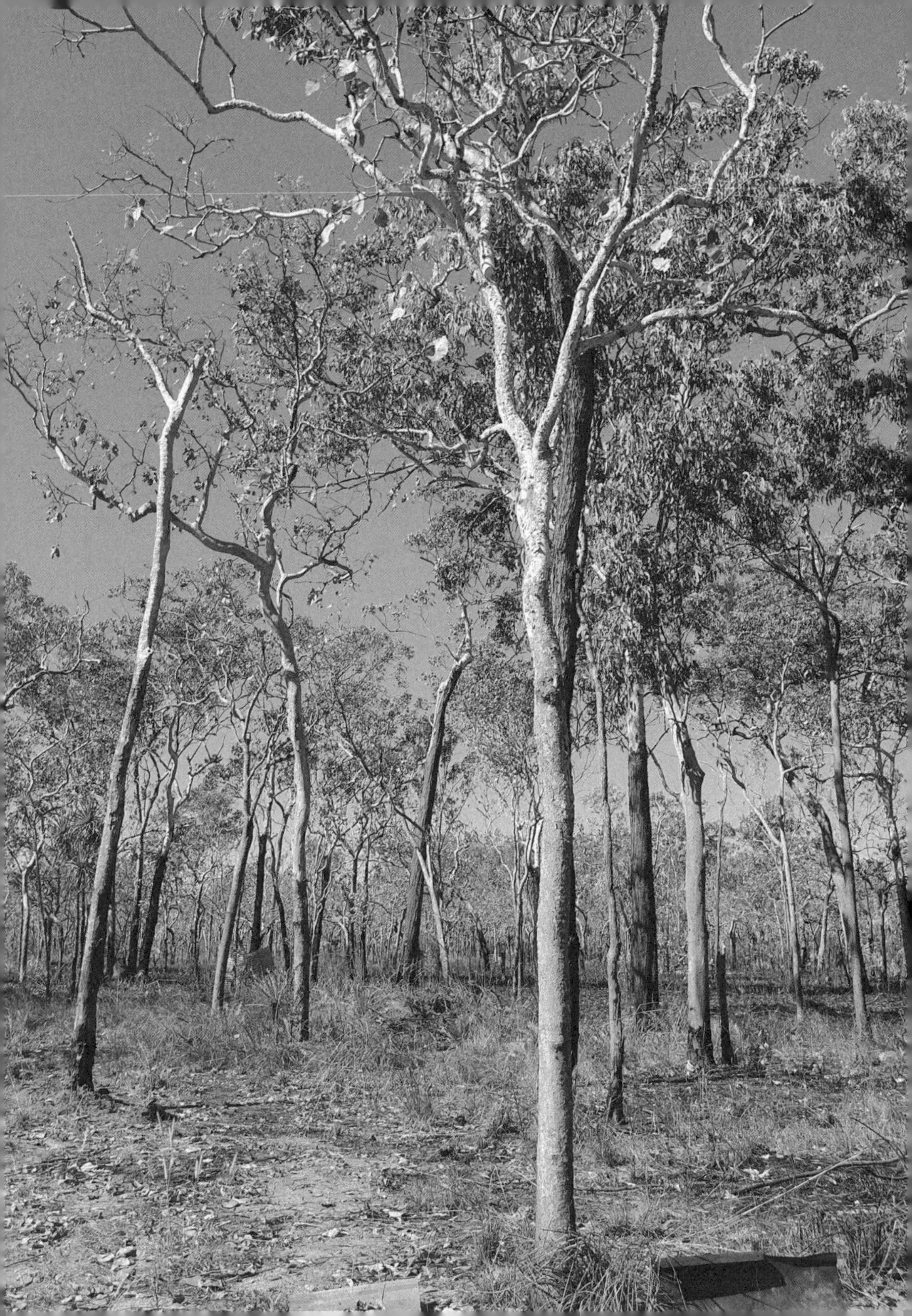

The Ancestral Present of Oceanic Illusions: Connected and Differentiated in Late Toxic Liberalism[1]

Elizabeth A. Povinelli

Seaside Conversations

It's March 1985 at a little coastal area called Madpil, in the Northern Territory of Australia. Marjorie Bilbil, Ruby Yarrowin, Alice Wainbirri, some of their children and grandchildren, and I are sitting on the beach at the edge of a mangrove talking over a meal of rice, sea snails, mud crabs, and sweet tea. The city of Darwin is shimmering across the harbour. I met these women, ranging in age from late forties to early sixties, soon after arriving in the Northern Territory in 1984, straight out of my BA in philosophy. Since 1975 they had observed and participated in a contentious land claim over the Cox Peninsula, where Madpil is located. At the centre of the peninsula was the community in which they lived, and, for the most part, had grown up and had children. Their parents and grandparents had travelled up and down the coast we were sitting on, dodging and taking advantage of a new virulent pestilence called settler colonialism while they maintained the connective practices undergirding the stability of people's different lands stretching along the coast to Anson Bay some two hundred miles south. These practices included formal rituals that reenacted the ancestral travels of specific *durlg* (in the Batjemalh language; 'therrawin' in the Emmiyengal language; 'totems' in Anthropological English; 'Dreamings' in public English) that created the topology of the region; formal rituals that acknowledged and reflected the *durlg*-infused landscape's response to the new conditions of the settler pestilence; and ordinary ways of looking out for and caring for land, such as our day spent sweating in the mangrove.

In the 1930s, the Northern Territory government doubled down on the forcible internment of Indigenous groups. Bilbil, Yarrowin, and Wainbirri's parents were forced into the Delissaville Settlement at the centre of Cox Peninsula. (With the passage of the Aboriginal Land Rights Act in 1976, the settlement was renamed 'Belyuen', after its waterhole.) From then on, all movement would be strictly monitored by settler superintendents as part of the federal state's new tactic to eliminate the Indigenous otherwise (than through murder and violence), through forced containment and assimilation. But the land and its peoples at Delissaville refused the authority of settler law. They came together around the Belyuen waterhole and its underground aquatic tunnels stretching to the seaside around the Cox Peninsula and down to Anson Bay. Belyuen was a *maroi* (in the Batjemalh language; 'mirrhe' in the Emmiyengal language; 'conception totem' in Anthropological English) site a place of dynamic interplay between the spirits of the deceased and the spirits of yet-to-be-born

1 This is an edited extract from a text which was originally published in *e-flux journal*, Issue #112, October 2020: https://www.e-flux.com/journal/112/352823/the-ancestral-present-of-oceanic-illusions-connected-and-differentiated-in-late-toxic-liberalism.

children. Belyuen would keep alive the connective tissue of dispersed places—the ways in which the land was specifically entangled—so that each place could stay alive.

As we rested from a long sweaty slog through the mangrove, Bilbil, Yarrowin, and Wainbirri described struggling to explain to the anthropologists and lawyers working on their behalf to have the lands around Madpil returned to their families how they could at one and the same time have and hold specific coastal lands that hugged the coast of Anson Bay, much further south, and still be irreducibly connected to the lands around Belyuen as well. The creole phrasing that they used to describe the situation was 'Mebela got roan roan country, yeah, but they imjoinedupbet got that Belyuen waterhole. Belyuen, im now been make mebela properly bla dis country.' (We have our own lands, but they are joined to others in an original and ongoing way through the Belyuen waterhole. Belyuen made us properly from here.) Their 'roan roan' countries were within Marritjaben-, Marriamu-, Menthayengal-, Emmiyengal-, Wadjigiyn-, and Kiyuk-speaking countries, and included nearly twenty *therrawin*, (in Emmiyengal; 'durlg' in Batjemalh; 'totems' in Anthropological English). Yes, some of the connective tissue was derived from the topologically formative effects of ancestral *durlg* who moved across the region, but the effects were not done and dead. They were present and dynamic.

Bilbil used her eldest daughter, AA, as an example. AA was a Murrumurru (Long Yam *therrawin*) Emmiyengal woman through her father. From notes, Bilbil told me:

> Your edje, im picks up that murrumurru from Mabaluk from im father, though im also think back la my Redjerung (Red Kangaroo therrawin), Marritjaben side. But im got ingaraiyn maroi (in Batjemalh; 'mirrhe' in Emmiyengal; 'conception totem' in Anthropological English) from Belyuen, and must be here langa other side, Imaluk. That Belyuen waterhole been smellim sweat when me I ben bogey there, and im think, 'yeah, gonna send baby spirit into that sea turtle.' So when that old man got that ingaraiyn langa Milik, imself been look and think, 'im different this turtle. Too many seaweed tangled up lei im back.' Then AA been come out gamenawerra. Too many hair lei im back. We sebe. Im sign.

She gestured east toward where an Ingaraiyn *therrawin* sat in the tidal zone as the likely source of the turtle spirit Belyuen sent into an actual sea turtle, which acted as a material conduit into her husband and then her and then her child. As she did so, AA's body stretched and extended (*ex-tendĕre*) into and across the topological shapings of the ancestral present, folding and pushing inward (*in-tendĕre*) an immanent spacing.

Leave aside hoary anthropological debates about totems and animistic cultures for a moment.[2] Note instead the porosity of modes of embodiment (water, organic bodies) and the multiplicity of connectivities posited as potentially codetermining them substantially. Some are actual, some immanent, all to a more-than-human world that is constantly signing to its human co-participants, who must weigh what is and isn't a sign of a manifestation. A Long Yam site, located at Mabaluk some 150 kilometres as the crow flies from where we are sitting, passed to AA through her father's body ('What this word? What they say, perragut for this kindabet? Here look, Beth, "patrilineal".' [What is this word? What do white people say for this kind of connection to land? Here, look at this, Beth. 'Patrilineal'.]) A sea turtle *mirrhe* passed into AA from a saltwater encounter between a human, a sea turtle, and a waterhole during a hunting event, creating a connection to a Sea Turtle site proximate to where she was born, did the ceremony, and hunted (all sweat). And a waterhole inside the community acts as a material communication. It is a site through which ancestral beings travel across aquatic underground tunnels to nearby and far-afield places.

Bilbil, Yarrowin, Wainbirri, and the other Belyuen elder men and women were right. They faced a state law that only recognised (i.e., that *demanded*, as the basis for the return of stolen property) a singular form of human-land relations—some form of a 'local descent group' (Anthropological English for 'socially inflected biology such as patrilineality and matrilineality'). They also faced the theoretically conservative consultant anthropologists who wrote reports adjudicating their claim, and the lawyers who read the reports. Both the anthropologists and the lawyers remained puzzled, if not downright skeptical, in the face of questions like: how could these women, and the men of the community, say that their *therrawin* were always where they were, and were continuing to engage in the same events? How could the unchanging be dynamic, the permanent alterable, and the persistent eventful? Not all anthropologists were confused in this way. Barbara Glowczewski describes a similar reality among her Yuendemu colleagues, in which ceremony pulls into actuality the immanent cartographies that transverse human and more-than-human worlds.[3] These actualisations are the consequences of previous sedimentations that remain beneath and across the overlay of the settler state.

2 Philippe Descola, *Beyond Nature and Culture*, Chicago: University of Chicago Press, 2014.

3 Barbara Glowczewski, *Totemic Becomings: Cosmopolitics of the Dreaming*, Edinburgh: Edinburgh University Press, 2015.

What troubled Bilbil, Yarrowin, Wainbirri, and other older men and women was that anthropologists and lawyers saw all forms of dynamic permanence as somehow less important than the frozen framework of a settler law that recognised only one kind of relation—the descent of man. This was a biological reduction by which their thick relations to the more-than-human were nothing more than a question of what man birthed what person. It was like trying to maneuver across an endless series of funhouse mirrors. As these women described a *durlg*-determined but dynamic relation to their country, the state and its anthropologists would attempt to re-determine the dynamic by reducing its complexity to a stunningly hermeneutically stupid biology lesson that cut the ties across people and place to produce an enclosed mini nation-state. The land claim dragged on for twenty-plus years; forests were plundered to produce all the law and consultant reports and formal evidence. But under the guise of liberal recognition, no conversation was actually allowed to occur. As Aimé Césaire wrote in his *Discourse on Colonialism*:

> I admit that it is a good thing to place different civilisations in contact with each other; that it is an excellent thing to blend different worlds; that whatever its own particular genius may be, a civilisation that withdraws into itself atrophies; that for civilizations, exchange is oxygen ... But then I ask the following question: has colonisation really placed civilisations in contact? Or, if you prefer, of all the ways of establishing contact, was it the best? I answer no.[4]

4 Aimé Césaire, *Discourse on Colonialism*, trans. Joan Pinkham, New York: Monthly Review Press, 2000, p. 33.

Some twenty-five years after our conversation at Madpil, I am sitting near a tent camp with many of the now-adult children of Yarrowin and Wainbirri, their partners, and their children. We had grown up side by side as I commuted back and forth from the US two or three times a year. They are living at the edge of the northern coast of Anson Bay, having decided to leave Belyuen. Belyuen had been engulfed by violence, caused in large part by the aftereffects of the same land claim that kicked off the conversation among Bilbil, Yarrowin, Wainbirri, and me in 1985. A piece of federal legislation celebrated as recognising Indigenous law refused to acknowledge one side of the dynamic that the older women struggled to explain. The Land Rights Commission found one small section of the community to be the legally recognised 'traditional Aboriginal owners', even while stating that the entire community had the same rights to the area through Indigenous cultural and ceremonial law. Indigenous law could be rec-

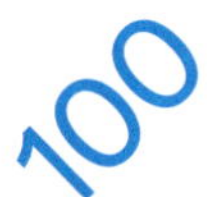

ognised as existing but would not be allowed to determine the operation of the state. The divisions settler law sliced into the community had enormous social and economic consequences. All decisions about how the surrounding lands would be developed were made by only a small group, which also reaped all the benefits flowing from such decisions. The tensions that the state created did not affect the state; they went inward and then exploded.

Told they were strangers in their own land, the fifty odd men, women, children, and I were discussing how to keep from sliding into destitution but also refuse to open their land to mining. Mining is like a phalanx of circulating capitalist scavenger birds, promising to separate and extract while preserving and enhancing—science fiction inversions of ancestral *durlg*. Everyone had seen the consequences of such promises: gaping holes from previous mines, poisoned rivers, and unexplained cancers. Liam Grealy and Kirsty Howey describe 'the politico-bureaucratic edifice of uniform drinking water governance and service provision across the NT [Northern Territory]' as 'a state-curated fiction' that 'produces a racialised "archipelago" of differentiated islands of drinking water governance'.[5]

A couple of people suggested running a green tourist outfit and creating a corporation for it through the Office of the Registrar of Indigenous Corporations.[6] Very quickly, everyone struggled with the state-set trap inherent to this plan. If they selected a place name, say Mabaluk, then the state would immediately consider other family members from adjacent countries and languages as outside, or subsidiary. 'Karrabing' was proposed as much as for its semantic content as its conceptual pragmatics. 'Karrabing' is an Emmiyengal word referring to when the vast regional tides are at their lowest. Karrabing opens possibilities as it connects distinct places—it opens fishing, crabbing, and clamming as it shows and makes available the reefs, mangroves, and shore banks connecting ('joining up') the countries of the Indigenous inhabitants of the shoreline. 'Karrabing' was not merely a referential term. It was intended as a concept, foregrounding the dynamic process of emerging and submerging connections across places. For the people who would become the Karrabing, 'karrabing' signals how families best strengthen their relationship to, and the health of, their 'roan roan' country by keeping robust the connective tissue between them (*joinedupbet*). They learned this from their parents, who had learned from theirs. This learning is a practice.

Karrabing would become the framework through which a set of land-oriented filmic practices would embody an ongoing resistance to

5 Liam Grealy and Kirsty Howey, 'Securing Water Supply: Governing Drinking Water in the Northern Territory', *Australian Geographer* 51, no. 3, 2020, pp. 341–60.

6 See Elizabeth A. Povinelli, 'Routes/Worlds,' *e-flux journal*, no. 27, September 2011.

the state's effort to divide and pit Indigenous people and their lands against each other. In other words, making films would not only represent the Karrabing members' views about the irreducible condition of connectivity among the different countries. It would also practise this counter-discourse intergenerationally.

Property Relations, Oceanic Feelings

The frustrations that the older women described to me in 1985 when trying to explain to *perragut* (white people as a general category for settlers) how they had their own distinct countries—even while these countries could not be separated into small sovereign fiefdoms—have been mirrored by the surprise many Karrabing members have expressed after encountering audiences for their films inside and outside Australia. No one expresses anger, nor even the anguish of Bilbil, Yarrowin, and Wainbirri. But the problem remains, persisting across time and space—the struggle some *perragut* have in comprehending these simultaneous statements: 'Each of us got our roan roan country from our fathers. Places can't be made separate separate.' Two general responses to this kind of statement suggest what is still at stake as critical theory continues to try and break with the concept of sovereign objects. On the one hand, when they describe their *durlg* relations to their land, Karrabing members are often taken to mean that they own that land. On the other hand, when they discuss the undergirding connectivity between them and the more-than-human world, they are heard to be describing an undifferentiated oceanic feeling, sometimes compared to a colloquial understanding of the Buddhist falling away of all difference.

The first misunderstanding has been under constant pressure in critical theory and Indigenous theory. Aileen Moreton-Robinson has powerfully critiqued the 'white possessive' whereby the settler state's gift of self-determination is a demand that Indigenous people mimic the psychosis at the heart of Western liberalism: namely, the fantasy of a sovereign body that determines itself, has final say over its use and the use of things within it—that speaks on the basis of its own sovereign self-possession. When Karrabing members describe being a group with multiple lands and *durlg* stretching across the coasts of Anson Bay and beyond, they see audiences hearing them as saying something like: 'I' have a country that is

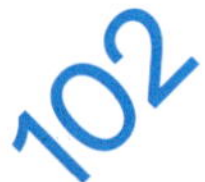

different from his or her country, much as a citizen would say his or her country was distinct from another, or capitalists would say they owned what was theirs. That is, some in the audience hear members evoking a liberal property relation. I often use Mikhail Bakhtin as a counter to this misunderstanding. For him, all words, including 'I', are mere rejoinders to a world within us, because it formed us, before we were us. We can quote him at length from his 'The Problem of Speech Genres':

> The very boundaries of the utterance are determined by a change of speech subjects. Utterances are not indifferent to one another and are not self-sufficient; they are aware of and mutually reflect one another. These mutual reflections determine their character. Each utterance is filled with echoes and reverberations of other utterances to which it is related by the communality of the sphere of speech communication. Every utterance must be regarded primarily as a response to preceding utterances of the given sphere (we understand the word 'response' here in the broadest sense). Each utterance refutes, affirms, supplements, and relies on the others, presupposes them to be known, and somehow takes them into account.[7]

But often at such film screenings I don't get into long Bakhtin quotes, since Karrabing members, like Cecilia Lewis, powerfully describe their form of belonging to their own lands as an ethical position irreducibly stretched through the other more-than-human worlds of other Karrabing members. In a conversation upending the Judeo-Christian narrative about Babel, Cecilia and other Karrabing members describe not merely an original linguistic multiplicity, but an original ethical relation to the other's language:

> Yeah but here where you talk to det person le you joinimupbet det tubela—and det nuther language where you speak le, that other person dem inside you again. You think bla det person.
>
> (Yeah, but here we think that when you speak to that person in this way, you connect or articulate, you and him—when you speak their language to them the other person comes inside you and you go inside of them. You are thinking of/with/through that other person.)[8]

7 M. M. Bahktin, 'The Problem of Speech Genres', *Speech Genres and Other Late Essays, Austin:* University of Texas Press, 1987, p. 91.

8 'Australian Babel: A Conversation with Karrabing', *Specimen: The Babel Review of Translations,* October 31, 2017.

The land claim legislation clipped all the connecting tissue that provided conditions for holding lands. Karrabing would work to restore this tissue. For Karrabing member Rex Edmunds, this is the connective tissue without which proper caring-for cannot be done. It is materially analogous to how ceremonies must be held:

> Well, you need your uncle or aunt or cousin, in our way it's a cousin, like your mum's brother's kids or your dad's sister's kids to do the burning of the clothes. Because they are your aunt (father's sister) or uncle (mother's brother), they are always from another clan, so another country. Best if the uncle, aunt or cousins are close, but as long as it's connected in this way it's okay. How could I burn my mum's or sister's or father's clothes myself: no one who is in my totem group can touch those things during the ceremony. I am boss of them, but I cannot do it myself. I need my relations from that other totem or country.[9]

Ironically, in the lead-up to the establishment of the land rights law in 1976, the Land Rights Commission noted how this principle fucked with Western notions of property without negating the fact that people knew which lands belong with and to them. One can say that 'religious rites [are] owned by a clan,' but the rites 'could not be held without the assistance of the managers whose essential task it was to prepare the ritual paraphernalia, decorate the celebrants and conduct the rite.'[10] And lest readers reduce the importance of these managers to something analogous to hired labour, the Commission notes that the 'agreement of managers had to be secured for the exploitation of specialised local resources such as ochre and flint deposits and for visits by the clan owners to their own sacred sites.'[11] Rex Edmunds understands this as a strategy by which recognition is a trick severing the relations between groups in order to create hostilities across them.

Karrabing foreground the connective or joint nature of themselves and their lands as they fight against the reduction of their sense to a contractual logic which presupposes the very thing they are fighting against, the irreducibility of the sovereign subject. The contractual imaginary may be explicit, as in a monetary or compensatory debt between two subjects. It can also be affective, such as the feeling of what one owes a mother or a nation. The contractual subject can be a mass subject, such as a nation-state connected to other nation-states by treaties. And it can be an abstract person, as in a corporation. Everyone acknowledges that the realities of such sovereign bodies are messy, and hardly sealed. Human bodies leak inside out and absorb

9 Rex Edmunds and Elizabeth A. Povinelli, 'A Conversation at Bamayak and Mabaluk, Part of the Coastal Lands of the Emmiyengal People', in *Living with Ghosts: Legacies of Colonialism and Fascism, L'Internationale online*, 2019.

10 Report from the Aboriginal Land Rights Commission, 1973, p. 5.

11 Report from the Aboriginal Land Rights Commission, 1973, p. 5. See also Andrew Schaap, 'The Absurd Logic of Aboriginal Sovereignty', in Andrew Schaap (ed.) *Law and Agonistic Politics*, Farnham: Ashgate, 2009, pp. 209–25.

the outside in. State borders become distended, their organs laying on foreign grounds, as governments stretch hearings offshore. How did Australian migration enforcement end up on Christmas Island, on Nauru? How did Haitian interdiction become a maritime affair?[12] How did existential desperation result in the ideology of the political treaty? Moreover, mass subjects bear all the traces of the racial and class logics that compose the proper subject. But whichever way you look at the contractual subject, it has nothing to do with the heart of what Karrabing are saying.

12 Jeffrey Kahn, *Islands of Sovereignty: Haitian Migration and the Borders of Empire*, Chicago: University of Chicago Press, 2019.

In a video commissioned by the Art Gallery of New South Wales, Cecilia Lewis, her daughter Natasha Bigfoot Lewis, and Rex put it this way:

CL Like we have Suntu group wuliya Kiyuk and wuliya roan. They got their roan place and roan story le they roan country. We got Trevor mob. They got their own country, roan language, roan story. Bwudjut mob, they got their own story. Emmi mob got their roan story here la Mabaluk. Methnayengal got their roan story la Kugan mob. But we're still one mob. We different language group.

RE ... but we're one mob.

CL All one big family down the coast. Married family relations.

NL Because we're connected by the coastline.

RE And by those stories (ancestral paths crisscrossing countries).

This position of interdependent respect extends to the more-than-human world. In a part that didn't make it into the broadcast, Cecilia, Natasha, and Rex discuss some of the ancestral dynamics that demand human attention and commitment. Natasha notes that if Karrabing do not continue to care for ancestral lands by coming and being with them (in the concept of 'sweat') then the 'land dies; it shuts itself up.' Note the qualification of death—the divergence from a geontological understanding. Karrabing understand the 'dying' of the more-than-human world as an active withdrawing, a going under, a withholding that in turn can catastrophically transform the human world. Karrabing understand that like they themselves, *durlg* persist in an ancestrally past, frozen, but ancestral present. *Durlg* are responsive to the forces torqueing topology and ecology, now especially the pestilence of extractive consumptive capitalism.

If Karrabing must continually correct those who might unwittingly collapse their understanding of 'roan country' into the Western concept of property, they also must combat a second, perhaps stranger, evacuation of all specificity between various human and more-than-human worlds. Addressed through the imaginary of People-at-One-with-Nature, Karrabing find themselves cast into an undifferentiated sea, heard to be saying that they are connected to everything, rather than to specific multilayered territories and relations.

...

When Natasha Bigfoot Lewis noted the consequence of neglecting one's ongoing relationship with the more-than-human worlds of Karrabing lands, she referenced Karrabing's film *The Mermaids, or Aiden in Wonderland* (2018). *The Mermaids* is an exploration of Western toxic contamination, capitalism, and human and nonhuman life. Set in a land and seascape poisoned by capitalism where only Aboriginals can survive long periods outdoors, the film tells the story of a young Indigenous man, Aiden, taken away when he was just a baby to be a part of a medical experiment to save the white race. He is then released back into the world to his family. As he travels with his father and brother across the landscape, he confronts two possible futures and pasts embodied by his own tale and the timely narratives of multinational chemical and extractive industries. Natasha also knows that the contaminations of colonialism can secrete and sediment below human perceptibility. In a three-channel video work commissioned by Natasha Ginwala for the 2017 Contour Biennale, Natasha and others describe how, in making our second film, *Windjarrameru, The Stealing C*nt$* (2015), Karrabing learned that lands they had long hunted and camped were contaminated by the toxic remains of an abandoned military radio installation. The nearby *perragut* community had been informed years before, but not the members of Belyuen. As the older women, their children and grandchildren, and I sat eating our hard-won crabs and sea snails at Madpil, we—but they more than I because I didn't arrive until 1984, and then came and went—were ingesting in these coastal foods the sedimentations of toxic colonialism. Oceanic tides bring in and out these toxicities in all too predictably distributed patterns—the world poor continue to act as the kidneys of the world rich.

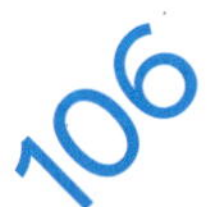

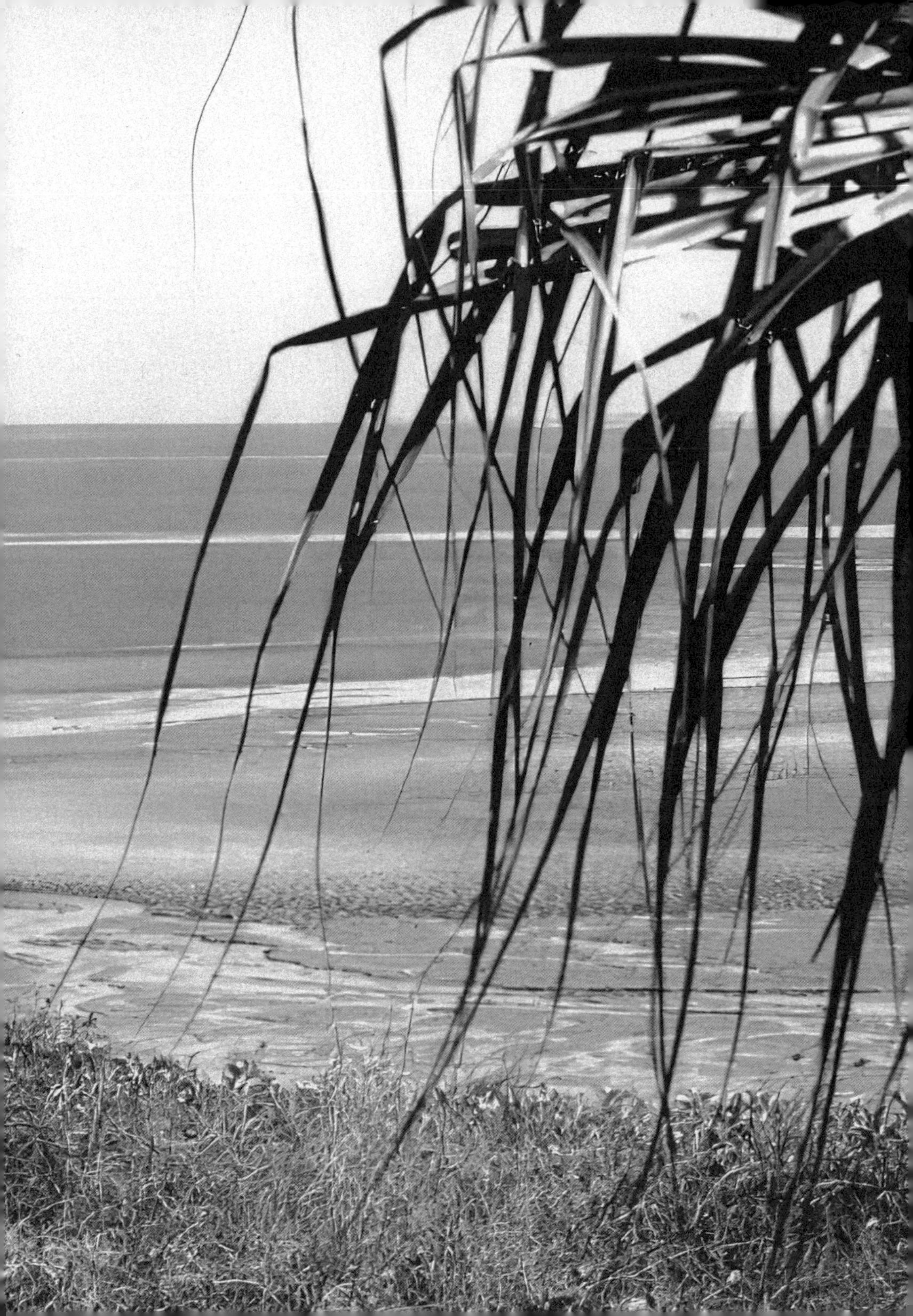

The Karrabing Film Collective: Seizing the Means of Interpretation

Vivian Ziherl

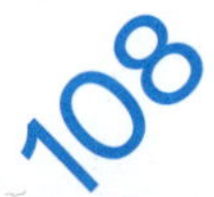

The Karrabing Film Collective is without doubt one of the most remarkable artistic forces emerging from Australia over the past decade and, from around 2015 onwards, they have been warmly received and celebrated by major institutions across the United States, Europe, the United Kingdom, Asia, and the Middle East. From museums such as the Tate Modern in London and MoMA PS1 in New York, to Biennial platforms such as the Gwangju Biennial and film festivals such as the Berlinale, their work has been celebrated for its artistic innovations and its powerful contributions to international conversations on topics such as the 'decolonial' and the 'Anthropocene'. The circulation and reception of their work however is marked by two striking and intersecting paradoxes. The first is that while Karrabing's filmmaking has been extensively engaged among international networks, it has to date been less discussed in relation to Australian art history and is quite scarcely represented among Australian collecting institutions. The second paradox dovetails with the first, in that critical engagements with Karrabing have tended to focus on the analytic concepts generated through their work, for example in notions of the 'ancestral-present', or of 'toxic liberalism'. These lexicons orient readings of the work towards greater analyses of settler-colonial and carceral power in the first instance. Close study of their image-making and *mise-en-scène* in the more conventional mode of art criticism is a comparatively less common approach.

In a sense these paradoxes are far from necessarily undesirable, given the pragmatic emergence of Karrabing's filmmaking practice as an urgently needed survival strategy amid renewed cycles of dispossession that took place in Australia from around the time of the 2007 global financial crisis and towards the tail end of over two decades of conservative federal rule that was characterised by a punitive approach to social difference.[1] It is also a tendency that I've participated in personally over the past years. This has been the case in my engagements with the Karrabing Film Collective in forums such as *e-flux journal*, as well as through the Frontier Imaginaries curatorial platform with numerous talks and commissions. In part, this has also been on account of my deep admiration for the critical writing of one Karrabing member in particular, Elizabeth A. Povinelli, who credits her written analytics back to Emmiyengal knowledge and perspectives at every turn. On the occasion of their monographic survey at the Haus der Kunst München, and with near to a decade of filmmaking to reflect upon, it is not only timely but a matter of some accountability to engage the work of Karrabing as a unique, powerful, and historically significant artistry that is worthy of study for its contribu-

1 On the punitive relation to social difference, see: Ghassan Hage, *White Nation* (1998); Aileen Moreton Robinson, *The White Possessive* (2015); and Elizabeth A. Povinelli, *The Cunning of Recognition* (2002), which charts the Native Title court case in which Karrabing members were involved among a heterogenous group of claimants.

tion not only to an anticolonial and late-capital-era *ethics* (by which I mean a study of obligation vis a vis geometries of power), but also in regard to their significant contribution to *aesthetics* (by which I mean the same, albeit studied in relation to cultural archives, art histories, and 'sense-making' practices rather than through concepts per se.)

In the following notes I will spend some time with Karrabing's indelible image-making—reflecting upon its irreverent humour, its dizzying montage overlays, its deft scripting as well as its distinctly non-romantic structures of characterisation. Among other things I hope to place these innovations among artists such as Tracy Moffatt, Vernon Ah Kee, and earlier Aboriginal art movements in painting, as well as amid broader predicaments in contemporary art in its post-1989 globalising phase. In doing so, these reflections will focus on a sequence of films produced from 2014 to 2018. It was during this time that I was intimately involved in supporting the mediation and internationalisation of Karrabing's work, including their nomination to the Visible Award in 2015, their first overseas travel to Palestine in 2016 and in commissioning their two-channel film and sculptural installation *Mermaids: Mirror Worlds* in 2018.[2]

Over this period Karrabing flourished swiftly as artists. Amid the grinding drain of the settler colony and against the terminally dispossessive function of global markets and the art-world gaze, Karrabing's cinema has—with artistic brilliance—struck out to seize the means of interpretation.

Indigenous Video and Survivance, an Australian Chapter

One of the greatest masterpieces of Australian contemporary art, let alone of video practice, is surely Vernon ah Kee's 2010 multi-channel installation *tall man*. Across four channels the video opens up the compressed time of political crisis through densely inter-cut footage sourced from an uprising that took place in 2004 in response to the death in police custody of an Aboriginal man, Mulrunji Doomadgee. The historical layers surrounding this event and its mediatised shockwaves highlight the recombinant carceral logics of Australia's psyche. Its location, for example, of Palm Island, was originally settled as a prison in which to incarcerate agents of Indigenous resistance during the transition from convict colony to settler self-rule.[3]

Ah Kee's montage drew on a cache of video assembled by lawyers who brought a case of manslaughter against a Police Officer in-

2 Co-commissioned with the Van Abbemuseum, Eindhoven; the Institute of Modern Art, Meanjin/Brisbane; and Publics Helsinki.

3 In particular, the present day state of Queensland is marked by the brutality of a piece of legislation known by shorthand as 'The Act'. Established in 1897 and on the eve of Federation, the legislation granted the state total authority over its Indigenous subjects, who were cast as wards under the authority of a state-appointed 'protector'. The full title of legislation was 'The Prohibition of the Sale of Opium and the Protection of Aborigines Act'. Under its auspices, a paternalist regime was established, forcing Indigenous people into a network of government-managed missions throughout the state, while deporting dissenting or rebellious agitators to the carceral mission of Palm Island. The conditions of deprivation on the missions were extreme and entirely recent, remaining intact to some degree through to the 1970s and 1980s.

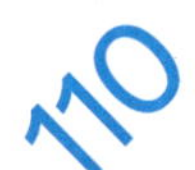

volved (murder was too ambitious a charge for the Australian courts and, in any case, the Officer was not found not guilty when medical evidence was discarded).[4] In particular the work comprised a large amount of hand-held mobile-phone footage taken during the chaotic moments of the uprising. Elsewhere political theorist Judith Butler has described the surge of video images that emerged from and propelled the 2010 Arab Spring as 'a kind of countersurveillance of military and police action', defined in relation to 'bodily action, gesture, movement, congregation, persistence, and exposure to possible violence'.[5] Butler's point here was to stress the footage as documenting not just the events of Tahrir square, but in conveying a heretofore occluded social and political possibility. What the video represented, Butler implied, was not only the protestors but their mode of resistance.

As Aboriginal historian Michael Aird reminds us, the recognition of Indigenous Australian aesthetics as contemporary art was sharply foreclosed until extremely recently. In Meanjin/Brisbane for example, up until the 1980s there had been only two places to see Indigenous art.[6] One was in the unreconstructed ethnographic displays of the local museum (unchanged from 1911–1986), while the other was in the 'Native Creations' that sold painted boomerangs, among other items, to a tourist market.[7] In 1988, the late great painter Gordon Bennett put the existential dimension of this foreclosure to canvas in his early masterpiece *The Outsider.* With incredibly deft and layered brush-strokes for one still in art school, the acrylic painting depicts Bennett standing in the famous Arles bedroom of Vincent van Gogh. Bennett, however, does not survive the interpellation. Hauntingly he is pictured brutally decapitated, a marble head fallen among Van Gogh's bedsheets while his bloodied torso merges with the 'starry night' above.

It was also in the 1980s that some of the first Indigenous students undertook and graduated from formal art training in Australia. Graduating the Queensland College of Art in 1982, a few years prior to Bennett's study at the same institution, the photographer and filmmaker Tracy Moffatt rose quickly to national attention. Her work too, was preoccupied with self-representation albeit not in painting but in photographic and moving image. Deftly grasping the libidinal work of the gaze, Moffat's feature films such as *Night Cries: A Rural Tragedy* (1990) and *beDevil* (1993) struck a stance of loving irreverence towards the camp heroines of Hollywood cinema, the cultural archives of European and American photography, as well as towards Australian art history such as the arid landscapes of Russell Drysdale.

4 Cosima Marriner, 'Calm in Palm Island after verdict', *The Sydney Morning Herald,* 21 June 2007, https://www.smh.com.au/national/calm-in-palm-island-after-verdict-20070621-gdqfks.html.

5 Judith Butler, *Notes Toward a Performative Theory of Assembly,* Cambridge: Harvard University Press, 2015, p. 75.

6 Michael Aird, 'Gordon Hookey: Another History, Another Reality,' in *Gordon Hookey: Summoning Time, Painting and Politikill Transition in MURRILAND!,* Brisbane: Griffith University, Kassel: documenta 14, Amsterdam: Frontier Imaginaries, Eindhoven: Van Abbemuseum, p. 13.

7 As Yamatji scholar Stephen Gilchrist has pointed out, this is consistent also with the South Australian Museum, which went unchanged from 1914 to 1986. Stephen Gilchrist, 'Indigenous Curation: Now and in the Future', in *Djalkiri: Yolngu Art, Collaborations and Collections,* Sydney: Sydney University Press, 2021, pp. 22–29.

Where mainstream art criticism at the time still struggled to recognise the mere possibility of an 'Aboriginal contemporary artist', Moffat was driven to locate her own psyche behind the lens, her own desires unfurling before it. One of the artists' most memorable works, *Heaven* (1997), is a tour de force of hand-held camera work and knowing eroticism. Crouching behind a car, Moffat captures clandestine views of young tanned and toned surfers, a white Australian icon of masculinity, witnessed in various stages of nakedness as they change out of clinging wetsuits.

Both Vernon ah Kee's and Tracey Moffat's Indigenous video art-making push at, splice up, and reframe modes of representation (or erasure) of Indigenous subjects in the Australian popular imaginary. Produced from the 1980s onwards, they intervene in a televisual construction of national consciousness as well as its place in greater global constructions of race. Although his practice was primarily as a painter, Gordon Bennett also produced a striking video experiment in 1994 titled *D.U.H! (Down under Homi)* (1994). In this hypnotic and looping piece, the artist dances masked and dressed in a tuxedo amid a field of static. The soundtrack to the work, Los Angeles rapper Ice T's 1993 track 'Race War', was produced in the wake of the 1992 Rodney King riots—an apogee of mediatisation and racial violence. Its lyrics include the striking internationalist call: 'Back to the facts, What about Australia? A fuckin' failure, The Aboriginal people are black, So they got jacked, You ask me about free speech and the Riots? So what's in store? I'm talkin' bout a race war.'

As many have noted, the particular political-social ferment of the riot is also foundational to Karrabing as a filmmaking praxis. Their experiments in digital media were spurred as a tactics of survival following the group's displacement in the wake of riots that took place in 2007 within the Aboriginal community of Belyuen in Australia's Top End. In a sense, these riots are the natal scene of Karrabing's video-aesthetic drive. They gave its particular conditions of necessity.

At the same time, the events of the riots point to issues of artistic composition and require a lens that is more mobile in time. By this I am referring on the one hand to the composition of Karrabing itself as a film/video-making assemblage of Emmiyengal and non-Emmiyangal, or complicatedly-Emmiyengal actors. On the other hand, I am referring to the symmetry between Karrabing's natal story and the experiences of other, earlier, Aboriginal art-making movements in Australia such as those that spurred the 'dot painting' style of Aboriginal aesthetics expressed as paint on canvas or board.

Seizing the Means of Interpretation

To start with Karrabing itself, a pre-history of the group in its current art-making formation would have to go back at least to the 1980s and to scenes in which a young American philosophy graduate was approached by Marjorie Bilbil and other Emmiyengal *wulgamen* (women elders) to help out in preparing a funding grant for a women's social centre. Obviously, this would be prefigured by scenes of white arrival to the country and its entire colonial rearrangement through occupation, devastation, and dispossession. In this case, however, the young graduate was progressively recruited into Emmiyengal resistance. Eventually the graduate would agree to become an anthropologist so as to serve in a highly significant land rights case—the Kenbi land claim—the first in the country effecting white urbanised areas.[8] The outcomes of that case would reiterate all the perversities of circular colonial logics. Many groups of people who were forcibly displaced would be judged, by settler-colonial authorities, as to whether they were authentically connected to country they'd been removed from. Through a decades-long legal battle some families would receive recognition and a certain degree of enfranchisement, while others would remain in poverty. Imposed ethnographic division would fuel social disharmony. And by the time of a renewed crackdown in policing and dispossession in 2007 the situation would be set to erupt. When it did, members of a particular Emmiyengal family group fled the violence, attempting to maintain jobs, social-security arrangements, and schooling for children while camping in tents outside of the township.

Karrabing was born as a means of survival amid these grim circumstances. Its first incarnation took form as a 'geo-tagging' GPS (global satellite positioning) project. The maintenance of ancestral knowledge and sites was, as ever, entwined in efforts to raise material and financial support—to hold a world together. Famously, the idea to expand the project into filmmaking came at the end of a particularly exasperating day at the edifices of Australian bureaucracy and its economies of denial. Returning to camp having failed to overcome dizzying and overlapping hurdles, one Karrabing member Linda Yarrowin looked at the others gathered and said in effect; 'they should make a film of this, no-one would believe us what we have to deal with.'

Some years later their first feature, *When the Dogs Talked* (2014) achieved exactly this. Its plot centred on a central character—Cecilia Lewis—who one day goes missing having reached her limits with the over-crowding and socio-economic impossibilities of township life. Shortly thereafter, the Department of Social Services comes knock-

8 A particularly striking scene from the court hearings of the Kenbi land claim became the focus of a notable early essay by Elizabeth A. Povinelli that questioned the capacity of the Australian legal system to recognise Indigenous land rights along with the strain that this places on Indigenous communities to render themselves legible within them. Elizabeth A. Povinelli 'Do Rocks Listen? The Cultural Politics of Apprehending Australian Aboriginal Labour', *American Anthropologist*, New Series, vol. 97, no. 3, Sep 1995, pp. 505–18.

ing and an intergenerational group of Karrabing members must try to find Lewis or face eviction. As they branch out in search parties, however, young Karrabing members also confront their place amid Emmiyengal and settler worlds. Under unremitting pressure by authorities to enter into 'mainstream' economic relations, they are challenged as to whether they still 'believe' the Dingo-dog dreaming that inscribes a series of large holes at a particular site into law and inheritance structures.

The film is an early masterpiece by the group. It deftly frames enormous social and existential questions amid the backdrop of crowded car-rides, failing mobile phone reception, red-dust roads, tidal inlets, and the brutally sterile curbsides of suburbia. Contemporary Indigenous film and TV-makers such as Rachel Perkins and Warwick Thornton have also captured these settings for the stark contrast and sheer scales that they command. Their respective seasons of the *Mystery Road* TV series are a monument in Australian screen culture, auguring in a new era of confidence in storytelling out of the shadows of the heroic 1970s wave such as directors Peter Wier and Fred Schepsi, who plumbed the anxious colonial psyche of Australian identity, and the 1990s cinema aftermath which clung to camp, comedy, and the 'little guy' in much loved films such as *Strictly Ballroom* (1992), *Priscilla Queen of the Desert* (1994), *Muriel's Wedding* (1995), and *The Castle* (1997).

In the hands of Karrabing, scenes of an Australian Indigenous 'everyday' become the raw material of a challenge to the basic scripts of official social life. The stilted professional tone of the departmental social workers' 'Who lives here?' finds its true weight and scope as a mother asks her child 'You believe that?'. The mother, Cecilia Lewis, is referring to her dog Dreaming story and the distant and uncertain stare in response is a haunting, indelible image. It's an image that is for no white filmmaker to capture in the current time, and yet it speaks to the paradoxes with which the greater nation grapples. To become something else or not. To acknowledge genuine title, or to double-down on half measures.

Certain aspects in the style of *When the Dogs Talk* would be fleeting, while others would go on to shape Karrabing's future work. Already, at this early stage, the film features a collaborative script-writing structure that has since been dubbed 'improvisational realism'. In this methodology Karrabing members introduce character and plot ideas, usually based in real-life experience, and adapt narrative structures around each other and the circumstances that they encounter. Dialogue is then developed as the films are shot yielding a phrasing,

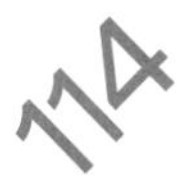

immediacy, and a sense of comic timing that would be beyond the reach of even a finely trained and drilled cast.

In one scene from *Wutharr: Saltwater* Dreams (2016), a Karrabing Member Sandra Yarrowin tries to figure out how to fill in a form, in response to a $30,000 fine for setting off a flare without proper safety equipment. In the film this incident drives the narrative, having occurred during a motor-boat breakdown far from shore and when a passerby fisherman refused to offer water or help. 'What does this say, Gigi?' Yarrowin asks, 'When event occurred, where you ... what's that word? ...' Another member leans over: 'It says, when event occurred where you "alien juris"? Yes or no. You two?.' The camera pans across to a backyard shed with a mix of male members. 'No!' says a chorus, before pausing, and then again in chorus, 'Yes ... yes,' before another pause as members glance left and right.

As a script-making device, Karrabing's collectivised methodology also produces frequent and incisive articulations of the political-symbolic meta-structures faced by Karrabing. And it is often these that have been so noted within critical and scholarly discussions. A good example comes in the detourned suspense thriller/stake-out drama of *Windjarrameru, Stealing C*nt$* (2015), the follow-up to *When the Dogs Talked.* The film plays on the formation of dispossession from an Indigenous Australian perspective, and stages a drama in which a group of young boys is chased by police when they uncover and make off with a stash of beers hidden in the bush by illegal miners who are, no less, endangering a sacred site. Fleeing from police pursuit, the boys find refuge in an area of radioactive contamination. Having finished off the beers, they turn to reflections on their predicament and share stories of incarceration; one drawing a map of the local prison in sand for the others. When a car parks nearby some among the boys are anxious and flighty, tempted to run. One of the hide-outs, Kelvin Bigfoot, however, reassures them: 'It's ok, we're safe here. We're inside this radiation area. Police won't come in here. We're safe.'

Character and Narrative Causality

Compared with their mutual script-writing however, some areas of Karrabing's filmmaking shifted markedly from the impressive opening salvo of *When the Dogs Talked.* In particular, their structures of characterisation and narrative drive transformed swiftly and in tandem with new filming techniques based upon hand-held devices. *When the Dogs Talked* was produced with the help of an external producer/director who had brought an industry-based system of planned camera shots and narrative framing. As a result, the film is anchored quite closely in two particular characters—Cecilia Lewis (the mother) and Telish Binanmu (her daughter). Between them we are invited to explore psychological depth in the romantic narrative mode, and in psychoanalytic typologies of parent/infant subject formation.

Very quickly however, this structure dissolved. Karrabing took over the role of director and camera operators, directors of photography, et cetera, which was enabled also through a shift from expensive high-end camera equipment to the use of mobile phones. Whatever 'loss in image quality' this created was amply made up for in far greater fidelity to Karrabing's storytelling modalities. This trajectory culminated in the group's third major film, *Wutharr, Saltwater Dreams*—an absolute triumph of narrative layering and multi-focal critique. In a truly precise diagram of social power enviable by Foucault, Agamben, or any of the great post-structuralist critics, the film posits its protagonists between three overlapping regimes of governance: the moral system of Judeo-Christian values that underpins the juridical structures of settler society; the capitalist system of material extraction and deprivation that determines mere possibility; and finally, the geo-ancestral system of obligation to which Karrabing are also fundamentally bound.

Among these dense layers, Karrabing members are captured struggling through conditions of staggering incommensurability. It is also in this film, *Wutharr,* that Karrabing developed a unique style of colour-saturated montage. Through its hallucinogenic layers totemic animals and deceased relatives appear in the present-day. At the time I referred to this style as a kind of critical psychedelic.[9] By this I meant a visual form that could convey the dizzying gaps between official court record or market presupposition and the realities of Emmiyengal life. The style strikes a strong resemblance to certain scenes in the television satire *Atlanta*, where, for example, a character will suddenly and surreally be flung into the air by a car that is heard but that does not appear anywhere on screen. These disorienting disjunctions convey the gaps between official worlds and Emmiyengal realities, or the racialised experiences of debt and unemployment in the case of Atlanta.

Common between these styles is a storytelling structure in which character, narrative, and causality have become recombinant. Characters no longer drive narrative through their conscious, or perhaps unconscious desires. Instead mysterious forces intervene, throwing things off course. And in the case of Karrabing, character is altogeth-

9 Vivian Ziherl, 'Karrabing Film Collective 'Wutharr: Saltwater Dreams', *Vdrome,* https://www.vdrome.org/karrabing-film-collective-wutharr-saltwater-dreams.

er more spectrally defined. In the late 1980s the irreverent, gay American anthropologist Eric Michaels undertook research into the popularity of VCR technology and viewing among Warlpiri communities some ways south of Belyuen. Working together with Leonard *Japanangka* Granites, the research confirmed the overwhelming take-up of video screenings and remarked: 'Of all the introduced Western technologies, only rifles and four-wheel drive Toyotas have achieved such acceptance.'[10]

Delving further into the types of video cassettes being consumed, the study found that Hollywood genre film was particularly popular along with serialised TV programs such as *The A-Team*. As well as being focused on a Black hero, in the case of the latter, Michaels argued that this genre-based narrative is compatible with Warlpiri storytelling in which 'personal motivation is unusual ... characters do things because the class (kin, animal, plant) of which they are members is known to behave in this way.'[11] The classical structuring of plot points around impasses or events of adversity is also affected by these logics: 'It (character exposition) is more likely in Aboriginal accounts to be supplied by what we would consider supernatural reasons, consistent with the reasons misfortunes befall people in Aboriginal cosmology.'[12]

Thus, in *Wutharr*, when the motor-boat disastrously breaks down and sets off a chain of events culminating in an unpayable fine, there are multiple explanations. For Linda Yarrowin, the group is being punished by Jesus for having gone astray from their pious and self-improving devotion. For Trevor Bianamu, the breakdown was caused by jealous ancestors whose country and rites had been left unobserved. For Rex Edmunds, the failure was a case of rusty wiring, and the lack of expensive mechanical parts. Each causality suggested a different, disciplining regime of power. In later films and commencing from *The Jealous One* (2017), Karrabing would increasingly structure their narratives through ancestral layers. In that film, the story of a jealous sea-monster and a hawk is combined with the mundane events of two family members holding those totems. From these early works forward, Karrabing's seizure of the means of script-making has thus flowed together with a recomposition—or what Denise Ferreira da Silva would call a de-re-composition—of modes of character and causality.[13] It is a formation that contrasts the exterior event as driver of psychological interiority, with enmeshed and temporally interconnected layers of character by type and territorial site. Either mode says much about who or what a subject is, and of how they are to relate to the world around them.

10 Eric Michaels, 'Hollywood Iconography: A Warlpiri Reading', in *Bad Aboriginal Art: Tradition, Media and Technological Horizons*, Minneapolis: Minnesota Press, 1993, p. 90.

11 Ibid, p. 91.

12 Ibid, p. 91.

13 Denise Ferreira da Silva, 'The Racial Event or, That Which Happens Without Time', in *The Two-Sided Lake: Scenarios, Storyboards and Sets from Liverpool Biennial 2016*, Rosie Cooper, Sandeep Parmar, and Dominic Willsdon (eds.), Liverpool: Liverpool University Press 2016, p. 247.

Untraditional Media

It is hard to estimate exactly how influential or widely received Karrabing are, let alone exactly what their international impact means in the context of Australia. In the most mundane sense, the many commissions and prizes have meant an influx of real and much needed economic resources, and to be fair, national and state funding bodies in Australia have contributed generously to the production of new work. This work has less often stayed in the country, however. In their reception Karabing are, as I've mentioned, something of a paradox. In 2021 I reached out to Povinelli to alert her that Karrabing had been rated #8 in *Art Review* magazine's much watched annual 'Power 100'. Jokingly I suggested that gallerist David Zwirner, placed at #23, might have a spare BMW to send them in honor of the achievement.

To conclude then, in reflection on the place of Karrabing in Australian art history it is worthwhile revisiting a topic that has been defining of twentieth-century Euro-American art history more broadly: that of 'medium specificity'. Much ink has been spilled on the topic, especially in the pages of the American journal *October*.[14] In short, the idea is that each European art 'medium' has its own set of parameters that define the potential meaning and significance of any given artwork. Whereby painting is concerned with pigment and representation relative to flatness, and sculpture is concerned with phenomenologies of space and bodily perception. Unsurprisingly, this theory was adopted in the wake of formalist movements and Minimalism in particular.

How, then, to come to terms with such 'medium' specificity at the interface of the inscription of Indigenous aesthetics into European or modern media? Here, the video-making of Karrabing bears striking resemblance not as much to other Indigenous filmmaking such as by the urban-based artists Vernon Ah Kee and Tracy Moffat. Rather, there is an uncanny echo with earlier twentieth-century Indigenous art movements that forged a path into the European ur-medium of painting.

Specifically, I have in mind the 1950s to 1970s Papunya Tula movement which is broadly considered a watershed of 'traditional' Indigenous art styles in Australia. It is certain that in terms of market value the Papunya Tula movement changed the shape of Indigenous art with a striking sequence of resale auctions through the 1990s and early 2000s. In these celebrity events, works that had been bought in and nearby the Central Desert community for prices of around $60–220 sold at prices that the artist Richard Bell remarked 'look like telephone numbers'.[15] This rocketing market culminated in 2007 with the

14 The book-length essay 'Journey on the North Sea' published in 2000 by Rosalind Krauss culminated this tendency. Rosalind Krauss, *A Voyage on the North Sea: Art in the Age of thePost-Medium Condition*, London: Thames & Hudson, 2000.

15 Richard Bell, 2002, 'Aboriginal Art: It's a White Thing!', http://www.kooriweb.org/foley/great/art/bell.html.

sale of Clifford Possum Tjapaltjarri's *Warlugulong* (1977) for $2.4 million. Meanwhile none of the benefits of this market adjustment returned to the artists who produced work from and remained in impoverished conditions and ongoing cycles of dispossession.

The Papunya Tula painters, for example, had been forced off their lands in the 1950s by a combination of policies of assimilation and traditional water springs being interrupted by pastoralists boring new wells during a drought.[16] It was in the context of the reserve school that a group of senior men began experimenting in transferring images usually ceremonially inscribed on bodies or in sand into paint on board. In hindsight, it should not be possible to look at the appearance of Aboriginal art as paint and canvas without bearing in mind the assimilationist period that it arose through and the acts of survival that it inscribes.

There is a striking symmetry between the story of Papunya Tula painting and Karrabing video. Whereas the Papunya Tula artists had been forced off their lands and onto a reserve however, the art of Karrabing emerged when they were forced again off a former mission and back onto traditional country that was by then fenced off, contaminated, and heavily exploited. The innovation of Karrabing's Emmiyengal aesthetics into video bears a resemblance of Papunya Tula's innovation of Pintupi, Luritja, Walpiri, Arrernte, and Anmatyerre aesthetics into paint. Neither can be fully grasped without substantively challenging the assumptions of a western art history and its presuppositions of the art-making or art-viewing subject. This impasse crosses both visual and narrative dimensions. Narrative, we can be reminded, was the great bugaboo of the formalists and advocates of the medium specificity approach.

Karrabing's work accordingly sits somewhere astride Australian Indigenous image-making practices that have often been considered connected and yet distinct; between urban-based image-making in technologically based media and remote or non-urban based image-making in paint. Their work troubles the ethnographic lenses by which these practices have often been separated, and which artist Richard Bell for example vehemently opposed in his classic 2001 critique 'Bell's Theorem'.[17] In doing so, their work points back towards much more attentive and sophisticated approaches towards Indigenous aesthetics—both in terms of the powerful insights that they entail politically as well as in appreciation of what are inadmissibly significant, brilliant, and historically remarkable image-making practices.

16 Here I'm referring to the case of the Papunya Tula movement in particular, where a body of small painted panels were created in the former Western Desert mission settlement of Papunya in 1971–72. The art movement was inseparable from a real movement of Pintupi, Luritja, Walpiri, Arrernte, and Anmatyerre peoples from their lands to a government managed settlement. There, a school teacher at the community encouraged the painting of images in the style of body and sand painting used in ceremony. A detailed history of this art movement and its political circumstances can be found in Vivian Johnson's *Once Upon a Time in Papunya* (2010).

17 Richard Bell 2002.

Porous Jurisdictions: Sacrifice Zones and Environmental Law in the Northern Territory of Australia

Kirsty Howey

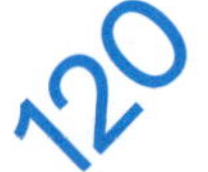

Introduction: A Special Mine

In March this year, I went hunting for a new lithium mine on Karrabing country. Pegmatite, the hard white rock where the mineral is typically found in Australia, is seen in rocky outcrops throughout the region. It has been targeted before by prospectors for its embedded quantities of mica, tin, and tantalum, albeit without great commercial success. Yet pegmatite's value has recently skyrocketed. The lithium it contains is in demand for the batteries needed for the necessary energy transition from fossil fuels to renewables. The mining company has blanketed much of the region—around five hundred square kilometres—in exploration tenements in anticipation of the promised green economic bonanza. The company also announced a deal with Tesla, one of the most valuable companies in the world. Its share price skyrocketed. It is, according to its boosters, a special mine, sorely needed by society to confront and transcend the climate crisis.

Given the esteem in which it was held and its lofty corporate connections, I felt that the mine should have been easier to locate. As I drove along the Cox Peninsula Road, about an hour's drive from the Northern Territory's capital Darwin, the savanna bushland on either side all looked the same to me. When I searched for the mine on Apple maps, it didn't show up. Using GPS coordinates, I eventually found it. There was no sign, just a dirt track from the bitumen highway. A chain across the gate indicated I couldn't go any further without risking prosecution. I got out of my air-conditioned four-wheel-drive and felt the furnace of late wet season heat and humidity assault me. I could hear bulldozers close by, but the Eucalypt forest with its grassy understory shielded me from what was going on. Defeated, I returned home to Darwin.

Zombie Mines

While my attempts to visit in person had failed, I did in fact know this mine. It was made legible to me via the hundreds of pages of environmental assessment documentation that accompanied the mining company's application for regulatory approval under applicable environmental and mining laws. As I pored over the paperwork, the infrastructure and its impacts were immediately familiar to me from my work on the impacts of other environmentally disastrous mines in the Northern Territory. There was a waste rock dump, a tailings storage facility, storage ponds for wastewater, and an open pit. Reading further, I discovered some common red flags: limited baseline studies, the drawdown of the local aquifer to dewater the mining pit, the pollution of local waterways by mine waste, among other possible impacts.

The most concerning risk was perhaps acid and metalliferous drainage. A common problem in mines in the tropics, this process is caused by the 'weathering' of mine waste by natural processes. The quotidian essentials for life on earth—water and air—are the agents by which acid mine drainage takes hold. The oxidation of metal sulphides in waste rock dumps, pits, and tailings storage dams, primarily caused by infiltration of rainwater, converts sulphides into sulfuric acid and iron oxy-hydroxide and creates intense heat. Thus converted, the water-turned-acid can dissolve heavy metals and salts, creating a toxic chemistry for living things.[1] Acid mine drainage is characterised by its slow emergence, incremental movement, and longevity, seeping into soil and water systems for millennia when it is uncontained. The true extent of acid mine drainage may not become evident until well after ore reserves are depleted, and mines closed and rehabilitated. Such a revelation would represent a perverse kind of best-case scenario, with unplanned abandonment of mine sites the earlier occurring norm. These dormant legacies are 'zombie mines',[2] technically deceased but still possessing lethal capacities. One way to mitigate the risk of acid mine drainage after closure of a mine is to ensure that mining infrastructure—the main source of such contamination—is rehabilitated to the maximum extent possible. As a matter of good mining practice, this generally involves 'backfilling' the open pit with the waste rock dump and whatever toxins remain in the tailings storage facility, to reduce the surface footprint of potentially toxic infrastructure. However, in the case of the lithium mine on Karrabing Country, this mining infrastructure would remain in the landscape permanently, including an evocatively described 'open pit lake'. Such an approach usually increases, rather than mitigates, the risk of acid mine drainage. It is especially problematic in a region prone to cyclones, predicted to become more intense as the world warms. It is an antiquated approach to mine closure that nonetheless still prevails in the Northern Territory, with toxic impacts on waterways from legacy and currently operating mines the norm rather than the exception.

1 Gavin Mudd, 'The McArthur River Project: The Environmental Case for Complete Pit Backfil', 2016, https://www.mpi.org.au/2016/08/the-mcarthur-river-project-theenvironmental-case-for-complete-pit-backfill.

2 John Sandlos, and Arn Keeling, 'Zombie Mines and the (Over)burden of History', *Solutions Journal*, 3(3), 2013, pp. 80–83.

Environmental Law and Slow Violence

Despite these evident failings, the mine was duly authorised by the regulators under relevant Northern Territory laws. An acid mine drain-

age management plan should be developed by the mine at a later date, said the regulator, which would involve careful monitoring of the site. The problem could, and would, be contained.

That industrial actors (including governments and mining companies) have difficulty dealing with such insidious toxicities as acid mine drainage across vast scales of time and space is well-recognised. Scott Nixon[3] has revealed the incremental 'slow violence' of events with disastrous environmental, social, and ethical impacts including the Bhopal chemical explosion in India, the damning of India's Narmada River, and the Chernobyl meltdown. But the violence caused by these spectacular disasters is 'not confined to the immediate time-space of the event itself. Rather, the effects slowly reverberate across affected spaces and populations.'[4] Slow violence thus 'occurs gradually and out of sight, a violence of delayed destruction that is dispersed across time and space, an attritional violence that is typically not viewed as violence at all.'[5] These drawn-out impacts are often invisible because they lack the explosive immediacy of typical public configurations of disaster, and they are structurally hidden through regimes of imperceptibility.[6] They are also racialised, acting unevenly to 'disproportionately jeopardise the livelihoods, prospects, and memory banks of the global poor.'[7]

My contention here is that the ostensibly rational, technical, uncontroversial, and mundane workings of 'legal jurisdiction' are one key regime of imperceptibility whereby law provides the structures to facilitate slow violence. Jurisdiction is a 'hidden architecture' that is nonetheless the 'organising principle behind the distribution of state power'.[8] It bestows legal authority on the state and its institutions (be they courts, the parliament, the executive, or other entities) to judge or act in a defined field of responsibility: that is, it also sets the limits of that legal authority. While the assertion of sovereignty by the settler state has been the focus of analysis of the foundation of the doctrine of native title, Dorsett and McVeigh suggest it is jurisdiction that was the primary legal technology used by the settler state to 'supplant other sites of adjudication and authority', including those founded in Indigenous law and custom.[9]

The laws that govern acid mine drainage, for example, shape its possible pathways through time and space. While ostensibly directed towards containing the creation of toxic wastes and safeguarding against environmental impacts of mining, they in fact do the opposite. As de Sousa Santos has pointed out, while the law gives the impression of universal application, this is a distortion. We in fact 'live in a time of porous legality or of legal porosity, of multiple networks of

3 Rob Nixon, *Slow Violence and the Environmentalism of the Poor*, Cambridge, MA: Harvard University Press, 2011.

4 Ben Anderson, Kevin Grove, Lauren Rickards, and Matthew Kearnes, 'Slow emergencies: Temporality and the racialized biopolitics of emergency governance', *Progress in Human Geography*, 41(4), 2019, pp. 524–33.

5 Rob Nixon 2011, p. 2.

6 Michelle Murphy, *Sick building syndrome and the problem of uncertainty: environmental politics, technoscience, and women workers*, Durham, NC: Duke University Press, 2006.

7 Nixon 2011, p. 5.

8 Jeffrey Kahn, 'Geographies of Discretion and the Jurisdictional Imagination', *PoLAR: Political and Legal Anthropology Review*, 40(1), 2017, pp. 5–27.

9 Shaunnagh Dorsett and Shaun McVeigh, 'Conduct of laws: native title, responsibility, and some limits of jurisdictional thinking', *Melbourne University Law Review*, 36(2), 2012, pp. 470–93.

legal orders forcing us to constant transitions and trespassings'.[10] The trick of law is to make incommensurate legal orders, 'each of which has its own scope, its own logic and its own criteria for what is to be governed, as well as rules for how to govern' seem to 'coexist without a great deal of overt conflict'.[11] It is jurisdiction which performs this classificatory magic, sorting different and often contradictory governance regimes into separable categories, including the what, where, when, and who of governance.[12]

Timescapes of Environmental Law in the Northern Territory

There is a bias in environmental law towards a very specific temporal juncture: when authorisation of a project looms. A combination of different legal jurisdictions interlock during this window in time: the grant of mineral titles under the Mineral Titles Act, the environmental impact assessment of the mine under the Northern Territory's Environment Protection Act and its federal counterpart the Environment Protection and Biodiversity Conservation Act, the approval of mining management plans and authorisations under the Mining Management Act, waste discharges under the Water Act, and the grant of authority certificates regulating access to sacred sites under the Northern Territory Sacred Sites Act (NT). Land rights and native title regimes also box Indigenous people into the dominant temporality of project approval. Agreements struck under the Land Rights Act and Native Title Act authorise the grant of mineral titles, typically granted as part of the regulatory architecture of project authorisation and negotiated before projects begin. Project approval is also when public access to otherwise opaque environmental and scientific data produced by miners is required by the legislation, largely via the environmental assessment process. Public and media attention is thus skewed towards the time of project authorisation, largely because that is when they might know some of what is going on. Finally, a range of other private legal contractual arrangements, usually conditional upon regulatory approvals being obtained, attach to the regulatory approvals described above—for instance, finance and security agreements to build capital infrastructure, and off-take agreements through which prospective miners agree with prospective buyers to purchase yet-to-be-mined commodities.

There is thus a cluster of legal, political, and institutional arrangements that concentrate pressure on project approvals triggered

10 Boaventura De Sousa Santos, 'Law: A Map of Misreading: Toward a Postmodern Conception of Law', *Journal of Law and Society*, 14(3), 1987, pp. 279–302, p. 298.

11 Mariana Valverde, 'Jurisdiction and Scale: Legal "Technicalities" as Resources for Theory', *Social & Legal Studies*, 18(2), 2009, pp. 139–57, p. 141.

12 Ibid., pp. 144–45.

by mining companies. This period can vary, from a few months to many years. Of course, this period seems lengthy, particularly to governments who are bound by three to four year political cycles and companies captured by a capitalist conception of time as money, where 'speed becomes a competitive advantage, as the faster an activity can be produced, traded, and consumed, the shorter the period in which an economic resource is tied up'.[13] Yet, compared to other timescapes, not least of which is the latency of the projected impacts of the mine, it is a short period. According to environmental law scholar Benjamin Richardson, environmental regulation has 'become a victim of the cult of speed as pressure from political and business elites intensifies to quicken licensing decisions, environmental assessments, and other procedures that may delay economic development'.[14]

Mining executives, politicians, bureaucrats, scientists, bankers, lawyers, even the media, are complicit in this time compression, their expertise and attention front-ended via ostensibly separate yet overlapping legal jurisdictions. The law produces the sense that these are the moments that really matter, and they do matter, in the sense that this is when projects with the potential for unleashing environmental destruction are given the tick. But the weighting is deceptive. Outside of these periods, the mine and its impacts go on, unconstrained by the same legal timetable over which the public and other players fret.

Permable Pathways and Trespassing Toxicities

So, what laws do apply after the time of project approval, both during the mine's operations and post-closure?

The laws regulating environmental pollution from mine sites in the Northern Territory make a crucial spatial distinction. On the mine site (that is, within the mining lease), a government department called the Department of Industry, Tourism and Trade (DITT) has almost exclusive regulatory jurisdiction. The Waste Management Pollution Control Act, the principal Northern Territory legislation regulating industry and individuals who conduct potentially polluting activities, does not apply to contamination caused by mining activities that is confined to a mine site. Similarly, the general criminal prohibition on polluting a waterway is carved out from the Water Act if the contamination is confined to the mine site. There is one key exception to DITT's exclu-

13 Benjamin Richardson, *Time and Environmental Law: Telling Nature's Time*, Cambridge: Cambridge University Press, 2017, p. 38.

14 Ibid., p. 285.

sive regulatory jurisdiction on the site: the mine has a waste discharge licence issued by the Controller of Water Resources under the Water Act which permits the mine to discharge mine-derived contaminants into the river at times of high flow.

Within DITT's on-site regulatory jurisdiction, the Mining Management Act permits pollution on the mine site as long as it is done in accordance with approved documentation. Yet the environmental protection obligations in this legislation are qualified. Mining management plans must only 'as far as practicable' operate effectively in protecting the environment. Compliance with them protects mining operators against polluting activities that might otherwise constitute offences under the legislation. For example, the general offence in the Mining Management Act against releasing waste or contaminants on or off mining sites is neutralised as long as the operator complies with its plan. Thus, on the mine site operators have wide parameters as long as mining management plans are complied with. This is a jurisdiction of discretion, where whatever the government department decides is acceptable, based on mining company advice, becomes what is legally enforceable.

To pull out from the technical detail, the key point is that environmental impacts are temporally contained (that is, for now) and spatially confined to the mine site. The materialities of groundwater and surface water systems, and their connectivities, of course make a mockery of this neat legal spatial and temporal partition. Acid mine drainage gains uneven traction across a huge timescale, facilitated by the perfect carrier that itself defies fixity: water. Its impacts are often hidden or delayed, as water systems are slowly infiltrated. Nor are these water systems comprehensively understood. Surface water systems in the wet season and groundwater systems all year round are the pathways by which mine contaminants are potentially transported.

However, as Ballestero notes, aquifers are not closed tanks or containers, but more like sponges, collapsing rock, water and air, and facilitating oozing water flows and seeping migrations.[15] The technical definition of aquifer is, quite literally, a saturated rock or sediment that is also sufficiently permeable to transmit water elsewhere. Aquifers are movement, in a ceaseless push and pull in different directions.[16] There are recognised knowledge gaps about potential and actual connections between groundwater aquifers and surface water in the region. Data on groundwater and surface water connectivity is deficient. There may be other watery connections occurring underground and linking up in unknown ways that provide a path-

15 Andrea Ballestero, 'Living with Aquifers', *e-flux journal,* 2019, https://www.e-flux.com/architecture/liquid-utility/259651/living-with-aquifers.

16 Ibid.

way for contaminants far from the current monitoring points and far into the future. Aquifers transgress spatial, temporal, and legal boundaries, their 'overflowing borders challeng[ing] any seamless infrastructuralization'.[17]

An array of checks and balances has been approved to assess, monitor, and ideally prevent these eventualities. However, such measures can only work if they are actively implemented. Problems in enforcing environmental monitoring and compliance are not limited to the Northern Territory, nor even Australia. This has long been recognised globally in the context of environmental law.[18] Slippage between environmental 'regulatory standards and the actual conduct of regulated parties is far from being a peripheral element of the legal regime'.[19] A lack of environmental monitoring, compliance, and enforcement post-approval, when the project is on foot, is thus not a kink in the system, but a core feature. It is what allows mining to be a lawful pollution machine. While the scrutiny of multiple intersecting laws rains down during the temporal window of project approvals, the legal screws are taken off for the duration of a project's operations. The law is there but has little purchase.

The management systems and oversight mechanisms deployed to manage the mine's impacts—even if effective—have their own bounded temporality, that of the project's operating phase. The legal situation is more dire post-closure. Many possible impacts may not occur until after the mine is technically closed and rehabilitated. Acid mine drainage may not manifest for centuries, far away from the mine site.

What happens then? The law may provide some recourse via the retrospective gaze of compensation for environmental and property damage, but if the mine is abandoned then who will be prosecuted for contamination offences? Post-closure, and post-abandonment, the law peters out.

Conclusion – bracketed

In writing about the forms of existence that are sacrificed by settler colonialism's progress towards its own ever-shifting horizon, Elizabeth Povinelli notes that it is 'the black and brown bodies, the subaltern and the indigenous, interned in the brackets of recognition' that are thrown overboard.[20] What do the technical manoeuvres of legal jurisdiction tell us about these brackets?

As mentioned above, when it comes to mines on their country, Indigenous people are boxed into a particular spacetime configuration.

17 Ibid.

18 Leonard Ortolano and Anne Shepherd, 'Environmental impact assessment: challenges and opportunities', *Impact Assess*, 13(3), 1995, pp. 3–30,

19 Daniel Farber, 'Taking Slippage Seriously: Noncompliance and Creative Compliance in Environmental Law', *Harvard Enviornmental Law Review*, 23, 1999, pp. 297–325, p. 298.

20 Elizabeth Povinelli, ' Horizons, Frontiers, Late Liberal Territoriality, and Toxic Habitats', *e-flux journal*, 2018, https://www.e-flux.com/journal/90/191186/horizons-andfrontiers-late-liberal-territoriality-and-toxic-habitats.

This is the land rights or native title agreement, which gives them the ability, in certain defined circumstances, to negotiate a deal with the mining company. The furious activity of deal-making is temporally constrained to the time of project approval, as are a range of other environmental approvals. For the crucial temporality of the project itself, when the potential for environmental catastrophe is greatest, the law loiters safely within latent discretionary jurisdictions.

By comparison, the state has all the time in the world: 'apart from its apparent benevolence, its other weapon is to wait'.[21] Once the lithium deposits on Karrabing Country were discovered, the state sprung into action with a prefabricated interlocking set of legal jurisdictions and confected urgency to facilitate the required transaction(s) and give the appearance of genuine regulatory scrutiny and risk assessment. Individually, each piece of legislation looks cogent and fit for purpose. This law for protecting water, this one for waste, this one for mining. Analysed together, and considering the unpredictable seeping materialities of acid mine drainage through time and space, they are actually permeable pathways for contamination. The game of legal jurisdiction is expertly navigated by the corporations and the state to dispossess and disempower Indigenous people in favour of extractive imperatives with poisonous consequences, all the while retaining the sheen of objective apolitical legality. Understanding the spatiotemporal machinery of jurisdiction thus moves us towards an understanding of the how of slow violence, and law's role in it. As it turns out, despite the bold assertions that this mine is different due to its vital role in the energy transition, the lithium mine on Karrabing Country is in fact a clone, a sacrifice zone created in part by the environmental laws meant to make it safe.

21 Arundhati Roy, 'The algebra of infinite justice', *The Progressive*, 65(12), 2001, pp. 28–30.

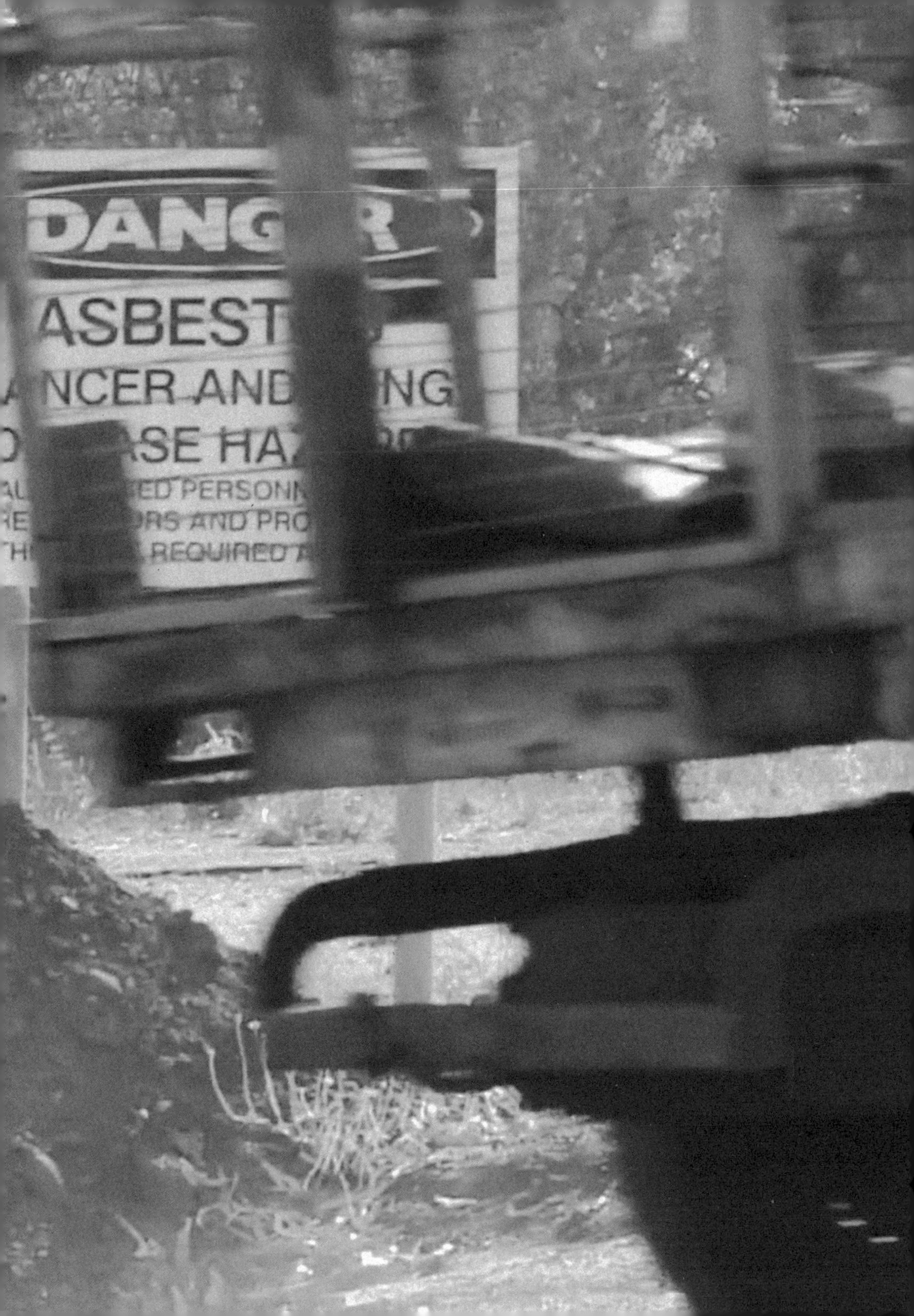
DANG
ASBEST
NCER AND ING
SE HA
ED PERSONN
ORS AND PRO
REQUIRED A

Bell's Theorem: ABORIGINAL ART – It's a White Thing![1]

Richard Bell

1 This text was originally published in November 2002 on the webpage of Richard Bell, found at http://www.kooriweb.org/foley/great/art/bell.html.

This paper has been written to articulate some thoughts on this subject that may not yet be in the public domain. I am the primary source for most of the information gathered (often through personal experience or discussions with numerous people).

I must say here that I am not an academic. Consequently, the style and tone of delivery will chop and change. It will be conversational, playful, serious, tongue-in-cheek, moralistic, tolerant, sermonistic, and informative.

Aboriginal art has become a product of the times. A commodity. The result of a concerted and sustained marketing strategy, albeit one that has been loose and uncoordinated.

There is no Aboriginal art industry. There is, however, an industry that caters for Aboriginal art. The key players in that industry are not Aboriginal. They are mostly white people whose areas of expertise are in the fields of anthropology and 'Western art'.

It will be shown here how key issues interrelate to produce the phenomenon called Aboriginal art and how those issues conspire to condemn it to non-Aboriginal control.

Western Art: Its Effect

During the last century and a quarter Western art has evolved into an elaborate, sophisticated, and complex system. This system supplies venues (museums, galleries, et cetera) teaching facilities (art education institutions, drawing classes, et cetera). and referees (art critics) and offers huge rewards for the chosen few elite players in the game (including artists, curators, art critics, art dealers, and even patrons). This arrangement is not dissimilar to modern spectator sports. It is also not unlike ancient religions—substitute gods, sacrificial offerings, high priests, et cetera.

Like some voracious ancient god, Western art devours all offerings at will. Sometimes the digestion will be slow and painful. However, it is resilient and will inexorably continue on its pre-ordained path that is to analyse and pigeonhole everything.

Western art is the product of Western Europeans and their colonial offspring. It imposes and perpetuates superiority over art produced in other parts of the world. For example, the African masks copied by Picasso. Westerners drooled at Picasso's originality—to copy the African artists while simultaneously ignoring the genius of the Africans.

Any new 'art movement' is, after the requisite hoopla and hype, named and given an **ISM**, that is duly attached to the end of a noun, e.g. 'modernism'. This 'nounism' doesn't transfer to non-Western art. Words like primitive, ethnographic, provincialist, or folk-art suffice. Below the ISMs are 'Schools'. A noun followed by School. For example, the Heidelberg School.

Aboriginal art is considered a 'movement' and as yet has not graduated to ISM status by being 'named'. I shall do so now. I **NAME** Aboriginal art **HIEROWISM**. It is the modern hieroglyphics. Also, there is always controversy (lotsa rows) so I think it's appropriate. So. How is it that an unqualified Black **CAN'T** name an art movement?

Prior to the twentieth century, art produced by Westerners from former colonies was not considered to be up to the standard of art produced by resident Europeans. The North Americans demanded, and begrudgingly attained, parity with their European cousins. In fact, the axis of power has actually shifted away from Paris to New York and their artists are at the forefront of Western art today. Not so their Antipodean counterparts, who struggle with what has been called 'The Provincialism Problem' (Terry Smith in his 1974 article of the same name). This

has produced a cultural cringe of massive proportions that requires artists from provincial outposts to be able to merely aspire to mediocrity.

Provincialism permeates most levels of Australian society. Consequently, it weighs heavily on the industry catering for the art of Aboriginal Australians and renders most of those involved in that industry unworthy of the roles they have given themselves. It is unwise to market Aboriginal art from the Western Art aesthetic and *attach* an Aboriginal spirituality (an exploitative tactic that suggests that the purchaser can buy some). Perhaps it would be wiser to market this form of art from a purely Western construct. Demand that it be seen for what it is—as being among the world's best examples of Abstract Expressionism. Ditch the pretence of spirituality that consigns the art to ethnography and its attendant 'glass ceiling'. Ditch the cultural cringe and insert the art at the level of the best in Western art avoiding the provincialism trap.

Spirituality and Ethnocentricity

There is no doubt that attaching spirituality during a sale of Aboriginal art helps greatly in closing a deal. Western dissatisfaction with Christianity since the 1960s has sharpened focus in this area. However, important matters haven't been given due consideration. Matters such as:

> The number of artists holding the knowledge is declining rapidly and the younger people are reluctant to take up the 'old ways';
>
> Given the above. A dying, soon dead, culture is being raked over;
>
> The image of the 'noble savage' (from whence comes the spirituality) implies a position of racial superiority (consciously or not);
>
> It is not necessary to invoke spirituality when promoting artists as individuals. Who they are. Where they're from. What they know. What they've done. These things become crucial. Perhaps the curators of the early shows were in such a rush to show the works that they hid their unprofessional (and superior) behaviour behind the 'collective CV';
>
> That a proliferation of white experts is belittling the people who own the culture. For example, the **NAMED** white expert is far better known than the mostly unnamed Aboriginal artists from the famous **PAPUNYA SCHOOL** of painters.

That the lack of Aboriginal input into areas of concern is continually overlooked has created the feeling that the culture is being stolen, et cetera.

Other important issues arise out of the 'ethnographic' approach to Aboriginal art. Anthropologists play a crucial role in the *interpretation* of Aboriginal art. Their approach is, by definition, ethnographic, and its classification system fits cosily into ethnographic art. Consider the classification of 'Urban Aboriginal art'. This is the work of people descended from the original owners of the heavily populated areas of the continent. Through a brutal colonisation process much of the culture has disappeared. However, what has survived is important. **THE DREAMTIME** is the past, the present, and the future. The Urban artists are still telling Dreamtime stories, albeit contemporary ones. The Dreamings (of the favoured 'real Aborigines' from the least settled areas) actually pass deep into Urban territories. In short, the Dreamings cannot be complete without reciprocity between the supposed real Aboriginals of the north and the supposed unreal or inauthentic Aboriginals of the south.

Many Urban artists have rejected the ethno-classification of Aboriginal art to the extent they don't participate in Aboriginal shows. They see themselves as **ARTISTS**—not as *Aboriginal* artists.

The real problem arises out of the very nature of Western art. Westerners need to sort and categorise everything in order to make sense of the world. That they do so in an ethnocentric manner is academic. The world of music is not dominated by Western classical music—different styles stand alongside each other with extensive cross-fertilisation from different cultures. Not so in visual art.

The Art Centres

Aboriginal art has foreshadowed the establishment of community art centres throughout remote areas. These centres assist by providing advice, marketing opportunities/strategies, art supplies, and documentation. The contact person is the art advisor who is almost always white. These centres are run according to the community's needs and aspirations.

The art centre takes a one third commission of the (wholesale) price for the services it provides. It consigns work to a network of galleries throughout Australia and overseas at an agreed retail price. For example, the art centre values a work at $600 and its share is $200. The gallery takes a 40 per cent commission for selling the work; therefore the retail price is $1000. Thus the artist receives $400 or 40 per cent plus the applicable service provided by the art centre.

That scenario works well for artists operating on that level of income. If the artist is on a ten fold larger income, the level of costs incurred by the art centre may be the same, or comparable, yet the artists' cut remains at 40 per cent. Well below the 60 per cent (minus costs) that other Australian artists receive. In any event, the amount of money an Aboriginal artist gets, rarely, if ever, stays in his/her pocket. Generally, it is shared among family and friends or their community.

The government's continued financial support of the art centre movement ensures some level of government control over the industry that caters for Aboriginal art. Their considerable contribution makes it look good. They think it justifies their appropriation of Aboriginal imagery in advertising campaigns, et cetera. They think that they have bought our culture. Well, soorrreee. It never happened.

The New Tribal Order

It is now approaching the fourth decade of art centres and they have spawned a new tribe of people called **BINTS** (been in the Northern Territory). It must be said however that the largest tribe in Australia is the **LYARMEE** who get their name from their ability to tell very convincing lies—especially to themselves. There is emerging, as we speak, a tribe of honorary BINTs known as the **BOOKEE** (because they learn everything about Aboriginals from books and fully fledged BINTs). The bookee rarely, if ever, deign their presence upon the Aboriginal people about whom they have become recently expert.

Bints get close to Aboriginal people and culture to ultimately return south where they proclaim their newly acquired 'pseudo-Aboriginality'. They believe this modern form of Aboriginality is superior to the Urban Aboriginality of the Blacks from these long-ago conquered lands. And, if they don't actually believe this to be true, they have a sneaking suspicion that it is.

This phenomenon further clouds the authenticity or 'realness' of Urban Blacks. That is, we (Urban Blacks) can be authentic Aboriginal people. We are not purebred *Aborigines.* Our culture was ripped from us and not much remains. Most of our languages have disappeared. We don't all have black or even dark skin. We don't take shit from you. We look disdainfully at you bringing our people from the north to parade them like circus animals to your audience. An audience ever curious to see a live version of the noble savage and one no less keen to congratulate themselves for not wiping out the entire Aboriginal race. We resent how you keep them away from us and we feel sorrow and sadness for OUR people. We have been consigned to the dustbin of history. Still, we survive.

The Regional System

You have erected and maintain barriers between us Aboriginal peoples. Those barriers serve to re-enforce the *regional system* (classification of Aboriginal art based on geographical areas—for example, Western Desert, Eastern Arnhem Land, Urban, et cetera).

Within this system does there lie an insidious, sinister coincidence to ponder? Whether or not, the racial purity of the artists is a serious consideration. Given the previously discussed issues of spirituality and noble savages it is difficult to believe that it is not. Then, is this system of classification not therefore racist? Or, should we believe that it is a coincidence and purely accidental? That it is not a postcolonial plot to divide and rule. That Australians are indeed the kindest, most humane colonialist power in the history of the world and that Australia is without doubt the best country on the planet Earth.

These questions are intricately and intrinsically enmeshed within the Australian legal system, its society and in its national psyche. The Native Title Act, 1993 (NTA) is the manifestation and embodiment of these issues—its flagship is Aboriginal art. It is the new symbolism of the new nation.

The Native Title Act

The NTA specifically requires Aboriginal people to prove that native title exists (in the claimed area) by means of song, dance, storytelling, et cetera. We have to prove that we are related to the birds, the animals, the insects, the microbes, the Earth, the wind and fire. This is an extremely difficult task even for the Aboriginal people with minimal 'white' contact.

The task for Urban Blacks becomes monumental and mostly impossible. To date, every determination by the Federal Court of Australia has been appealed to, or is on appeal, to the High Court of Australia.

The degree of difficulty facing Aboriginal people in proving their right of inheritance is in direct contrast to non-Aboriginal people who merely have to prove they are related to another human being. Is this not therefore racist?

The High Court, during its Mabo decision (which precipitated the NTA), overturned the legal fiction of *terra nullius*. Under both international and British law at the time of settlement of Australia there existed three methods by which sovereignty could be *acquired* by foreign states:

Conquest
Cession
terra nullius (Latin for 'land with no people' or 'empty land').

The British government chose the doctrine of *terra nullius* as its method of acquisition of sovereignty over Australia. It is safe to assume that they did this to avoid the need to negotiate with the native peoples about the terms of the exchange of sovereignty (treaties) which was required had they chosen to invoke either *conquest* or *cession.*

The High Court of Australia must be admired for its creativity. It invented a **NEW** element to enable acquisition of sovereignty. They called it **IMPLIED CESSION.** This element has no legal precedent in either British law or international law. It is another legal fiction. They have inserted a lie for a lie. As it must be admired for its creativity so the High Court must be condemned for its audacious land grab.

The relationship between the NTA and Aboriginal art is undeniable. The relevant requirements of proof are inextricably linked:

> The relationship to the land—with the
> song, the dance, the painting;
>
> The white interpreters—with the art critics, the anthropologists;
>
> Law versus lore—with lawyers, anthropologists;
>
> The legal industry and the 'industry', that caters for
> Aboriginal art trot out from within their respective ranks
> 'experts' who are interchangeable between them.

White Australia uses Aboriginal imagery and native fauna and flora to promote tourism and other industries. These things belong to the Black fella. However, an underlying assumption that arises out of this use of our imagery is that there has been a conciliation process through which an equitable partnership between Black Australians and White Australians has been created. Patently, blatantly, gratingly, this is not true. Never, ever has the white fella sat down and talked with us about all of the things they now call their own (they even call us *their* Aborigines—as if we are their chattels). It is true, however, that they have talked to and at us on many, many occasions. But only on relatively minor matters like native title.

Paternalism

The paternalism and social engineering of the old colonial regimes are cynically matched and even surpassed by the new postcolonial ones. The Australian government continues to assert Aboriginal people don't have rights—that we have privileges. Of course, this is also conveniently misconstrued to project to their electorate that Aboriginal people are somehow more privileged than are whites. Another recent example is the 'reconciliation' process that once again suggests conciliation at some prior date. It never happened. Reconciliation was a con. Now they find that they have to begin to re-con their silly nation. Denial is a crucial part of government strategy.

The underlying essence of land tenure in Australia is paternalism. That Aboriginal people don't own the land; couldn't own the land; never owned the land; that we don't understand ownership of land; that we couldn't/can't understand ownership of land. That Aboriginal people aren't/weren't fully evolved human beings. That we can't manage our own affairs. That we can't do without you. That we were lucky that the English 'settled' our lands. That you have been here too long to be denied your Land Rights. This IS the prevailing attitude in this country.

You don't believe this to be true?
Then ask yourself the following questions.

→

Now. Ask yourself what you believe. Then what you think the average punter believes. And don't bullshit.

Having confirmed your paternalism, if not racism, consider your view and position in relation to Aboriginal art and indeed Australian society. Perhaps you should also consider that you are an uninvited guest behaving like a 'Star Boarder'.

No one ever consults Aboriginal people on important matters. No one asked if they could take our gold out of our land. No one asked us if they could run up a credit bill for hundreds of millions of dollars. Little wonder then that people like Osama bin Laden think they can interrupt our peaceful resistance without having to consult the Aboriginal People. If you can do it. He can do it.

Do you believe, and I mean *REALLY* believe, Aboriginal people:

Please circle either Yes or No.

Once owned all of Australia?
Yes / No

Still own all of Australia?
Yes / No

Still have rights to land that have not been properly negotiated?
Yes / No

Had a recognisable form of land tenure?
Yes / No

Were 'civilized'?
Yes / No

Are 'civilized'?
Yes / No

Deserve to own all of Australia at any time?
Yes / No

Deserve to own all of Australia now?
Yes / No

Deserve to own any of Australia at any time?
Yes / No

Deserve to own any of Australia now?
Yes / No

Deserve to own any of the good parts of Australia?
Yes / No

Can manage their own affairs?
Yes / No

Should be thankful for everything you have done for us?
Yes / No

Should be thankful for some things you have done for us?
Yes / No

Appropria-tionism

It is time, now, to discuss the distasteful and discomforting subject of the appropriation of Aboriginal imagery. This practice has been accruing for centuries throughout the world (according to Jacques Derrida et al.). It has become an accepted movement in Western art called, appropriately, **APPROPRIATIONISM**. The Aboriginal People of Australia and people from other former colonies are most upset about Appropriationism and consider it to be stealing. We couldn't care less about Western artists appropriating one another. But we object strongly to the appropriation of 'our' artists' work by non-Aboriginal people.

There are several causes of distress arising from appropriation and its so-called 'death of the author' argument. Firstly, the artist may not be the sole owner of the copyright of the 'story' or the imagery contained in the artwork. Secondly, the 'sharing' of imagery between the coloniser and the colonised is suggestive of an equitable agreement between the artists. Not true. Otherwise, the works would be collaborations. Thirdly, Aboriginal people all over the world are adamant that their respective cultures are not for sale—that our cultures are the only things we still own and that we will own and that we will struggle mightily to maintain that ownership.

Aboriginal people have stated our case against appropriation. We are not asking artists to do the impossible or even to do something that is difficult. A vow never to pick your nose is impossible to keep. A vow for monogamy is difficult to uphold. That a desire by non-Aboriginal artists to overcome the aforementioned provincialism problem may urge them to appropriate Aboriginal imagery is not an excuse. Artists appropriate because they can. So too, a dog can lick his balls because he can. To all those artists who have resisted the temptation or who now desist, congratulations and thank you.

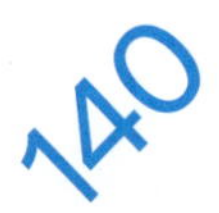

Anthropologists

Aboriginal cultures throughout the world have been infested by plagues of anthropologists down the ages. Never more so than during the last three decades here in Australia. We have been the most studied creatures on earth. They KNOW more about us than we know about ourselves. Should you ask an Aboriginal how they're feeling, the most appropriate answer would be 'Wait 'til I ask my Anthropologist'. They are stuck so far up our arses that they on first name terms with sphincters, colons, and any intestinal parasites. And behold, the DO speak for us.

Countless books have been written about Aboriginal people by white folks. All their information (including photographs) is taken as and for free. Come the book launch and the Aboriginal informants are nowhere to be seen, *naturellement!* Of course, this shabby treatment is readily rationalised thus: 'But they were so nice. I thought they didn't mind'. Or: 'But I didn't have any money then'. Whaatt! No advance from your publisher? Perhaps they're just bums. However, it is suspected that they and their publishers are of the opinion that we are so desperate to talk to them, that they are sooo kind to be even talking to us that we must be thankful. How superior! I should suggest that the Australian government advise publishers and the ologists with their praying mantras that it is prudent (and decent) for them to budget for these costs as a matter of due process. Information costs. The bank should also equip all Aboriginal people with an EFTPOS facility to rectify this blatant exploitation.

The work of anthropologists merely serves to perpetuate the prevailing hegemony inserting their anthropocentric-theological twist on the studied culture, thereby paving the way for their religious allies to wreak their havoc.

Essentially, it is felt among Indigenous peoples that the anthropologists really have better things to do than to delve into our cultures. For example, they could analyse the colonialist cultures to understand the relationship between the imposition of powerlessness and terrorism. This would be an extremely useful (and welcome) contribution that would go a long way towards redeeming anthropology's appalling reputation.

Exploitation

The most emotive issue to arise out of Aboriginal art is the 'E' word. No—not ecstasy. Exploitation. Despite or in-spite of the Aboriginal art centre system, exploitation of Aboriginal artists has proliferated. In fact, exploitation has become an art form that is so proficient that it is thoroughly deserving of an ISM. I give you **EXPLOITATIONISM**. There are numerous instances that can be quoted of artists relinquishing works at extremely low prices to unscrupulous dealers to resell to realise exorbitant profits.

One profitable and exploitative practice is to bring the artists to the 'Big Smoke' to paint for a wage. In these cases the artists are paid a weekly sum that negates any further claim for payment. The dealer is not required to set aside any percentage to the artists even though the works are sold for considerable sums of money. Don't believe it? Consider whether any dealer would bring to the smoke anyone other than the artists whose work is saleable and at good prices. This practice should be monitored and audited.

There is also the example of profiteering by accident. A teacher at a remote settlement is delightedly surprised at the artistic abilities of the natives and begins to collect (cheaply alright! Ridiculously cheaply) the earliest examples of those works. Some of those works surface decades later at auctions with reserves that resemble telephone numbers. The profit margin in the reserves of these works in some cases was upwards of one thousand per cent. Is the teacher the sole beneficiary of this 'accident'? Or, is there an arrangement in place where the artist (or their families) too benefit? If not, is this not also an example of gross exploitation?

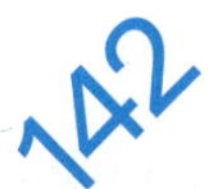

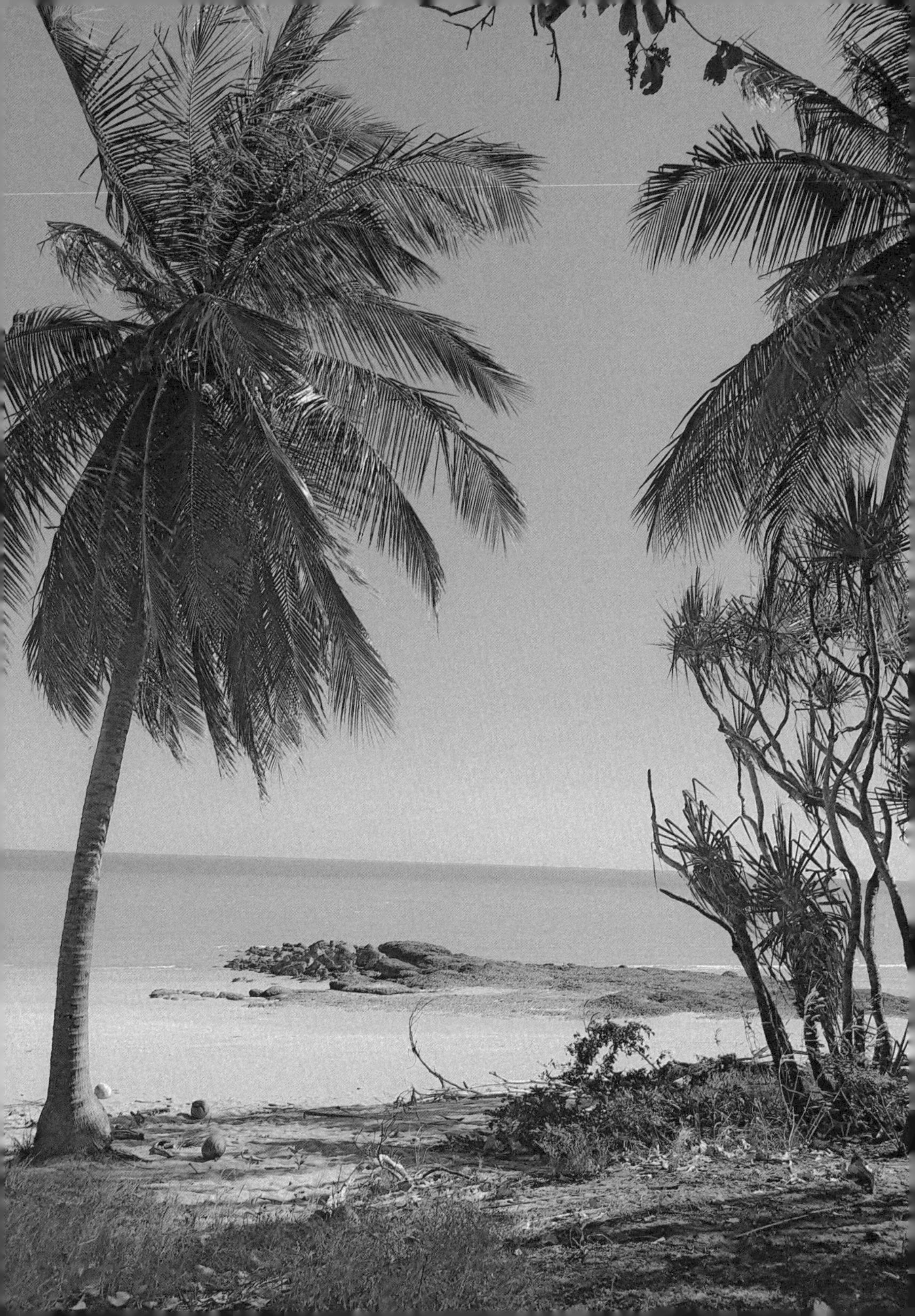

The Triangle of Discomfort

Earlier in this essay, reference was made to the fact that the artists (through the art centre system) receive 40 per cent of the consigned retail price for their work. While this is not ideal, there is a strong argument that it is fair. Let us assume it IS fair, for example, a work sells for $1000, the artists receive the obligatory $400, the art centre receives its $200 and the dealer gets their $400.
Diagram → 01

Of course, if the artist is directly involved the artist (Black, white or brindle) must receive 60 per cent (or $600) of the retail price.
Diagram → 02

Unfortunately there are severe variations to these scenarios. For example, a work retails for $1000. The dealer takes the requisite $400. A middleman emerges who takes the remaining $600 having already paid the artist (or promised to pay) $100 or 10 per cent of retail. Clearly, a case of exploitation. In this situation, what I have called the Triangle of Discomfort comes into play.
Diagram → 03

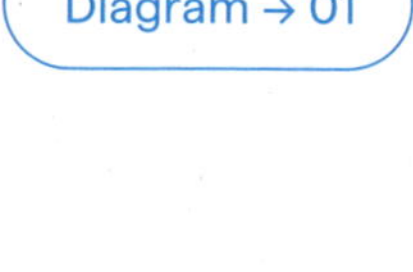

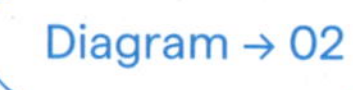

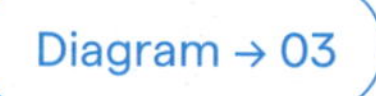

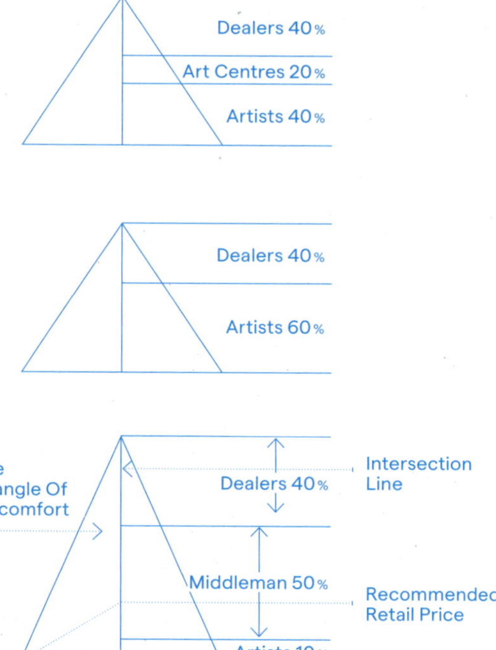

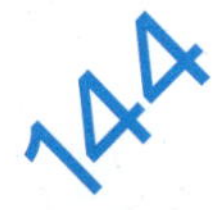

The Triangle of Discomfort

The Triangle of Discomfort measures the excess above the recommended retail price, which is 1.5 times whatever the artist receives. It can be seen in diagram 3 that the dealer and the carpetbagger do exceedingly well in comparison TO THE ARTIST. Ultimately the co-operation of dealers is essential to overcome these sorts of problems.

Should an art centre not be involved in the sale of Aboriginal art, and instead a middleman is involved, then that person should be permitted no more than 20 per cent of retail as commission. Please note, these middlemen are there in numbers and they won't go away. They need to be regulated in order to avoid the Triangle of Discomfort.

It might be said that this is difficult, almost impossible, to do. Not so. The art centres are well equipped, with the latest technology widely available to them. Due diligence towards the authenticity of the work would confirm the price paid to the artist should an art centre not be involved. There must be cooperation between the dealers and the art centres, even when the middlemen are involved. Any dealer or art centre not prepared to go though this process should be liable to legal sanction. Or, they must engage in some other activity.

Conclusion

It is a great source of discomfort to Aboriginal people that Aboriginal art is not controlled by Aboriginal people. Indeed that is so for many other people. It has been shown that there are numerous issues and mechanisms that impact on the phenomenon known as Aboriginal art. Its sustainability and the ability of the artists to re-invent themselves are not discussed here.

Aboriginal art is bought, sold, and promoted from within the system, that is, Western art consigns it to 'pigeon-holing' within that system. Why can't an art movement arise and be separate from but equal to Western art—within its own aesthetic, its own voices, its own infrastructure, et cetera?

Please permit the proposal for the recommendation of an **OMBUDSMAN FOR THE ARTS** in Australia to look after the interest of all of its artists. The Ombudsman must be able to intercede on behalf of artists with investigatory powers and with legal sanctions available to effectively deal with issues such as those mentioned above and any other important matters that may arise from time to time.

It is extremely doubtful whether Aboriginal people in Australia will ever be able to regain control of this important part of our culture. Obstacles and barriers have been cruelly and thoughtfully placed to deprive us of an equitable future.

For example:

The Native Title Act;

Stereotyping of Aboriginal people as lazy-good-for-nothing drunks;

Valorising one group of Aboriginal people whilst demonising another on the basis of racial purity;

Inflicting anthropologists upon us;

Sanctioning a new tribal order;

Subjecting us to paternalism and exploitation;

Appropriating our images et cetera.

All these crimes serve the purpose of dehumanising us to justify to ALL non-Aboriginal Australians that it's okay to deny us justice. Forever.

There is no hope.

Acknowledgment

I would sincerely like to thank all the Aboriginal people who have kindly shared their knowledge and experience and to whom I owe everything and I dedicate this to them.

Richard Bell
November 2002

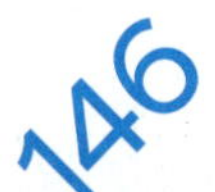

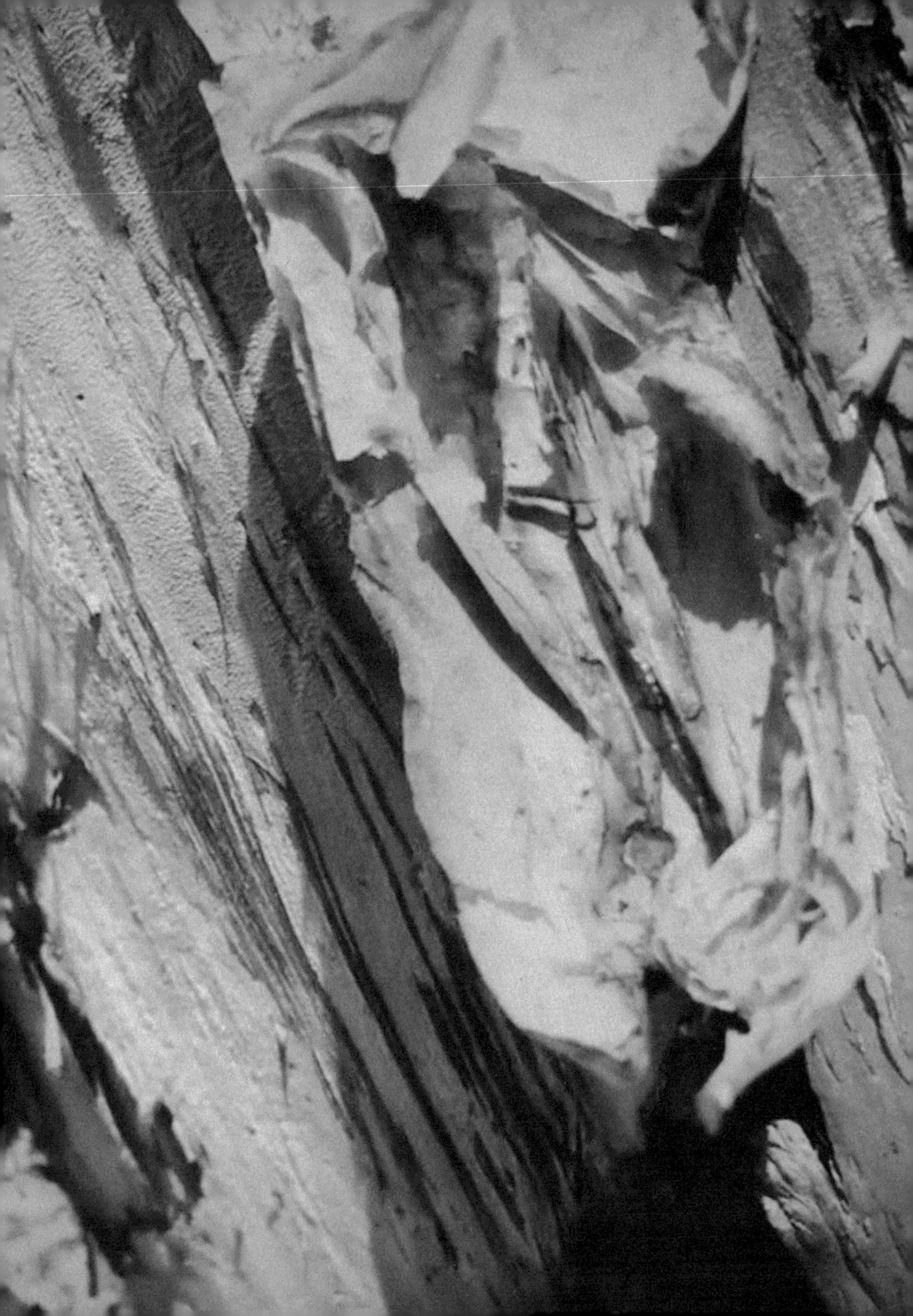

Across Australia, Artists are Disrupting the Colonial Mindset[1]

Paola Balla

1 A version of this text was originally published in *frieze* on 31 October 2018: https://www.frieze.com/article/across-australia-artists-are-disrupting-colonial-mindset

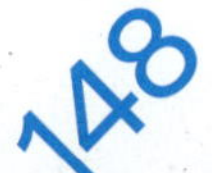

In the Australian art world, 'decolonisation' has become a buzzword in academia, galleries, and museums, yet Aboriginal and Torres Strait Islander artists have been calling for decolonisation and asserting Indigenous sovereignty for decades. The process of decolonising requires ongoing work and our peoples have created generational legacies of storytelling about surviving and denouncing colonisation through art, theatre, literature, and community activism.

Sovereignty is central to the identity and wellbeing of Indigenous peoples in our fight for justice. The arts are an accessible and engaging way of discussing these complex issues in a country where white colonial and patriarchal narratives dominate public spaces. In recent years, a social-media revolution has been mobilised by Indigenous activists, scholars, and artists who are part of a lineage of Aboriginal resistance from letter and petition writing like that of esteemed Yorta Yorta activist, William Cooper on.

There is also an emerging Aboriginal podcast culture: one of the first was *Wild Black Women,* which was hosted by Associate Professor Chelsea Watego, who went on to write the acclaimed and bestselling book *Another Day in the Colony* (2021), described as a ground-breaking call to arms, and the comedy writer Angelina Hurley, currently writing a PhD on Black humour as the first Indigenous doctoral candidate at Griffith Film School. The podcast was a Black women and community centred, sharply funny, and politically astute programme that took racism, whiteness, and the patriarchy to task.

Coming out of the new wave of Indigenous artist and activist collectives is This Mob, who went on to curate an outstanding survey show called *Collective Movements* at Monash University Museum of Art (MUMA) in 2022, and the continuing work of the Warriors of the Aboriginal Resistance (WAR), all predominantly led by young Aboriginal women and non-binary people, bringing thousands of people to Naarm/Melbourne's streets in mass protests against colonial oppression, violence, and Black deaths in custody. In 2021 during some of the toughest lockdown laws of the COVID-19 pandemic, they safely brought thousands of peoples to the streets to commemorate Black Lives Matter for Aboriginal People and to remind colonisers that this is a local reality for Aboriginal people.

Real Blak Tingz (Gabi Briggs x Arika Waulu) was a collective that aimed 'to destabilise the patriarchal society and its perpetual power structure that exists illegally on the land mass of so-called Australia.'[2] They curated and created a matriarchal exhibition of portraits, women's digging sticks, and installation at the Koorie Heritage Trust in 2017. Arika Waulu (they/them) a Gunnai, Gunditjmara and Djapwur-

2 See: https://koorieheritagetrust.com.au/whats-on/exhibitions/past-exhibitions/archive-2017/the-blak-matriarchy.

rung, visual artist and landback lover Wuurn Of Kanak–(Home of Digging Stick) has started a matriarchal movement of rematriating Country called WUURNOKKANAK-LANDBACK through land restoration and political actions, including an ethical fashion line.

Australia Day is celebrated on 26 January, but to sovereign Indigenous peoples it's known as Invasion Day, since it commemorates the landing in 1788 of the first fleet of British ships and the declaration of British sovereignty over Aboriginal lands. In 2018, WAR organised a march through Melbourne that attracted 60,000 people, demanding that Australia Day be abolished. (Some media reports confused this with other demands that the date be changed to a more inclusive day.) The protests also marked the 80th anniversary of the meeting of Aboriginal leaders in Sydney to request a national Day of Mourning in acknowledgement of the loss of Aboriginal lives during the country's colonisation and to speak out against their ongoing mistreatment. WAR have also created iconic protest banners that call for decolonisation, land rights, and the rights of Aboriginal children and women. (The banners were featured in *Sovereignty*, the exhibition I co-curated in 2016 at the Australian Centre for Contemporary Art in Melbourne with Director Max Delany.) The initiative of Aboriginal women is prominent in this movement; Aboriginal matriarchy is a driving cultural force.

The number of arts organisations, art schools, and independent galleries attempting to decolonise their spaces in various ways has increased, though the representation of Aboriginal staff has only barely increased. In great news, Yorta Yorta and Wemba Wemba woman Belinda Briggs was appointed as Curator for Indigenous Art at the Shepparton Art Museum (SAM) in regional Victoria, a figure who brings a wealth of knowledge not only in relation to art, but also from the Indigenous community and Yorta Yorta and Wemba Wemba cultures that she is part of, into the gallery itself.

Acknowledgements of Country have become more commonplace and the placement of Aboriginal-designed acknowledgement plaques has increased; Yinka Lerrk (gathering of women in Wemba-Wemba) has led the way with their Aboriginal-women-owned business in creating acknowledgement plaques featuring custom art for schools, galleries, retail spaces, and organisations.

Acknowledgement of Country as a first step has become regular practice by non-Aboriginal organisations and individuals to not only to recognise Aboriginal peoples as original owners of Country (land/s) and ongoing custodians, but to acknowledge their own complicity in colonisation and the privileges this brings white and settler people on

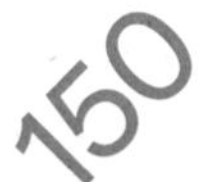

stolen unceded sovereign lands. The death of the Queen of England brought into sharp focus the ongoing nature of colonisation and the way it is revered in western nations like Australia.

An acknowledgment of Country, through spoken acknowledgment at exhibition openings, by installing plaques that name the traditional lands a building is constructed on, or by inviting Elders from traditional owner groups to conduct Welcome to Country ceremonies are all acts that demonstrate an attempt to decolonise.

At the least they are acts that ensure that Aboriginal contributions, land sovereignty, and recognition take place in public and formally.

These acknowledgments might also appear on gallery websites and in catalogues or other publications. Decolonisation also calls for Aboriginal artists to remind the public that they are continuing to resist colonisation and racism by speaking about trans-generational traumas, rebuking colonial narratives in public spaces and addressing institutional whiteness and privileges.

Other inclusive practices include inviting Indigenous artists, curators, writers, and activists to join museum boards, speak at events, and write for publications. In 2020 the Australian Centre for Moving Image (ACMI) supported the newly established First Nations Film Club for Indigenous community members to gather to view Black/Blak films and screen culture, and to discuss them with Indigenous directors, filmmakers, and actors.

The 2018 all Blak women's edition (BLAK BROW) for *The Lifted Brow* is still referred to as a standout example of an all-Indigenous women's mini-anthology and is yet to be replicated by a white or settler publication. This work is crucial in Australia, a country whose mainstream media is still dominated by white representation. Since the original publication of this article, for example, the immensely popular television show *Neighbours*, which has been on air since 1985 and finally ended in 2022, only to be re-announced and revived within months on another network!

So, *Neighbours* will continue with its vanilla version of suburbia: an area that in reality was founded on the dispossession of Aboriginal peoples and which is home to generations of migrants and people of colour. Non-white voices and faces are usually only seen and heard on non-profit broadcasters, such as National Indigenous Television, the Special Broadcasting Service, and the Australian Broadcasting Corporation, though this is slowly changing.

As of 2022, the majority of senior curatorial roles in galleries and museums are held by non-Indigenous people, predominantly white women and white men. This has led to calls for a decentring of whiteness, similar to the Decolonize This Place movement in the US. In Naarm/Melbourne, where I live, many artists and collectives work independently of mainstream galleries and collaborate with them in collective ways. Organisations such as Footscray Community Arts, which was established in 1974, have now had twelve years of Indigenous-led programming and projects.

Asserting sovereignty and self-determination can also be described as 'non-colonial', a term coined by the Indigenous Métis artist and scholar from Canada David Garneau, who speaks of creating a 'non-colonial trophy keeping place' by transforming museum collections with Indigenous communities, not on our behalf, and constructing non-colonial spaces within museums.[3] This was achieved in 2013 with the redevelopment of the Melbourne Museum's First Peoples Gallery as the Bunjilaka Aboriginal Cultural Centre by Indigenous curators and community members. Earlier this year, Museums Victoria, which runs the Melbourne Museum, appointed Genevieve Grieves as the first Indigenous head of First Peoples Collections in its 164-year history.

Contemporary political Aboriginal art is prolific and draws on tens of thousands of years of life and culture and occupation as sovereign people. In an article published in June in *Artlink*, Clothilde Bullen, just named as one of the most influential people in Power 100 by *Art Review* (along with the Karrabing Film Collective and Wiradjuri artist

3 David Garneau, 'From Colonial Trophy Case to Non-Colonial Keeping House', Museums Australasia Conference, 16 May 2016.

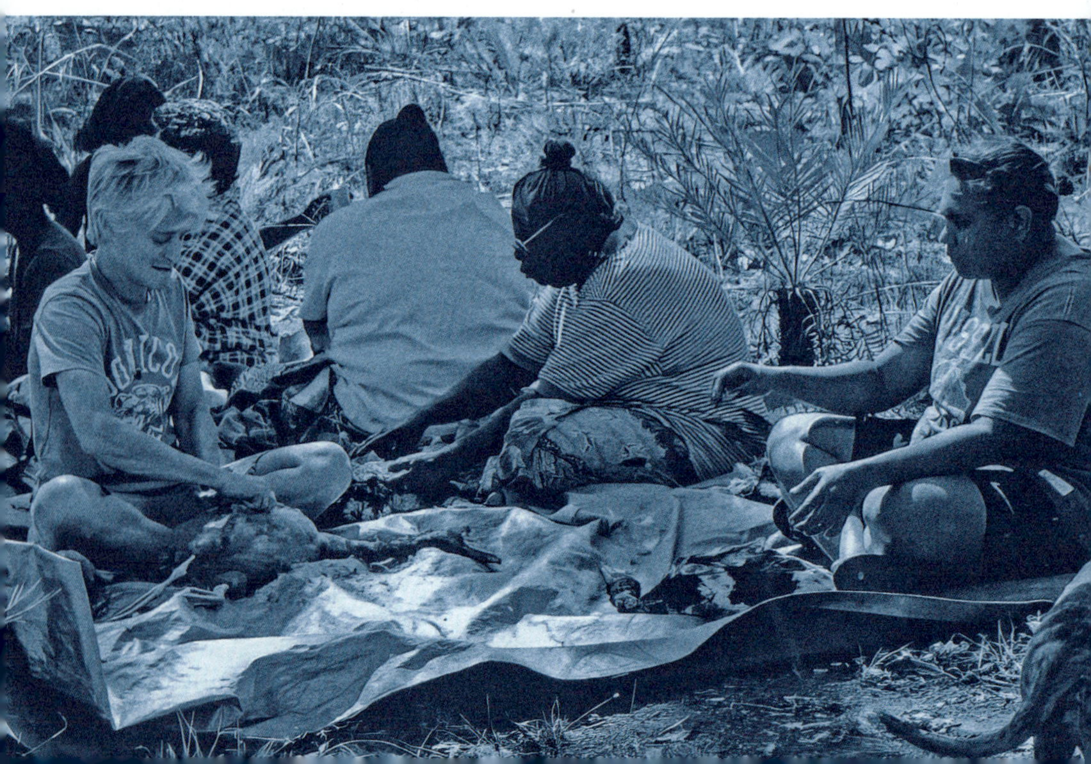

Brook Andrew), moved on from being the Indigenous curator of Aboriginal and Torres Strait Islander Collections and Exhibitions at the Museum of Contemporary Art Australia (MCA) in Sydney to the role of senior curator and head of Indigenous Programs at the Art Gallery of Western Australia (AGWA) in Perth.

In an article published in June 2018 in *Artlink*, Bullen described decolonisation as a contemporary process by which First Nations peoples 'reframe their own structures of thought, understand the history of their colonisation and re-invigorate tradition, language and cultural values and the simultaneous consideration of a new way of walking through the world'.

Some good examples of this approach include the disruptive and poetic performances *Bound and Unbound: Sovereign Acts (Act 1)* and *(Act 2)* (2015) by Unbound Collective, which took place in the colonial precinct of the state gallery, library, and museum in Adelaide in South Australia. (The collective comprises four Aboriginal women: Ali Gumillya Baker, Faye Rosas Blanch, Natalie Harkin, and Simone Ulalka Tur.) In Melbourne, Vicki Couzens and Maree Clarke are senior Aboriginal women revitalising traditional cultural practices, such as remaking possum-skin cloaks and creating memorials to honour lost Aboriginal lives. Brisbane-based Archie Moore creates immersive, sensorial works that invoke childhood experiences of Black life as living memorials. Also in Brisbane, Dale Harding's work pays homage to Aboriginal women's labour through subversive craft and installation work taught to him by family members. His installations speak of familial knowledge of place and history across his Ancestral lands. (His work was included in the Liverpool Biennial in the UK earlier this year.)

There are also practitioners from the Pacific diaspora who are contributing to the complexity of this debate, including curator Léuli Eshraghi and artist Lisa Hilli as well as several white Australian artists. Eshraghi and Hilli are critically self-aware of their viewpoints as settlers who are also Indigenous. Their work attempts to make sense of their place on unceded, stolen lands and to create spaces of contestation and resistance. Megan Evans's self-reflective work concerning her white historical privilege emerges from her collaborations with Aboriginal artists such as Peter Waples-Crowe. Their 2016 exhibition *Squatters and Savages* used humour and subversion to reflect upon the violence of the colonial frontier.

The white feminist female collective Soda_Jerk's *Terror Nullius* (2018) is a 55-minute film that collages iconic scenes from Australian cinema into a critique of white nationalism. It created controversy for its funders, the Ian Potter Foundation, which withdrew promotional support of the film just before its release, deeming it 'un-Australian' and 'a very controversial work of art'. The artists (Sydney-based siblings Dan and Dominique Angeloro) told *The Guardian* in March that 'if "very controversial" is another way of saying that the work is willing to start uncomfortable conversations, then we'll happily wear it.'[4]

Aboriginal art is a force that speaks back and *Blak*—a term coined by Destiny Deacon, the acclaimed photographic artist and KuKu and Erub/Mer Torres Straits woman. In the exhibition catalogue for the 1994 exhibition, *Blakness: Blak City Culture* at ACCA, in collaboration with Boomalli Aboriginal Artist Co-operative, curators Clare Williamson and Hetti Perkins wrote: 'The term 'Blak' was developed by Deacon as part of a symbolic but potent strategy of reclaiming colonialist language to create means of self-definition and expression.'[5]

It shares the lived experiences of Indigenous artists who resist the ongoing colonial project with acts of disruption to a white-dominated public discourse. As Kimberley Moulton, Yorta Yorta woman and Senior Curator South Eastern Aboriginal Collections at Museums Victoria states: 'There is strength in challenging the status quo, rejecting the pattern that our art, bodies, and culture are only noticed when recognised by the white centre. We do not need this: our First Peoples' ways of being and understanding surpass this. And we do not need to be defined within this canon as we can never fit within something that is constructed from our exclusion.'[6]

4 Luke Buckmaster, 'Terror Nullius review – dazzling, kinetic, mishmashed beast of an Australian film', *The Guardian*, 20 March, 2018, https://www.theguardian.com/film/2018/mar/20/terror-nullius-review-dazzling-kinetic-mishmashed-beast-of-an-australian-film.

5 Hetti Perkins and Clare Williamson (eds.), *Blakness, Blak City Culture*, Australian Centre Contemporary Art, Melbourne, 1994, pp. 20–31.

6 Kimberley Moulton, 'Sovereign Art and the Colonial Canon: Are We Lost Until We Are Found?', *Sovereignty*, 1995, Australian Centre for Contemporary Art, Melbourne, p. 31.

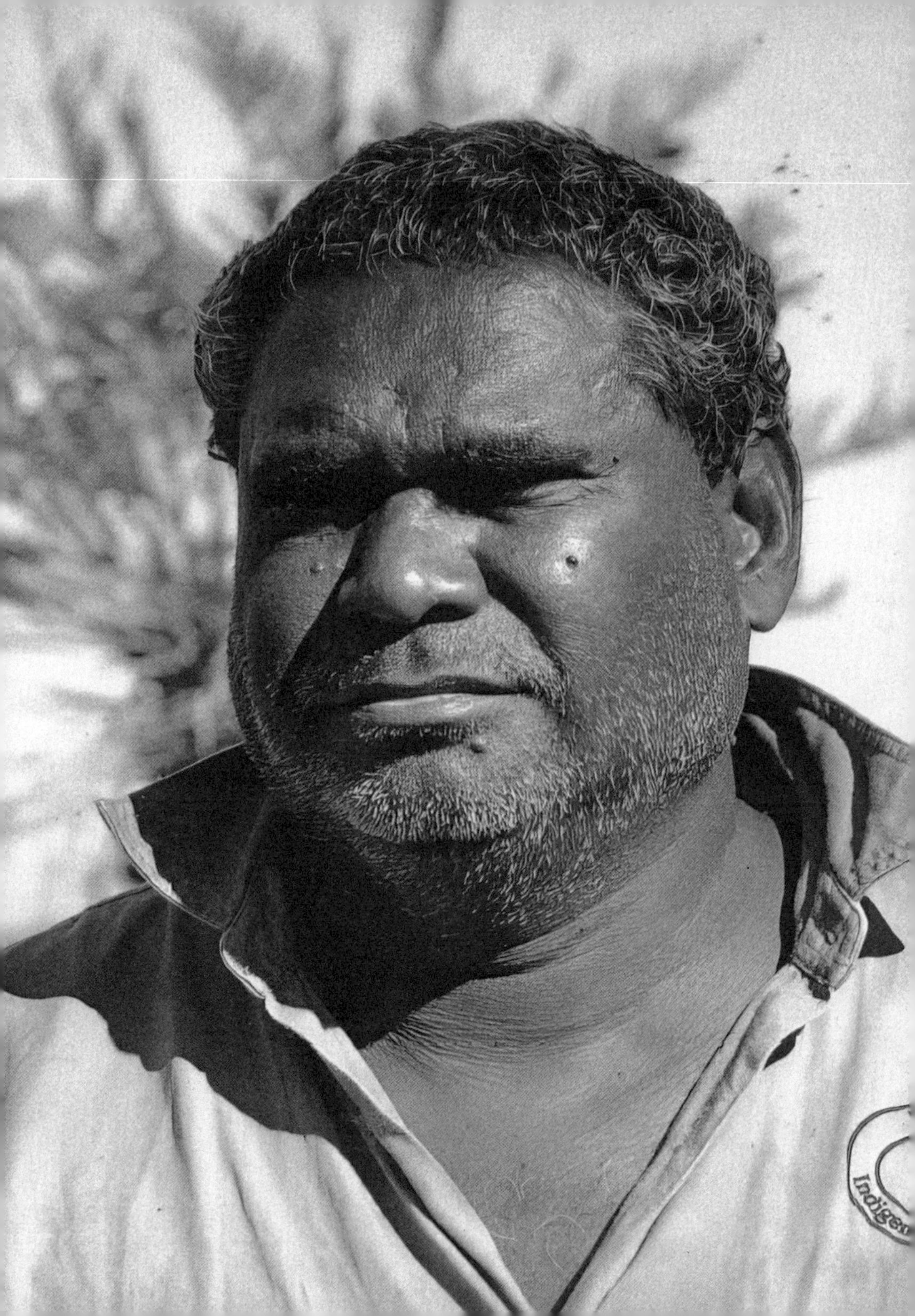

Growing up Karrabing: A conversation with Gavin Bianamu, Sheree Bianamu, Natasha Lewis Bigfoot, Ethan Jorrock, and Elizabeth Povinelli[1]

Karrabing Film Collective

1 This text was originally published in *un Magazine* 11.2, October 2017, http://unprojects.org.au/magazine/issues/issue-11-2/growing-up-karrabing.

GB → Gavin Bianamu
SB → Sheree Bianamu
NL → Natasha Lewis Bigfoot
EJ → Ethan Jorrock
EP → Elizabeth Povinelli

EP I am here at Buwambi on the coast of the Cox Peninsula with my niece and nephew, Sheree and Gavin Bianamu, and two of my grandkids, Ethan Jorrock, and Natasha Bigfoot Lewis.

Hey, youbela! I was thinking—I have known your parents since they were little kids and all of you since you were born. Like, Natie, I always picture you running around the yard across from Big Truck's house where I had breakfast and dinner so many times when I was still a young adult. Your house was where Kilili lived. She was Gavin and Sheree's *makeli* (Mother's Mother). You know that film we are finishing up for the Haus der Kulturen der Welt in Berlin? Kilili was with Ethan and your sister-girl (Great-Grandmother) when they escaped from the Katherine internment camp during World War II.

Youbela you were born oat Belyuen and grown up Karrabing. Maybe we should begin by talking about what Karrabing means?

NL The word means tide out—like low tide turning. But Karrabing is all the families around my grandmother side families and everyone married into it. We are all saltwater from the same coast—connected lands from the same coast.

EP How did it start?

NL Well we became homeless in 2007 because of a really bad riot at Belyuen. We went south, along the coastline, to a place called Bulgul, and lived in tents there. Most of us in Karrabing were there. You were there too! And we lived there to about 2010 when my mum got a government house in Darwin. We started Karrabing before then—but we really started making the films after that really, around 2011.

EP True.

SB And my dad always wanted to be a film star. His hero is Elvis Presley. True. But everyone said we should just tell our own stories since government wasn't listening to the problems we were having.

EP Ok, how old were all of you? I remember some of you were pretty little.

EJ I was born in 2002, so I must have been five.

SB I was nine.

NL I was fourteen.

GB So I must have been thirteen.

NL That's when Karrabing started.

EP So, see youbela really grew up inside of Karrabing.

SB Yes, as you can see from the first really first short film, *Karrabing, Low Tide Turning* to this film we making now, *Night Time Go (ngupelngamarrunu)*. From first, to second, to third, to fourth, and now this new one, you can see us turning from kids to teenagers to adults, making movies.

EP So what is it like growing up inside our film collective? Ethan, you first.

EJ It's fun.

EP Do you think you would know these stories inside these films if you hadn't been inside Karrabing?

EJ Nope. I didn't know about that Dog Dreaming no matter my mother's mum has that totem. I didn't really believe that Dogs stood up and were always trying to make fires with their own bare hands. At first when people kept telling me about Dreamings and totems and stuff, I didn't believe them until they took me up to the Dog Dreaming and I saw it myself and started listening to stories the old people were telling me—my grandma and grandpa's.

EP And you reckon making these films helps join together contemporary times, like today times, with those older times? Like films help stick that story to our bodies? Help me out. Like how does making film do that? How do we explain this to white people?

SB Like the story is in you and you can tell it from yourself.

NL Like that sweat is stuck to you. Like you don't want to believe that story but when you yourself tell that story, you believe that story.

EP Like when you yourself tell the story you look at yourself and find out that you are the story! Does that make sense?

SB, NL, GB, EB Yes.

NL Like the way we say, the country you go to, it has your sweat in it. It's like that with the films. The stories become stuck inside you because the films have your sweat inside them.

EP Yeah since I first came here in 1984, all these stories stopped being stories when I started to understand the deeper meaning. How they explain why this or that person acts like they do or this or that place. Like with my brother—your dad, Sheree and Gavin—is always jealous—it's his Dreaming, that *therrawin*, that *durlg*, from the story about the jealous sea monster. It's inside his body.

GB And that's why we made that film, *The Jealous One!*

EP Ok, Natie, so what has it been like for you growing up inside Karrabing, making films?

NL What do I like about Karrabing?

EP Sure, or what has it been like growing up making films since you were a teenager?

NL When we came together as Karrabing, all my grandmother side family, we were able to stick together. We all became as one during those terrible times. We never separated. We kept using film and making films to keep together and tell our stories. I like that idea. And when we are making the films they let me look at all those Dreamings—Dog and Mudi and *durlg* and where the Black Nunggudi water snake goes—with my own eyes, I learned much more. I was able to stick the places into my head.

EP You reckon making stories help keep the story in your head?

GB, NL Yes!

NL Because we go there. We see it. Our sweat is in it and it's in us.

GB And if we go there to make the films, and we really try to make the films true even though they are also just a story, we come to know the places and Dreamings because we come to know we are still there and we are still continuing the story. Then we have the possibility of passing all of this down to our kids or sisters' or brothers' kids.

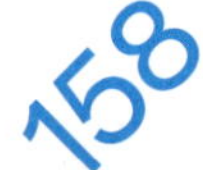

NL When we go there to make the films and everyone tells us the story about that place, then we pass that knowledge to all the young people, the little, little ones.

EP Do you think the knowledge is in the past or in the now?

NL In the past but …

GB In the past but we know it very well in the present time. Well the story is still there. If you go there you can see it—right there, staring at you. No matter what form of transport you want to go, by sea or by air, or by car, you can see it.

NL Doesn't matter what form of transport because you can still see it. But we play it in the now times so it is not just in the past; it is here inside us, like when we always say it's in our sweat. We work to make the film and the film also helps us make it really real to ourselves. It is now because it is still there.

EP And are your mob still here?

NL Yes we are still here. And that Dreaming is still here. And it's still true.

GB It was true in our grandparents' time and still in our time and still going to be in our kids' time.

SB For me, I like the films because they give me something to do and because when we're telling the story we're acting it out. Sometimes it's a bit rough and tough but in the end it can be pretty funny.

EP You shifted a bit from acting to shooting, aye?

EB Me too, Nanna. I do a bit of acting and bit of shooting.

EP Yeah, true.

SB Yeah when we did *When the Dogs Talked* and *Windjarrameru*, we used a really nice white man, Ian Jones, to shoot the films. But then we had to get up every morning and shoot all day for something like a week. And we thought, let's shoot our own film with iPhones then we can be more relaxed.

EB It's really fun when we get together and have a laugh with the family, because living on communities is really stressful a lot of the time.

EP Yeah, I don't think people realise how stressful it can be living in communities.

EB It really is. When people have nothing to do, and they are really bored, they can just start arguing, or drinking or whatever, and fighting is something to do. And people can get really hurt, people get really angry and family split up. But when we are making films, most of the time we are just cracking up laughing.

SB And to be honest that's the best thing I like, because when we're being Karrabing we can go out bush and do some cultural things and learn with the family and just get away from all the stress and relax and learn.

EP True. That's true for me too. Our films and art are being shown across the world now. Where have we been?

SB Well me, Natie, and my brother (Gavin), we went to Jerusalem where our film *Wutharr, Saltwater Dreams* was being shown in the Jerusalem Show. And we went to Ramalah and saw how the Palestinians had to live. And they were really interested in the Dreaming part and how we all have different ideas about the meaning—some Christian, some for Ancestors, some for just motors break down.

NL Yeah and yet we all still come together. They always ask us about that—you mob disagree? Sure. But we still together Karrabing.

EJ I only went to Sydney because I don't have a passport yet. But when we went to Sydney a lot of people were interested and wanted to know if our films were on YouTube.

GB Me, I'll go anywhere! I went to Jerusalem (Jerusalem Show-Qalandiya Biennale), Berlin (Berlinale, Forum Expanded), Mechelen (Contour Biennale), Brussels (Villa Empain), Netherlands (Van Abbemuseum), Paris (Centre Pompidou)—and we're all going to New York City and London—and Athens (documenta) in June.

EP Why do you think people are interested inside and outside Australia? Lots of people would pluck out their eyes to go to these places.

GB It's interesting for outside of Australia—they find it interesting because they don't know about Aboriginal people and how they live and what they do and believe in.

NL It's different from their environment. The way they live is in big city. We live in the bush area.

EP Yeah, but, I don't know how to put this, but like Australia has NITV, and they show a lot of good films, aye? So how you reckon our films fit into that?

NL Well they don't show the way, like true story, the way we live in everyday life and how it all connects to the generations and generations. They don't show it like that. They just show it little bit. The way it connects to past is that we listened to stories our old people told us, and passed down to us, the new generation mob. So the films have those stories inside them but we tell it the way we are living.

GB Yeah, they don't show much. Like some show old stories but they don't show how it fits with how we live, you know, in scrub, in and out of scrub to city, back and forth. Like real life, properly way how it all fits together. And like with this new film we are recreating what all those old people, our grandparents were going through in their lifetimes when they were living in the bush, and army and police tried to control them, we're trying to recreate that. But also it's true about our lives now. Different time. But police and government still are doing the same thing.

NL We are trying to show what is true, then and now, because these stories, these places and Dreamings and struggles are still here with us now. No matter, we are the new generation.

The Karrabing Film Collective is a film cooperative consisting of friends and family members whose lives interconnect along Indigenous coastal homelands northwest of Darwin, NT.

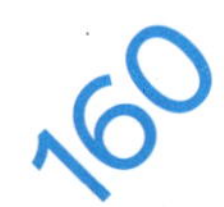

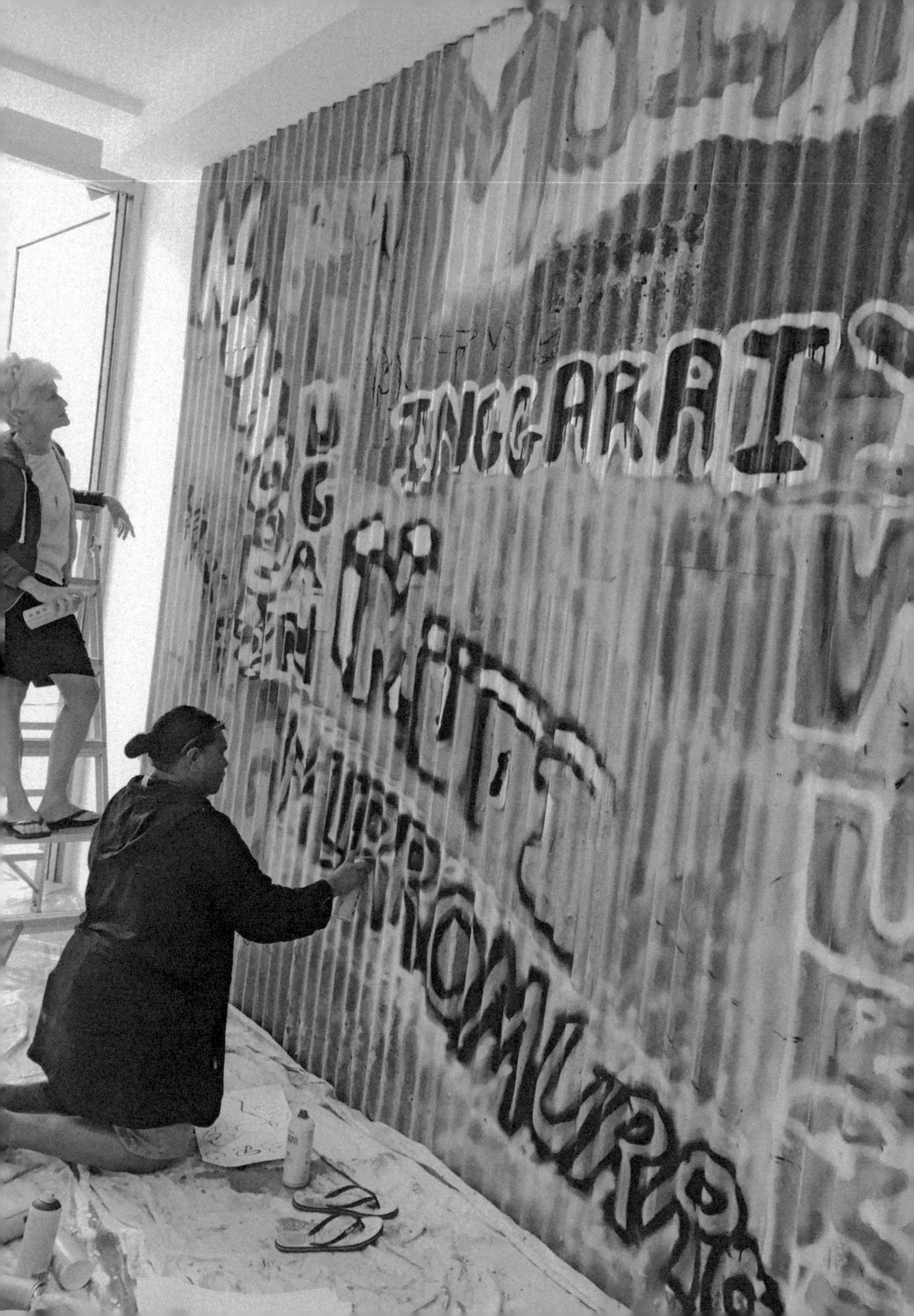

Karrabing: An Essay in Keywords[1]

Tess Lea and
Elizabeth A. Povinelli

1 This is an edited extract from a text which was originally published in *Visual Anthropology Review*, vol. 34, no. 1, 2018, p. 36–46.

Talking to Viewers, Talking to Karrabing: Lessons in Keywords

Whenever Karrabing members are present for questions after viewings, whether in Berlin, Jerusalem, Athens, Mechelen, or Canberra, audiences attempt to pin the meaning of what they are seeing to gain a better account of Karrabing intentions. The questions are usually provocative, genuine, and probative, invoking laughter, discussion, and interaction. As such, they are not wrong questions. Still, they are also indicative of a field of power in the kindly quest for meaning, a subtle, well-intentioned semantic plea, which here, in turn, we place into a dialogue around keywords, probing the audience for what they reveal about the politics of reception and circulation. For it is this play between conditioned expectations—what a liberal, educated, Western audience has been tutored to know about Indigenous existence and what Karrabing members want to say about who they are—that all Karrabing films make visible.

Ethnography/ Documentary

One of the continual questions the Karrabing are asked is one of genre (Povinelli 2016). Depending on where the films are shown, different suggestions are presented for members to select from: ethnography, documentary, surrealism, hyperrealism, fiction, or neorealist nonfiction. When Povinelli is available to the audience, the question often turns to ethnographic film, and more specifically, the tradition of Jean Rouch and his work in colonial French West Africa (Rouch 1978). Some are more insistent than others that the films be considered part of the ethnographic tradition (as opposed, say, to Augusto Boal's [2000] techniques otherwise known as 'theatre of the oppressed').

There are many things one might say about this. The first, importantly, is to note that contemporary ethnographic film is an incredibly rich and diverse visual field, one that is often more effective as a probative media than written ethnography, which nonetheless has been relentlessly critiqued as the ultimate form of colonial representation (Biddle 2008; Deger 2006; Ginsburg 2010, 2011; MacDougall 1998). As one of the founders of ethno-fiction—a genre that would spill into the written work of innovative anthropologists like Michael Taussig (Eakin 2001; Taussig 2004)—Rouch's own work broke multiple existing genres and helped to create visual anthropology as a field; but the problematics of representing 'the Other' simply to re-present ourselves remained. As Rachel Moore (1992) argued some time ago, 'Indigenous video' does not solve the problems which plague claims of ethnographic authority. Yet while these are important discussions, they misdirect Karrabing intentions. Working through issues of (mis)translation and (dis)orientation are key

Karrabing methods, yet members have never positioned their work as the empowered solution to issues of anthropological voice, raising the question of why ethnographic film is assumed to be the genre in which the Karrabing are working.

One answer is obvious: one of its members is an identified anthropologist, albeit one who became such at the request of the parents and grandparents of current Karrabing members (Povinelli 2016). Another answer is that the Collective builds their narratives out of their everyday lives, and representing the quotidian is the claimed space of anthropological work. What is more interesting to explore is the collapse of a collective form of creation into a form of being represented by oneself or another: by the anthropologist or by the group. In other words, the function of the film work is to be represented or to represent oneself to an audience. To show oneself for the other. As Linda Yarrowin has said, 'Our films show what it is really like, what's really going on, in our lives.' At another time, she restressed the point: 'A true story but story; real but got story.' Likewise, Natasha Bigfoot Lewis describes Karrabing films as 'true' in the sense that even though the most documentary of the films are fictional scenes mocked up out of reality, they are things that have or could have happened, a truthful capture of being Indigenous today. And yet what members also say is that these films are making true something 'in but as-of-yet unable to define' about the world. Sheree Bianamu and Ethan Jorrock, younger members of the Collective, describe this as a coming to understand, through the process of pulling into visibility through the needs of filming and sweating back into Country, how the stories their parents and grandparents told them are not merely 'children stories' but a means of framing their and their cohort's actions and land reactions (Bianamu et al. 2017). Here, the question turns from one of genre and classification to practice and formation: what practices bring forward a formation of social and land existence that Karrabing members struggle to (re)make as true, an issue which surfaces again with the question of collaboration.

Collaboration

The word collaboration, like ethnography, is not a word Karrabing tend to use, although it is a question routinely asked, perhaps as a front for the question people are too polite to ask: namely, what exactly is Karrabing? Either way, answers are not readily converted into the pithy statements different interlocutors are cued to hear, for they cut athwart the anthropologised definitions of land, kinship, and re-

latedness now enshrined in both legal and popular cultural recognition systems. The singularity of the concept also implies a mode of copresence that would otherwise not exist but for the deliberate intention of working together, raising the question: is it collaboration when the formation is already a set of relations among people who have lived with, loved, hated, and helped each other forever, relations of timeless *durée* and meaning? Here, we remember Rex Edmunds's statement that Karrabing means 'as the tide comes in, coming together'. This describes a group of people who, like the tides, come together and move apart as different functions of their lives converge and dissipate, neither as a once-off nor as a constant steady state, but as a continuation of relational practices.

Conceived in terms of funding systems, 'collaboration' might further assume members of the Collective represent discrete sovereign descent groups, as if these are an actual timeless entity—as if different descent groups discretely exist, having always done so in this type of form, who are now collaborating. Here too there is greater fluidity in practice. Let's say one way in which you get Country is through your father; but if your father dumped you ('just left his egg'), then you might reckon Country through your mother's father. Then, areas that might be one's country are always distributed and shifting. Tides come in and out, the sands shift, the fires rage, the rivers flood, banks erode, the Dreamings are crossed and push back with their demands, economic livelihoods ebb and flow, and people move and get married across different assemblies. There are absorptive modes of kinship and there are exclusive ones. For Karrabing members, absorptive modes dominate: blood relations and friends alike are enfolded. Of course, formal kin might be judged with different criteria: how good an aunty, or daughter, nephew, son is this one, in relation to affective ties met or failed? But this is as fixed as group boundaries might get; which is to say, affectively speaking again, hardly fixed at all, amid other histories of relating, responding, beholding, and feeling—and simply being present, returning, staying. It would be truer, but perhaps not clearer, to say the Collective collects relations between people who transcend the normative categories of liberal recognition. So another answer to the question of what is the Karrabing, or how does it collaborate, might be to say it is a formation that represents decisive self-organising prior to the imposed land council model of sovereign groups that preclude lively sociality. And this convoluted answer would be needed because all this inherent fluidity became administratively settled under systems of bureaucratic and anthropological recognition: the boundary and the heteronormative descent deemed by social anthropologists as being true for everywhere helped render all other modes of assembling secondary, meeting a government demand for certainty in the moment of exerting disciplinary muscularity out of old ethnographic forays (Povinelli 2002). Karrabing posit a mode of belonging to each other and to a stretch of landscape that runs counter and diagonally across this ethnographic burden, refusing it, as Audra Simpson (2014) might say, even as they foreground how this burden weighs down and deforms their lives—and deforms them according to a specific, if evolving, late liberal settler logic. Yet, just as a self-organising 'all one family' assemblage does not pull anthropologisms from the law's determinative carvings, so too Karrabing members are apprehended differently.

Povinelli: 'We can love each other as much as we want—but white people and governments interpret and frame us differently; we can't pretend the world is structured differently.'

Cultural Maintenance

If a general demand is often made of Indigenous collectives to produce narratives as forms of representation rather than as filmic innovation or straight play, a more specific demand is that Indigenous artistic effort be for something beyond the artistic production itself. Again, like the question of genre, or collaboration, the matter is complicated. After all, as a group the Karrabing Collective, including Povinelli, see filmmaking as a powerful means of actualising what is already potentially within the group. Telling and retelling narratives, analysing why scenes follow each other, figuring out how one generation's embodiment of their analytics of people and place is refigured in another, and arguing about what aspect of this analytic should be a part of a film: all these practices do indeed keep in the present, by making vital and compelling, what settlers would like to confine to the fading past. One could probably even quantify the effects of filmmaking and the continuing embodiment of Karrabing beliefs as a form of 'cultural maintenance'.

And yet, cultural maintenance per se is not why many Karrabing make films and artworks. Instead, they make them because how they now make them—on their own schedule; scenes shot periodically; in some cases one person playing one role, in other cases multiple bodies playing multiple parts—is fun and absorbing, a diversion in a boring week, a means to open travel interstate and overseas, a way of having something 'to show' in their lives, a pragmatic reason to come together, and a reason to co-create. Likewise, the success of Indige-

2 A question that is beyond the scope of this essay but deserves separate reflection is that of adoption and why specific art world curators have responded to Karrabing films so positively, citing Karrabing innovations in terms of length, addressivity, and aesthetic imaginaries, including their layering and articulating of images to demonstrate both the separation of Indigenous and non-Indigenous peoples and their irreducible interpenetrations.

nous film and art as a mode of production, and the vital roles played by regional art and media centres in Australia, does not necessarily pivot on grand intent or glorious capacities[2] but because they enable a way of doing, involving, and being together on country that is otherwise being strangled (for more on art centres, see Biddle 2016; on copresence as creativity in land care, see Vincent 2017). Film and art succeed for Karrabing when they take on board seriously the terms of everyday life and pragmatics. The multiplicity of reasons various members might make films opens the purposivity of filmmaking to an ever-widening set of ends and thus opens the possibility of what filmmaking might do for Karrabing members. In this sense, Karrabing filmmaking refuses the late liberal capture of all practices by economic rationality or cultural recognition, including the idea of filmmaking as an apprenticeship to a more industrious pathway in the name of individual or community betterment. But this, like any answers so far, cannot lessen audience and potential funder demands that the point of making films is transitional, a teleological quest for a self-disciplined and accredited future destiny.

Anthropologist in audience: 'So I noticed from the credits [for *Windjarrameru*] that Aboriginal people are not holding the cameras. Are they being trained to this work, so they can get jobs?'

Training

Particularly in Australia, where bureaucratised apperception of Indigenous possibility reigns even within anthropological circles, there is an ongoing demand that Aboriginal people adhere to reifications of their traditions. In terms of content, Indigenous sufferers must be obligated by their responsibilities to Country, and be thwarted by an uncaring State, in particularly recognisable ways. And as filmmakers holding the restorative device that now symbolises all racial and economic inequality, the camera itself, they should not only be representing themselves as ethnographic subjects but also as good citizens in the making. The work of being involved in films cannot be to simply provoke thought, mess around with meaningful purpose, have an excuse to get together, relieve boredom, or have fun, but has to be tied to an instrumental outcome. That is, beyond the demand that a film's political work be done according to narrative conventions, audiences want the additional reparative move of having black hands holding the camera: anything less is a diminution of Indigenous speaking authority, and a weakened platform for the ultimate goal of 'real jobs'.

That the marshalling of non-Indigenous resources, expertise, and mediatic technologies in order to rewrite how the profound inhospitalities of settler colonialism are survived and resisted is not a betrayal of one's indigeneity seems like an obvious point, one that has been powerfully made by scholars and practitioners alike.[3] But given the insistent demand that this playful work of critique and analysis instead be interpreted as a labour of self-improvement, oriented toward the fictive policy category called 'real work', it is a point worth reiterating. The instrumental demand has interpolative effects. Karrabing members will answer that they too are showing their agency. But when Linda Yarrowin tells a questioner: 'We actually doing something for ourselves. Not just being stomped down. People recognise we. Make us stronger,' this is not a statement of 'we are training ourselves for the purpose of securing tax-paying jobs as videographers,' but indicates a different pragmatism: one of confirming and creating social relations, activating new possibilities for ongoing and freely associating agency, in a situation in which land itself (and not only government) has desires for and designs on people's agencies.

There is another purpose of the filmmaking that the younger members note which could be categorised as 'development' oriented: the pleasure that comes from shooting scenes, and of showing them to appreciative audiences, travelling across their countries and the world. Indeed, the way Karrabing increasingly produce their films strains the military worker logic of film production with its harsh timetables, technical requirements, and shoot schedules. Moving to smartphone cinematography, as the latest productions do, scenes are shot whenever the time seems right—folks are around; moods are good; an iPhone is charged; the place is right. And why not? Living within late settler liberalism creates enough stress for anyone and everyone. What if filmmaking were at core to retrain the self to instead experience the ludic pleasures of co-making, of consciously co-being, without a disciplining agenda?

Behind the scenes, these different perspectives are given shape in outline form as people talk through various possible scenarios, sometimes in formal meetings, but just as often more informally, as people are driving somewhere, sitting around somewhere else. All scenes are improvised based on members' experience, desires, and mutual understanding. This said, while the above expositions suggest neither wholesale acceptance nor rejection of liberal settler terms and conditions but rather a grappling with its incessant demands and having fun in the process, Karrabing filmmaking is not about substituting an avant-Indigenous cinematic practice to replace that of Hollywood, or for that matter, government-generated truth claims, with counterclaims about Indigenous alterity. Instead, they are a practice of critical probing of the conditions (of continuation) within which the lived realities of Indigenous lifeworlds proceed. And herein lies the rub for reception politics. Karrabing films are better described as the residual artifacts, not quite secondary but not quite objects either, of ongoing living analytics that are expressed in multiple modalities, being playful, hanging around, environmental listening, and political scanning included.

Transparency

Rocky:
'Berragut [white people] got this way of talking;
what do they mean with that word "transparency"?'

It was an enjoyable conversation at the end of a film shoot. Tess, the policy ethnographer, was asking her foreign types of questions about Karrabing decision-making processes and what people meant by their term 'open book', mimicking audience interest in how the Collective operates as a collective. 'Open book', she learned, like transparency, had flexible valence, generating different kinds of synonyms, from 'nothing is hidden' or a shared problem ('what are we going to do with the money?'), to a probative sense of opening a topic in which everyone can participate, without a hidden agenda, without a fast looming deadline, with the pace, like that of using iPhones for filming, that allows multiple styles of chipping in. Open book means words do not veil intentions but disclose potential actions, establishing agentful possibilities.

It contrasts with—which is to say, in discussion it was contrasted with—how non-Indigenous people tend to deal with Karrabing members. An example was given. A land council representative might call, demanding to speak to a 'Traditional Owner'.[4]
Speaking to this new category of legal personhood clarifies the mechanism for individualising and hierarchising the negotiation of access to land, usually for non-Indigenous extraction and enterprise development purposes. The transparent consultation, already made opaque to anyone outside the introduced category of 'Traditional Owner', can further hide its agenda through an overabundance of impenetrable material, said too fast; as comprehensiveness in the service of obfuscation, delivered in thick documents; or as radically simplified brevity, as in a pipeline that is coming through, with no words on the two kilometre land clearances either side of the pipeline to be permanently levelled along its entirety (the hidden sting behind the actual consultation being recalled). Such transparency is relayed in *Wutharr*, where the 'why' of fines is conveyed through the administrative violence of impenetrable documents.

3 See Ginsburg 2004.
4 In the Aboriginal Land Rights (Northern Territory) Act 1976 (Cth), section 3, Traditional Aboriginal Owners are defined legally as 'in relation to a relevant tract of land, a "local descent group" of Aboriginals who: (1) have common spiritual affiliations to a site on the land, being affiliations that place the group under a primary spiritual responsibility for that site and for the land; and (2) are entitled by Aboriginal tradition to forage as of right over that land).'

Linda: 'That story [from Berragut], it cross-crosses. One story for this person; a different one for wepella [us people]. Like snake.'

Or, closer to the scene of global audience reception, via the background work of getting Karrabing members physically to such scenes of audience reception, we could take the moment of trying to get passports. After searching for birth certificates, creating repeat headshots to find ones which retained distinct facial features out of a booth's poor artificial lighting, and locating legitimate 'authorised' witnesses to sign these photographs as true, members discovered they had faithfully completed the wrong forms. Between earlier encounters with the passport authorities and the day of submission, another tectonic policy shift had occurred. Children born from naturalised Australian citizens could no longer assume their own Australian citizenship, a restriction that was announced in the negative, non-transparently: a line requesting proof of parent's naturalisation as part of a passport application no longer appeared in the otherwise identical forms, rendering our completion of the original, subtly more inclusive, document null and void. As the now incorrect documents of Indigenous applicants were torn up, the settler colonial nation-state asserted the non-national status of some, but not all, of its immigrant offspring.

So can the ongoing distance between Indigenous everyday lives and the desires of their interlocutors be bridged? We would say the answer is not better and better rendition. The Karrabing did not form themselves to be a translation machine or as a solution to the representational dilemmas of ethnographic description under continuing occupation. Rather, the gaps in interpretation and expectation are an inevitable outcome of the bureaucratised, ethnologised imaginations that many viewers bring to their interpretation, elicited by Karrabing media regardless of intention, revealing the power or force of the demand that Indigenous communicative forms be reformatted, or levelled, so as to be comprehendible and intelligible, while avoiding the implication that structural relations of power the films speak to sit inside theatre spaces too. Grounded in the desire for palatable, consumable difference, the films resist while accommodating the audience expectations they are speaking to, an accommodation that attenuates as Karrabing filmography moves further away from more readily readable ficto-documentary formats into the more real surreality enabled by smartphone technologies. In this, the audience reception loop is similar to that of policy expectation, permeating creative efforts even as it is sidestepped, simultaneously satisfying and resisting the desire for redemptive Indigeneity as a condition of audibility.

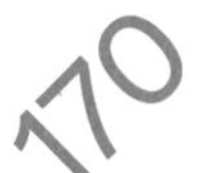

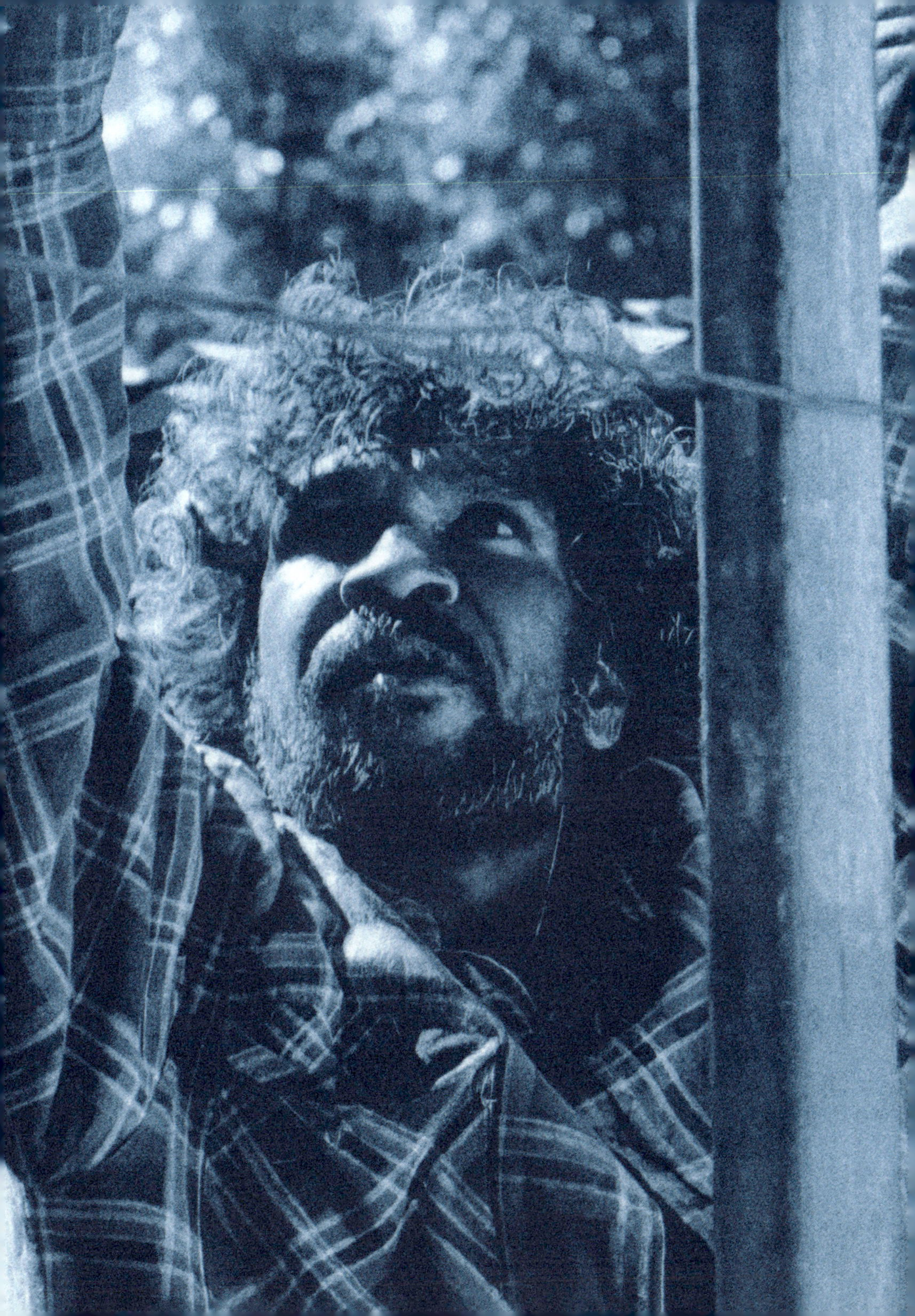

Comedy of Entanglement: Karrabing Film Collective[1]

May Adadol Ingawanij

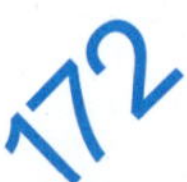

How to tell stories of relations and existence? This is a key question being posed across wide-ranging fields of practice to retune our imaginaries of ecological entanglement and possibilities of life in the Anthropocene. What processes of making, what expressive and combinatory forms, create affects and concepts that make tangible the connection between colonisation and environmental catastrophe, that embody imaginative futures and imaginaries of life for all? The novelist Amitav Ghosh speculates that the modern novel form itself, with its reality effects grounded in the investment in statistical probability and in the everyday of bourgeois ideology, is ill-suited to the contemporary urgency of narrating climate catastrophe.[2] In his recent study of artistic practices and environmental engagement, the art historian T.J. Demos surveys speculative uses of film documentary, installation, and artistic research to create different ways of perceiving the violence of state and corporate extraction and grasping moments of resistance and possibility.[3] The multi-authored book *Arts of Living on a Damaged Planet* (2017) proposes the figures of the ghost and the monster, an ethics of creation and expression lived as curiosity and attentiveness, and the cultivation of skills of foraging and gathering rather than conquest, as components of ways of living and creating symbiotic stories within landscapes haunted by histories of human destruction and past intimations of different possible futures.[4]

My article approaches the short films of Karrabing Film Collective as examples of audio-visual form and filmmaking praxis that use the comedic as a generative element. Humour strikingly shapes Karrabing's tactics of showing stories of an ongoing indeterminate existence in a damaged landscape of multiply intertwined and conflicted ecologies. In its self-description, Karrabing is a 'grassroots cooperative of friends and family members ... whose lives interconnect all along the coastal waters immediately west of Darwin' in Australia's Northern Territory, and across the Anson Bay, 'stretching outward into a global transnational network of curators, artists and filmmakers.'[5] To date, Karrabing has made a handful of short films whose stories and formal experimentations draw directly on the daily realities of Indigenous existence in Australia. In the past decade Karrabing members have been evicted from their homes and have had personal relations badly affected by state policies that have served to obstruct Indigenous claims to recognition of ownership of land. Experiences within and immediate to this intergenerational and dispersed group ground its filmic analysis of 'contemporary settler colonialism', and the purpose of its filmmaking is to use the process, event, and expressive capacities of film practice to keep moving within the corrosive and con-

1 This text was originally published in *Afterall* 48, Autumn/Winter, 2019, pp. 26–37.

2 Amitav Ghosh, *The Great Derangement: Climate Change and the Unthinkable*, Chicago: University of Chicago Press, 2016, pp. 15–24.

3 T.J. Demos, *Decolonizing Nature: Contemporary Art and the Politics of Ecology*, Berlin: Sternberg Press, 2016, pp. 167–98.

4 Anna Lowenhaupt Tsing, Heather Anne Swanson, Elaine Gan and Nils Bubandt (ed.), *Arts of Living on a Damaged Planet*, Minneapolis: University of Minnesota Press, 2017, pp. G1–G14.

5 Tess Lea and Elizabeth A. Povinelli, 'Karrabing: An Essay in Keywords', *Visual Anthropology Review*, vol. 34, no. 1, 2018, p. 37.

fined spaces of existence of Indigenous subjects in Australia—to make living a lively matter and to spot the potential to keep changing within the slow violence of settler late liberalism in order to 'challenge its grip'.[6] Over the past five years or so, Karrabing's short films have circulated widely within the transnational circuits of contemporary art, film festivals, and academic contexts. English-language publications accompany Karrabing's pragmatics of mobilising visibility within transnational arts circuits, mediated by high profile members—mainly Columbia University professor Elizabeth A. Povinelli.[7] References to the role of comedy and humour recur in these publications, most often in order to characterise the process and experience of filmmaking of the group as one of play and laughter, of spending and killing time, immersed in generating stories and filming them together.[8]

Rather than cover the same ground, I am interested in exploring humour in Karrabing's short films in terms of its strategy of enunciation and framing—as well as contextualising these works in relation to other moving-image practices whose formal strategies may be seen as adjacent to one another. Why take note of these formal aspects of Karrabing's filmmaking? Beyond the important if somewhat predictable point that humour remains an effective tool in countering clichéd portrayals of Indigenous existence as one of victimhood, conventionally drawn to the emotional tunes of the tragic, the solemn, or the melancholic, paying attention to comedic tactics in Karrabing's short films opens up avenues for juxtaposing and exploring resonances between the collective's audio-visual praxis and those examples elsewhere that would not otherwise be brought into proximity with each other. My life circumstances and research activities do not enable me to make meaningful comments about the significance of Karrabing's films in the context of Australia's politics of culture, land, and Indigenous subjectivity; rather, my take on its praxis is shaped partly by my continuing leftist attachment to the thoughts, styles, ambivalences, and afterlives of those films and written works of Third Cinema.[9] Karrabing's films capture my attention because they use humour and explore group dynamics, yet in different ways than do some of the canonical works of Third Cinema. Their experiment with unruly framing, creating disorientation through superimposition and shifting scales and directions of movement of objects and body parts in the frame, also resonate in rather unexpected ways with some works by contemporary artists in authoritarian regimes in Southeast Asia. Somewhat more randomly, the female elders in the films remind me of a fleeting figure of possibility among the extinguished and soon to be forgotten Red Shirts in Thai politics. That figure is *manut paa*, which liter-

6 Ibid.; see also Elizabeth A. Povinelli, *Geontologies: A Requiem to Late Liberalism*, Durham, NC: Duke University Press, 2016.

7 For instance, 'Karrabing Film Collective: Wutharr: Saltwater Dreams, Introduced by Vivian Ziherl', *Vdrome*, available at http://www.vdrome.org/karrabing-film-collective-wutharr-saltwater-dreams; 'Episode #18 Elizabeth Povinelli and Karrabing Film Collective', *Conversations in Anthropology@ Deakin* [podcast], January 2019, https://soundcloud.com/anthro-deakin/ep18-povinelli; 'Growing up Karrabing: a conversation with Gavin Bianamu, Sheree Bianamu, Natasha Lewis Bigfoot, Ethan Jorrock and Elizabeth Povinelli', *un Magazine*, vol. 11, no. 2, 2017, http://unprojects.org.au/magazine/issues/issue-11-2/growing-up-karrabing.

8 A conversation with a number of Karrabing members, which highlights the collective's valuing of the ludic qualities of their praxis, appears in a recent issue of *un Magazine* devoted to humour in art. See ibid.

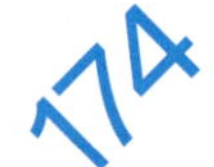

9 Key books on Third Cinema include Jim Pines and Paul Willemen (eds.), *Questions of Third Cinema*, London: BFI Publishing, 1990; Michael T. Martin (ed.), *New Latin American Cinema Volume 1: Theory, Practices, and Transcontinental Articulations*, Detroit: Wayne State University Press, 1997; Ella Shohat and Robert Stam, *Unthinking Eurocentrism: Multiculturalism and the Media*, Abingdon: Routledge, 2014.

ally translates as 'the auntie human type'—a figure that conjures the sturdy, mouthy, bumbag-slinging, stall-trading female of a certain age who no longer gives a shit and who every now and then makes disruptive noises and minor obstructions at the edges of protest situations.

Caricature of Circumstance

In *When the Dogs Talked* (2014), a visit by housing officials to the bungalow of a character, Gigi Lewis, based on a Karrabing member, triggers a reluctant journey. Young and old members of the extended family are surfing on whatever couch or floor surfaces they can fit in Gigi's small place. The officials have come to check up on reports of overcrowding; to buy some time, Gigi's sister goes to the door to tell them that her sister is not home. The officials demand that Gigi reports to them today, under threat of eviction, which leads the aunties to chivvy the group to get gas and phone credit so they can drive out into the country looking for her. A wayward, fractious search party eventually gets going. No one wants to be the first to offer to use their welfare card to fill the beaten-up truck. The vehicle breaks down on the red dirt road. A few of the men want to make a stop and go hunting instead. Family members they come across give contradictory information about where Gigi has gone and do not seem bothered by the situation. In any case, who can say for sure what the better outcome is, between hanging on in the cramped bungalow or losing the house and living an itinerant existence in tents in the country? More deliberations occur in *Wutharr, Saltwater Dreams* (2016), which entertains multiple possible causes for a boat's breakdown: Rex says the wiring just needs changing; Trever's story is that it is the ancestors' punishment; and Linda says the Christian church is testing her faith. It could equally have something to do with the state. An official walks up to the low fence demarcating the scuzzy yard of the house where a group of older Karrabing characters are passing time; the women are sitting on the wooden bench by the tree and the men are gathered to the other side under the porch. The official hands Linda Yarrowin, the registered owner of the boat, a thick form that she must fill in for not meeting the safety measures required to light a flare. She goes through each of the sections one by one. By the time the official is done reading out section five, 'settling [from welfare] payment', Linda's response is a sardonic mutter: 'far out.' She takes the form and passes it to another female to keep on reading. The question, peppered with legalese in Latin, demands a yes or no answer. The elder

10 Tess Lea and Elizabeth A. Povinelli, *Geontologies*, op cit., p. 39; Gabrielle O'Brien, 'Keeping Country Alive: Dreaming, Decolonisation and the Karrabing Film Collective', *Metro Magazine*, no. 199, 2019, pp. 108–13.

11 See Pramoedya Ananta Toer, *Tales from Djakarta: Caricatures of Circumstances and their Human Beings*, Ithaca, NY: Cornell University Press, 1999.

12 Benedict R. O'G. Anderson, 'Introduction', in ibid., p. 14.

calls out across the yard to the men: 'What's the answer?' 'Yes', 'no', is the casually disorderly reply. Whatever answer goes down on paper, there will likely be a fine to add to the existing toll that the accused already can't afford to pay.

Acts of unruly wandering, group undertakings, and journeys that go awry recur across Karrabing's short films. The Indigenous characters' digressive journeys are often triggered, or made illicit, by Kafkaesque state administration. In *The Jealous One* (2017), Rex Barramundi needs to cross the country to get to the spot on the beach where a funeral ritual will take place. He passes a sign prohibiting entry into Aboriginal territory without written permit and thus becomes a trespasser in his own country, pursued by an official. In the ensuing movement, commotion, digressions, and detours, these journeys and their wanderers slide and spiral in overlapping time-space dimensions and indeterminate states. Such spiralling structures *The Mermaids, or Aiden in Wonderland* (2018), a speculative story set in the near future when white people must protect themselves by remaining indoors—only Aboriginal people can survive outdoor contact with contaminated land, water, and creatures. The authority banishes the young Indigenous man Aiden, who had been captured as a child and turned into a test specimen, to the outside where he meets two male family members. The older men initiate his wandering across his contaminated homeland and tell ancestral Dreaming stories that contradict each other, yet seem connected. Stories of creation become stories of ancestral rivalry and shifting alliance, where entanglements of Dreamtime spawn variant speculative scenarios of surviving or surpassing the destruction of the whites. The trope of wandering, as Povinelli and others have observed, becomes Karrabing's method of representing landscape and embodying land, signalling affects and imaginaries of belonging and entanglement that differ from the settler colonial logic of land ownership and totemic recognition of Aboriginal land claims.[10]

The way these journeys unfold might be described as a kind of situational caricature. While the notion of caricature usually applies to those comedic modes that send up social types through exaggerated, parodic, or grotesque portrayals of their bodies, I am thinking here of the translated English-language title of a collection of short stories by Indonesian writer Pramoedya Ananta Toer, *Tales from Djakarta: Caricatures of Circumstances and their Human Beings* (1999).[11] In his introduction to the stories, Benedict Anderson notes an inversion. The caricaturist here 'works from his or her experience of life ... [and] ... announces her presence exactly as a teller of tales.'[12] Yet at the same

13 To borrow from Robert Stam's useful summary, see Robert Stam, *Keywords in Subversive Film/Media Aesthetics*, Hoboken, NJ: Wiley-Blackwell, 2015, pp. 79–86.

14 See ibid., pp. 68–100.

time what is being exaggerated are the circumstances, in this case of the newly independent Indonesia, which created absurd situations for its human beings. The storyteller directs his or her satirical barb, drawn from life experiences, at the circumstances rather than their social types. Moments in Karrabing's films capture a parallel dynamic. In the scene in *Wutharr* where Linda hands the far-out form to another female, the camera catches a glimpse of an irrepressible laugh coming from one of the other women; another delivers a line of dialogue in a voice cracking with laughter. These moments charmingly heighten caricature's capacity for cutting to the quick, when the performers are simultaneously acting in character and laughing from experience at the fictional circumstance, highlighting the routinised absurdity of state administrative delegitimisation of Indigenous existence.

Discordant Relations

Another distinctive way that comedy functions in the Karrabing's short films can be observed in comparison with the carnivalesque, an established trope in the films and theories of Third Cinema. Carnival creates ritualistic intervals of suspension of the rules of domination of the colonisers and the authorities. The carnivalesque creates utopian imaginaries of relations characterised by sensuous contact, carnality, conviviality, and suspension of hierarchy.[13] In its utopian duration the bodies of the oppressed intermingle and intertwine in collective waves, rhythms, and energy.[14] Time's texture and speculative power in Karrabing's films does not take on the form of the suspension of norms and institutions of domination. Instead, time figures through patterns of framing as riotous superimpositions and rescaling of object parts and body fragments within the frame. There is no outside of the everyday time of settler late liberal violence, yet that time of routinised administrative denial of life beyond the bare survival of Indigenous subjects intersects with and rubs against multiple other temporal scales, the deep time of partially connected and at times rivalling versions of ancestral Dreaming with the deep time of geological change and the accelerated time of capitalist extraction. And instead of the carnivalesque's investment in and utopian images of energetically intertwined, libidinous collective bodies, the group in Karrabing's films is a fractious yet somehow inexhaustible entity.

The group in this context consists of generations of humans, and humans with relations to a multiplicity of ancestors with situated presence in the environment and embodied as animal forms. The portrait of intergenerational and kinship relations in Karrabing's films is one of discord easily and at times frivolously triggered. In *Windjarrameru, The Stealing C*nt$* (2015), a group of young men open the cans of beer they stumble upon in the bush. They spot two male relatives painting a sign on the rock below and, with a mix of playfulness and aggression, chuck the empty cans at them. The argument between the old and young men spins out into multiple strands of claims, conflicts, and subterfuge. Police officers turn up; so too does the sister of the rock painter, who as it turns out is freelancing for miners digging illegally in the area. Her grandchildren are among the young men hiding among the trees from the police. Brother and sister get into a noisy argument, and while the police are trying to calm this conflict another grandmother tries to free one of the young men who she had sent to spy on the miners who has already been arrested. *Night Time Go* (2017) departs from other Karrabing films in incorporating archival actuality footage with fictional scenes sometimes presented in black and white and set in the past, to tell a speculative story of Karrabing ancestors as 'freedom fighters' who, with wooden sticks and bush survival skills, escape from an internment camp after World War II and force the retreat of the Australian army from their country. In the story, life in the camp is riven with conflicts. The inmates fight and accuse each other of stealing drinks and molesting their women. Gauging that their life in the camp is likely to be one of physical harm, death threats, petty rivalry, and mutual suspicion, the Karrabing ancestor characters escape in small groups. These miraculously effective 'freedom fighters' wander and disappear in small clusters, uninterested in grand gestures of Indigenous sovereignty and bearing no evident symbol of collective solidarity, unaided by purposefully connected maps, underground networks, or tunnel systems associated with the model of guerrilla resistance.

The camera held by someone who is familiar to the person being turned into an image can license a different degree of proximity and intimacy, and with results that may transgress the ethics of display or at least the etiquette of the publicly displayable. Martha Atienza's video *Anito* (2012), which records the carnivalesque duration of the annual Christian-animist Ati-Atihan procession on her home island of Bantayan in the Philippines, plays on its ambiguous status as simultaneously, a neighbourhood movie and an artist's moving-image work. The woman behind the camera is in the thick of the procession and her body in synch with its wild rhythm. Her lens gets very

15 See 'Growing up Karrabing', op. cit.

close to the visibly drunk children staggering as they swig from liquor bottles. What is the difference between playing this footage in the neighbourhood the evening after the procession ends and projecting it elsewhere on the circuits of contemporary art and film? Anito speculatively superimposes neighbourhood and dispersed sites of projection, enacting an ambiguous elision in its trajectories of display. The video's indeterminate directions of address are simultaneously internal, addressed to fellow islanders in the neighbourhood who would recognise the kids and the context of festivity, and also external, available to strangers on art world circuits who may or may not reach beyond reading such images via the cliché of Philippine exotica. Atienza's work parallels in this sense the multidirectional expressive trajectories of Karrabing's films, which are simultaneously internally addressed as artefacts from an Indigenous group's praxis of play, and externally addressed as mobile works presented on transnational art and educational circuits.

Unruly Superimpositions

The earlier Karrabing films, *When the Dogs Talked* and *Windjarrameru*, were shot on digital cameras by professional cinematographers accustomed to the pace and method of an industry-focused production schedule. From *Wutharr* onwards the group shifted to shooting with iPhone cameras, with some of its members doing the cinematography, and adopting a different schedule, seemingly closer to the casual pace of home movies.[15] Shifting to the phone camera apparatus has expanded the scope for portraying unruly group relations and entangled habituation. With these later films, the sense of subversiveness and disorientating energy are less derived from bodily performance than from enframing. The more recent films use extreme close-ups to a much greater degree, creating decentred images where body fragments take up a margin of the frame filled with earth, mud, water, sky, or all of these superimposed at once in saturated ochre or blue and pink palettes. A part of a foot occupies the lower left corner of the frame in an extremely low shot, with the camera at virtually ground level, such that the dry earth and trampled weeds fill the frame extending into depth of field. A medium shot presents only the torso of a body moving towards the camera person, the head itself cut off the top frame line. A white 'Hand of State', as the end credit of *The Jealous One* puts it, taps a keyboard. A dark hand marks incisions in the mudflats with a stick.

16 See James Penney, 'Zooming Out: Sembene's Ceddo and Third Cinema Aesthetics', *Canadian Journal of Film Studies*, vol. 24, no. 1, March 2015, pp. 2–24.

17 See Daniel Morgan, 'The Afterlife of Superimposition', in Dudley Andrew (ed.), *Opening Bazin: Postwar Film Theory and its Afterlife*, Oxford: Oxford University Press, 2011, pp. 127–41.

Karrabing's experimentation with what may be termed unruly framing and superimposition resonates interestingly with a number of contemporary works of the South exploring parallel themes of political ecologies, intersubjective relations and environmental entanglements. Compared with the approach to representing human bodies in examples from the canon of Third Cinema, Karrabing's camera phone enframing situates relations among bodies, and between bodies and matter, as embodying partial and fragmented connections—this is characterised by fluctuations and multidirectional ooziness and tensility of contact surface. In comparison, historical examples such as the dialectical film praxis of Ousmane Sembene's *Ceddo* (1977) shifts between long-distance shots visualising tableaux of bodies in circular groups and lines, and rapid zooms into close-ups of particular faces. As James Penney points out, such vacillation signals the dialectical relationship and movement between the circumstances and scope for agency and action of contending social groups and the perspectives and desires of individuals in them.[16] In this earlier example, human bodies are figured as agents that make history under circumstances not of their choosing, and they do so with feet on stable ground and bodies in solid landscape.

In Karrabing's recent films, notably *Mermaids* and *Wutharr*, rather than figuring intersubjective relations as the dialectics of long-shot tableaux and zooms, the compact phone camera aesthetics frames Indigenous human entanglement in multiple ecologies and situated relations via unruly superimpositions of images, in aggregate layering a part of this face with a part of this human or the body of a fish, a bird, a mud crab, a fly. Often, the framing superimposes fragments of a human, animal, or mythological body on land with images of the mass and motility of water, mud or swamp. The elements intermingle through unruly superimposition in the frame, such that earth, water, and fire, or salt and fresh water, do not so much meet at a certain threshold but pile and stack on top of each other, undermining the impression of gravitational pull and territorial volume and solidity. In film history, the technique of superimposition has typically been used to portray an individual's dream, fantasy, or altered psychological states, or it has been used to create effects of the supernatural and the uncanny. And some early film practitioner-theorists approached film's capacity for superimposition as indication of the potential of cinematic consciousness and thinking independent of and beyond the capacity of the human brain.[17] In the case of Karrabing's films, superimposition does something different. It figures multiplicity of times and versions of existence, and interconnection of ecologies, as the elemental medium of the characters' present-day existence. Superimposing extreme close-up images of the sparrow hawk and sea monster and a fragment of a human face situates the presentness of ancestral presence and people's ongoing relations with rivalrous but connected ancestral stories. Superimposition's transformation of landscape, sites, and matter into gravitationally suspended layers is also a kind of dialectical figure. It ambiguously figures the potential for radically altered existence recalibrating human agency within ecologically multiple and entangled time-space. At the same time the enframing of de-solidified ground and unearthly movement of liquid alludes to the contamination of the environment as the now ubiquitous circumstance of existence.

Lastly, we might also note a striking affinity between the disorientating super-impositions in Karrabing's recent films and a number of artists' moving-image works of the South. Eduardo Williams's short film, *Could See a Puma* (2011), follows the wandering of a group of teenage boys from rooftop verandas to a flatland strewn with abandoned and half-demolished concrete buildings, onto the edges of a swamp and into a forest. Over the duration of the film, the boys walk, scramble, and tumble in this eerie landscape of multidirectionally elastic time-space whose hues shift between mauve and a pinkish glow, dusk and nocturnal shadows. The film gradually renders the boys' languorous wandering in a manner transgressing the cinematic norm of showing humans walking laterally across the frame, a routine sight of human bodies traversing solid, inert space in gravitationally credible directions. The penultimate shot in *Could See a Puma* creates a vertiginous sensation when one of the boys exits the screen via a casual subterranean step, seemingly dipping through solid dark ground, and beyond the bottom frame line. A similarly incredible direction of movement down the bottom frame line also occurs in the works of Khvay Samnang and Taiki Sakpisit. Samnang's two-channel video installation, *Preah Kunlong* (2017), features a body with a headdress shaped from twigs and vines into forest creatures such as a peacock, an elephant, or a crocodile, moving in an animistic dance in the Chong ancestral forest in Cambodia currently threatened with a hydro-electric megaproject. At times the disorientating extreme close-ups show a fragment of the human-animal's head in the bottom area of the frame. The flow of dance movement makes the head disappear offscreen, down past the bottom frame line; in a similar manner, Taiki's archival assemblage, *Time of the Last Persecution* (2013), recuts and slows down fragments of early 1980s Thai mythological films, intensifying the sense of a cosmos unmoored with psychedelic shots of swaying bodies sliding offscreen in a downward slow-motion stroboscopic pulse. Less evidently excessive yet no less unruly in its conceptual approach to enframing are the exaggeratedly symmetric patterns of elegant camera movement linking Charles Lim Yi Yong's short film *All the Lines Flow Out* (2011) with his *SEA STATE 6* (2016). In the former, Lim repurposes a slow, aquatic version of early cinema's phantom ride shot to figure the movement of water along the Singapore River out to the surrounding sea, the vast volume of water whose agency, liquidness, and motility the official imaginary of Singapore's capitalist expansion tries to leave behind. In *SEA STATE 6*, the camera glides vertically down a tunnel system, moving smoothly yet strangely to the mellow rhythm of a retro pop tune down a massive underground tunnel system below an artificial island created from land reclamation in Singapore, developed for storing liquid hydrocarbons.

...

The formal expression and enunciation of humour in Karrabing's films corresponds with all of these techniques: centred around images, durations, and processes, celebrating the unruliness and liveliness of beings across temporal and environmental scales. Their films are grounded in what we might call post-carnivalesque repertoires and potentials of ecological relations, and in creating forms with human and nonhuman bodily modes of performance. As such, they are part of a contemporary ensemble taking reflexive approaches to the possibilities of cinematic movement and framing to explore human conducts—whether gigantic endeavours of mastery or microscopic wanderings—in entanglement with treacherous, indeterminate, and politically shaped ecologies, and within tumultuous cosmologies unmaking humans at the limit of their power and capacity.

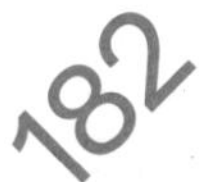

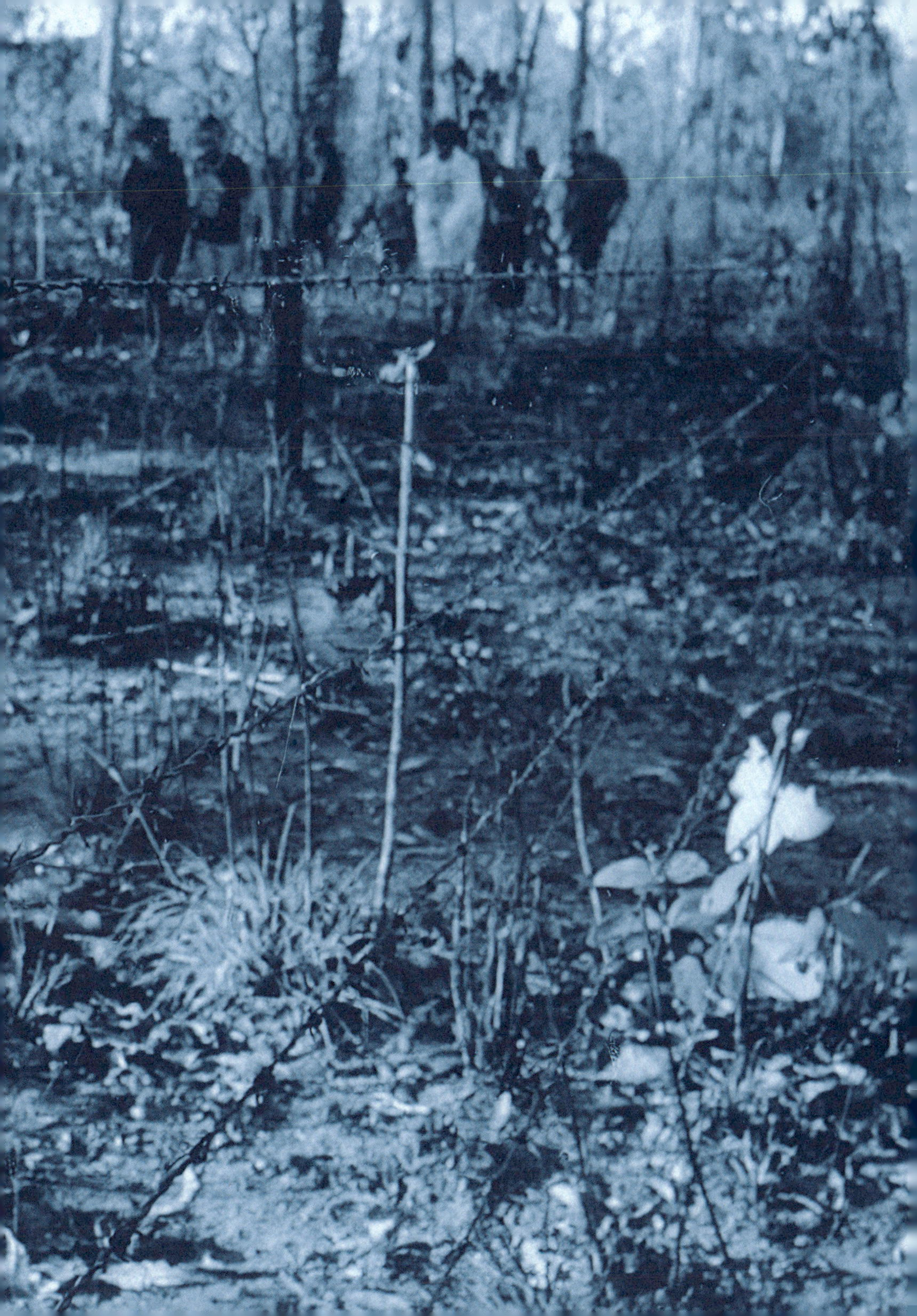

A Conversation at Bamayak and Mabaluk, Part of the Coastal Lands of the Emmiyengal People[1]

Elizabeth A. Povinelli and Rex Edmunds

1 This text was originally published in *L'Internationale online* on 3 October 2019, as part of the e-book *Living with Ghosts: Legacies of Colonialism and Fascism,* edited by Nick Aikens, Jyoti Mistry and Corina Oprea: https://www.internationaleonline.org/people/elizabeth_a_povinelli_and_rex_edmunds.

The following conversation between Rex Edmunds and Elizabeth A. Povinelli took place at Bamayak and Mabaluk, part of the coastal lands of the Emmiyengal people. They reached this remote territory by both bushwhacking a road through the area's highland forests and swamps with a group of Karrabing; others in the group come from adjacent coastal lands. Their conversation has been translated into English from the local Creole.

EP → Elizabeth A. Povinelli
RE → Rex Edmunds

EP I got an invitation to write a piece from some folks in Europe, *L'internationale online,* a mob of art European museums in Spain, Slovenia, Belgium, Turkey, Poland, the Netherlands, Sweden, and Ireland, I think. They have a project called 'Our Many Europes'. They are interested in non-fascist forms of belonging to country. So I thought, why not have a conversation with you about our different patrilineal countries?

RE Why would they be interested in that?

EP Well, in Hungary that have this guy called Orbán; and in Turkey, Erdoğan; and Russia, Putin; and the US, Trump; and Italy, Salvini. All these guys are pushing this idea that their nation should be just for 'us', not 'those other' people. They say that there is an original American or European or Turk or Russian and that the government should be protecting and advancing these people first and foremost (or only). America First, Hungary First, Russia First, Turkey First. When they say this, what they really mean is white Americans, European Hungarians, Russian Russians, et cetera. And it's not just these nations. Lots of other European nations have right-wing political parties gaining ground over the same idea. And so everyone is worried about fascism re-emerging. They wonder, can people have strong feelings for country, forms of belonging to a place, without becoming a fascist?

RE Well, the first thing I would say is that really the whole of Australia is Indigenous. It belongs to us mob, to different Indigenous groups and the different ways they belong to their country. So what do they mean 'fascist'? What does that word mean?

EP People use the word both precisely and loosely. In a really simple way, I'd say that 'fascists' are those who believe that a place is only for one kind of person, like white or Christian or Hindu, or whatever. And that the government should work only on behalf of this one kind of person. Also, fascists spit on—English has the word 'denigrate'—others in order to build themselves up. And fascists claim that they are the original, true people of the place. The 1930s was when fascism took over Europe and other places: Hitler in Germany, Franco in Spain, Stalin in Russia, and Mussolini in Italy.

RE Your countrymen! So they think we are fascists if we say Australia is Indigenous?

EP That's why I wanted to talk with you—no, they don't. I don't either. I thought we could begin to show why by talking about what is similar and different between my village in the Alps and your country here at Bamayak and Mabaluk. We've talked about going to my village in the Alps for years now—as you know, Rex (Sing), Linda (Yarrowin) and Aiden (Sing) went there after our last Paris screening.

RE Yeah, Rex was telling me about it—how they asked about what clan you were from and how you picked it up.

EP I told them I was part of the Simonatze clan of Povinellis and picked it up through my father's father's side; it goes as far back as anyone can reckon, since around the 1700s.

RE White people have clans?

EP Some still do. Many did before, but then this way of life got wiped out.

RE These people who are interested in some other kind of belonging, do they think clans are or aren't fascist?

EP That's what I want to talk about. Like we've discussed before, there are a lot of similarities between Carisolo and Bamayak and Mabaluk. I pick up my relationship to Carisolo through my father's father and follow the father-line all the way back. You pick up your relation to Bamayak and Mabaluk the same way. Carisolo is and isn't inside the nation of Italy: it has been at the frontier of warring empires and nations since records were kept.

The Carisolo clans talk about the tourists who flock into the area for skiing, hiking, and biking as 'those Italians', because although Carisolo is now within the borders of the Italian state, Italians remain foreigners in some essential way. Bamayak and Mabaluk are also inside and outside Australia. Australia colonised them, but they remain yours and other Emmi's according to a way of belonging outside of nationalism. And I don't know, are settler Australians foreigners?

RE They kind of are. But I have a question for you, does your mob in Carisolo have totems? Dreamings? Like we do?

EP Not anymore, if we did. Some people say that before Catholicism we had sacred trees and spirits. But that was sometime in the eighth century. At the church Santo Stefano in Carisolo there is a mural dating back to 1534 which shows Charlemagne (Carlo Magna) coming to Carisolo to convert the natives. People were given a choice, either give up your superstitions or have your head cut off. Or that's the legend.

RE Remember when you, me, and Gavin were at Eindhoven that first time, talking with Annie Fletcher and Vivian Ziherl at Van Abbemuseum about maybe doing a show and we were looking at the artist's work ... what was her name? ... well, remember those pictures in the last room showing one group of white people slaughtering another group. It was wild. Like they showed what was going on in Europe during ... when?

EP The early part, eleventh century maybe, I think.

RE One group was slaughtering the other group like a herd of cattle. Leg up hanging from a tree, guts being pulled out, hearts in one bucket, livers in another. But human beings! I was like shit. And that really got me thinking. If they treat each other like that ...

And Annie said that this was part of the fighting between religions. So they were Catholics slaughtering other Christians, or the other way around—I can't remember. I started thinking, I've never heard any of the old people talk about this happening with us. Sure, people fought, speared each other, but mainly over a woman, or women might fight for a man with their fighting sticks. And if someone did something wrong like in a ceremony, they would definitely be punished, you know, the hard way. But just slaughtering each other like cattle. I was thinking, they did that and then they came to us and started doing the same.

EP That was the option Charlemagne supposedly gave to the villages in the Alps. Accept Catholicism or leg up. So no totems now, even if we had them.

Can we talk about why having a totem, or *durlg* in Batjemalh, *therrawin* in Emmi, might be interesting for the question of non-fascist forms of belonging to a country? Maybe you could talk about your totem and how it relates to your land?

RE I am Mudi or what white people call Barramundi, a kind of fish. I saw it once on the menu in New York City! Anyway, my Mudi sits on the tip of Mabaluk; it's reef-shaped, like the tail of the fish. The point of Mabaluk is shaped like a mudi. I get the totem from my dad and he from his dad. It's the same way my dad's brother and their kids, like Natie (Natasha Bigfoot), pick it up. And so it's been ours since before the white people and right back to the Dreaming time. And it still is. I don't know if it's right to say, but we're the chiefs. (*laughing*)

EP Ah, but smack on point. Maybe you can tell folks about what you and Linda (Yarrowin) were saying in the video we made for Natasha Ginwala's exhibition at the ifa-Galerie in Berlin, *Riots: Slow Cancellation of the Future* (2018). You talked then about 'separate-separate and connected'. Maybe you can also talk about your totem and ceremonies like rag burning, *kapug*?

RE Sure, my totem, my *mudi* is one of two sisters who were circling around a place called Bandawarrangalgen—this place is still there, as you know. As they were going around and around they made a dangerous whirlpool. They decided after a while—maybe they were jealous of something, maybe it was a man—that one would go upstream and become a freshwater barramundi and the other would stay in the saltwater; the saltwater one came to my land and sat down at Mabaluk. So these sisters are 'separate-separate'. They each have the place where they were and are now, but they are also connected because of this story and the land that their activity shaped into being the way it is today.

The film we did, *The Jealous One* (2017), is also about this kind of thing: why various ancestor totems ended up where they are today. But also how that thing, the spirit of the thing, is still in the people who come from that totem. So the *durlg* in the film, the sea serpent, is jealous for not being involved in a *corroboree* which the other totems were having, so he steals the fire and runs off into the sea and tries to drown it. And that's where the sea monster totem is today, belonging to the Bianamu mob. And that's why your brother Trevor has always been a jealous person. Other totems were involved and they are now in other places. (*both laughing*)

So it's like that: separate-separate but connected. You can and can't make them different. Like we talk about 'Karrabing' as meaning one of the tides, the low tide, which shows how various places are connected and different, as you can see the shape of the sand and the reefs and the deep channel waterways below the surface of the water. It's also what connects all of us. How can I take care of my land if you are destroying yours? I think white people are realising this with climate change and the poisons and plastic and radiation everywhere now. And fracking. They say, oh, we'll only frack in this little area, but the poisons might spread into the underground water.

EP I think rag burning might help outside people understand this idea of how everything was connected or joined together at the very beginning.

RE You mean like when someone dies and it's your mother or father or brother or sister or son or daughter?

EP Yeah, people wouldn't have a clue.

RE Well, if someone from your family dies we have the Christian funeral at the graveyard. If it's a ceremonial man or woman, then we also have a *wangga* to show respect. But, in any case, you keep the person's old clothes or stuff that has their sweat on them, the spirit of that person, you know. Then maybe after a year—should be a year or something like that—we have a rag burning. Like we did for Trevor's mum and Daphne's husband last year. Well, you need your uncle or aunt or cousin, in our way it's a cousin, like your mum's brother's kids or your dad's sister's kids to do the burning of the clothes. Because they are your aunt (father's sister) or uncle (mother's brother), they are always from another clan, so another country. Best if the uncle, aunt or cousins are close, but as long as it's connected in this way it's okay. How could I burn my mum's or sister's or father's clothes myself: no one who is in my totem group can touch those things during the ceremony. I am boss of them, but I cannot do it myself. I need my relations from that other totem or country.

I think you're right, white people don't understand this. White people, government law, they just look at the separate part. They give a little bit of land to this clan and a little bit of land to that clan. You're separated by this boundary—you are over here. So everyone has just a little bit of land and they don't think about all the connections which have always kept that land strong: ceremony; the actions of ancestors, like my *mudi* and her sister; and other things, like keeping the mangroves open and stuff. You can see how only recognising the separate-separate part fucks up everything when it comes to mining and royalties. Everyone just thinks about what they can get out of something. And as the poisons leak out, well, then, people start fighting each other, killing each other. Honestly, I think white people, lawyers maybe, or politicians, definitely miners, they do that on purpose: 'Ah, we'll let them rip each other apart.'

Before, we would settle the problem through ceremony, doing the ceremony or getting the marriage done which would create the possibility for bringing people together. People would fight, but then they'd get back together because they had to. This would make both countries stronger.

EP I have always found this super interesting when thinking about nationalism more generally and because of my own particular relation to Carisolo and Italy, or how I was raised by my grandfather and grandmother, who were both from the village. Grandpa, a Simonatze Povinelli, and Gramma, an Ambrosi (don't know which clan, but the Ambrosis were a smaller group).

Grandpa really drilled into our heads that we were in America and that was great for opportunity—he didn't think about the fact that our sense of possibility came from a genocidal displacement of Native peoples—but that we belonged to Carisolo. For him this was totally different from being from Italy or the US, because anyone could be from these places if they could get in and get citizenship. But we belonged to Carisolo on an entirely different basis: kinship and descent, the patrilineal, too. Maybe many would find that wrong, but there you go.

But the mode of belonging that the old people taught me and you and everyone in Karrabing, in which you have this foundational belonging, but also this foundational belonging that needs what is outside of it or next door or down the coast or inland, this was never a part of what my grandpa talked about.

RE Our sweat is also part of this, our spirit. Our ancestors are in us and we are in the ground as we hunt and look after the land. Land recognises us if we keep working for it. You know when you go hunting you can feel it, the ancestors—the land is a part of you. Or maybe they punish you first if you haven't visited for a long time. Our third film *Wutharr, Saltwater Dreams* (2016) was about this, aye?

EP Like the first go at making this road.

RE Yeah, so we were going really well, getting somewhere on that first day we were making it. And then, I don't know, I just felt the coast close by—and I knew not to drive over the pandanus trees—but something, someone, started spinning my head, playing tricks on me, come on just go. And then bang, my radiator bust. You ripped your fingers. Then you, Kelvin, and Kieran were stuck on the road getting back.

But this time, it was easy. They opened the space for us. Like, okay, so you didn't give up. You are willing to work for us, okay, we'll also make it easy. I think they think like that, the ancestors.

EP It's funny, because, again, so much resonates with what I hear about Carisolo and so much is different, too. For instance, the village and church are literally composed of our families' flesh and sweat, and no matter who dies everyone in the village has to walk up the hill to the original church, Santo Stefano, as a sign of respect to the family. And yet I have always said I am glad my grandparents migrated before World War II, because I don't know which way they would have gone under fascism. I just don't know. Part of me thinks you really have to have an idea of nationalism to have fascism.

RE Meaning?

EP Let's say my father married a non-white woman from outside of the Alps and Italy and then had us. We would still belong to Carisolo through him and my grandfather. I am sure there would be some serious commentary, but there would still be this other form of belonging underneath. But nationalism says, you are or are not an Australian. On what basis? Shouldn't it just be citizenship?

RE Aboriginal people didn't have citizenship till land rights, or before 1967 [reference to the 1967 referendum which gave the Australian federal government the power to count Indigenous people in the census and to legislate on behalf of Indigenous people].

EP Exactly, so if the original people aren't Australian, who is?

RE White people. Europeans. The same people who slaughtered each other and then shipped themselves here.

EP And they can't get over that. Neither can Americans. The day after Trump was elected, I was heading to the subway in New York, heading up to school—it was beyond horrifying for so many of us. Anyway, this white guy is passing me on the street and talking over my shoulder to another guy. He said something about 'an Arab' who he'd just told, Trump's going to send you back to where you came from, buddy. I was still deranged and said, 'Why don't you go back to where you came from? Why don't we all?' And he said, 'I am an American, full-blood.' I said, 'You're European, like me.' That's where it all started. I think nationalism starts as a European formation. It has always been about whites.

RE All I can say is that Europeans had their chance to show what they can do. It's our time now.

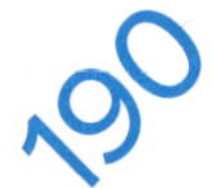

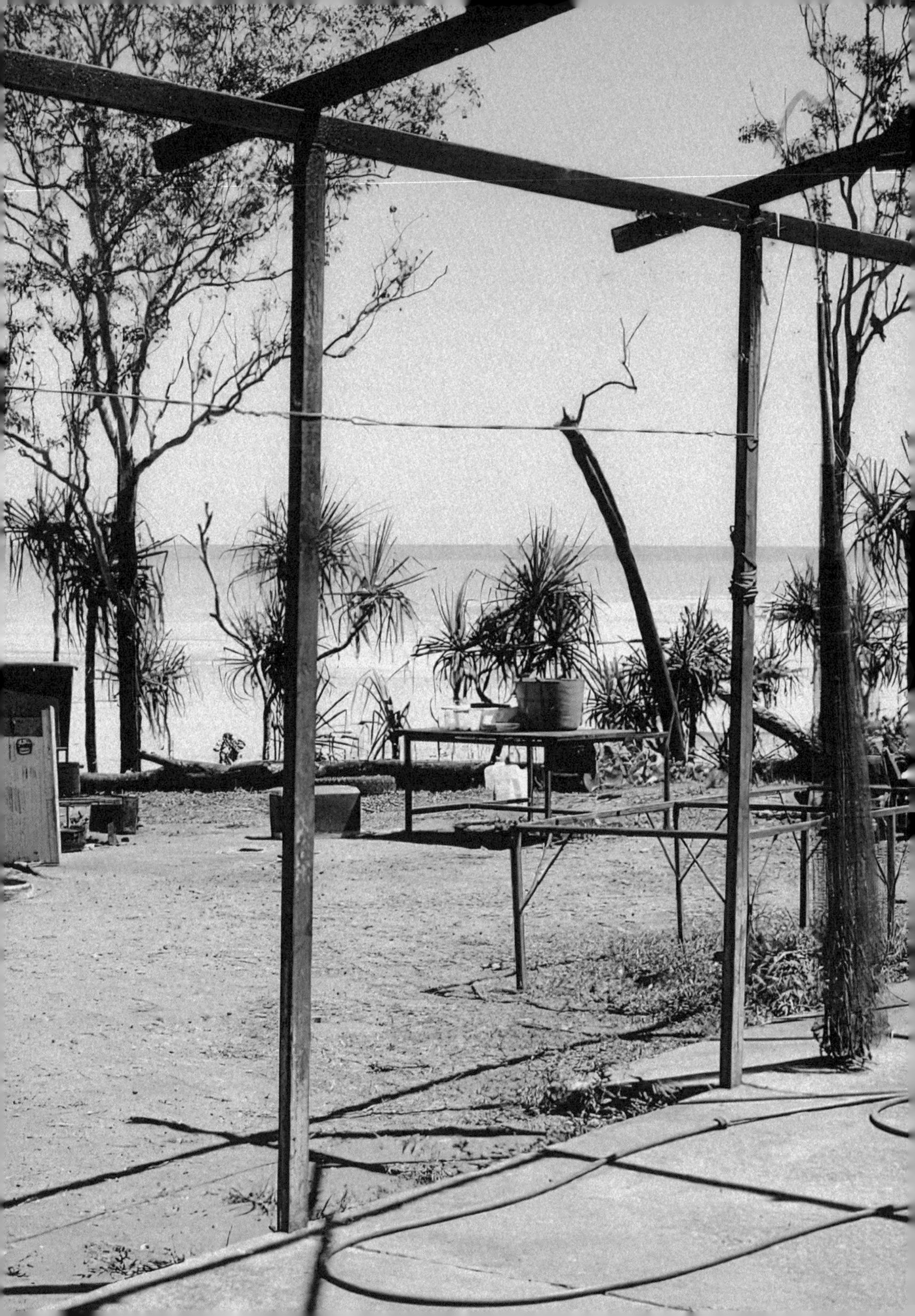

Karrabing Film Collective Tackles the Cultural and Environmental Devastation of Settler Colonialism[1]

Matariki Williams

1 This text was originally published in *Art in America,* 6 May 2020: https://www.artnews.com/art-in-america/features/karrabing-film-collective-day-in-the-life-1202686183. Copyrighted 2020. Penske Media Corporation.

The word 'karrabing', from which the Karrabing Film Collective takes its name, means 'tide out' in the Emmiyengal language, invoking the northwest coastline of Australia that connects the members of the collective, an intergenerational group of around thirty artists and filmmakers, most of whom are indigenous to the Northern Territory of Australia. Their use of the word offers an immediate insight into their work. As Karrabing member Natasha Bigfoot Lewis puts it, 'We are all saltwater from the same coast—connected lands from the same coast.'[2]

Karrabing's films are varied in style, but the group members have adopted an approach that they refer to as 'improvisational realism'. Shooting with iPhones or handheld cameras, they typically begin with a loose idea rooted in their everyday experiences rather than a fixed script, developing the plot and dialogue as they go, incorporating input from each participant. While their immediate community and environment are the foundation of Karrabing's films, often positioning viewers as fly-on-the-wall observers, these are not straightforward documentaries: realism is interwoven with alternative histories, speculative futures, and Dreaming narratives. As Nhanda and Nyoongar artist and curator Glenn Iseger-Pilkington explains, 'the Dreaming is the realm of ancestral spirits who formed Australia, giving plants, animals, language, lore, and law to the land. It operates beyond Western constructs of time, as a realm of cultural manifestation and unfolding that exists concurrently in our past, our present, and our future.'[3]

One main catalyst for the group's formation was the 2007 Northern Territory National Emergency Response, commonly known as the 'Intervention', a set of policies implemented by a federal government task force in response to a report commissioned by regional authorities on child sexual abuse and neglect in Aboriginal communities. The federal government enacted broad new legislation that gave it heightened control over Aboriginal communities, including restrictions on alcohol consumption, mandatory child welfare inspections, and a significant rise in policing.[4]

The Intervention coincided with the fallout from a riot at the Belyuen settlement, a rural Aboriginal community where many of the Karrabing members lived. The riot had attracted the attention of mainstream media outlets, and the members—many of whom had been left temporarily homeless—decided to produce their own accounts representing their perspective on issues affecting their communities. Along with American anthropologist Elizabeth A. Povinelli, a professor at Columbia University who first visited Belyuen in 1984 and has main-

2 'Growing up Karrabing: a conversation with Gavin Bianamu, Sheree Bianamu, Natasha Bigfoot Lewis, Ethan Jorrock and Elizabeth Povinelli', *UN Magazine*, 2017, unprojects.org.au.

3 Glenn Iseger-Pilkington, email to the author, April 6 2020.

4 Elizabeth A. Povinelli, *Geontologies: A Requiem to Late Liberalism*, Durham, NC and London: Duke University Press, 2016, pp. 24–25.

tained a close relationship with the community since, they formed the Karrabing Film Collective and made their first short film, *Karrabing! Low Tide Turning*, in 2011.

As a Māori person from Karrabing's neighbouring country, Aotearoa (New Zealand), I have certain historical commonalities with Aboriginal Australians and Torres Strait Islanders, Australia's two distinct Indigenous groups. We are all also citizens of Commonwealth countries with a long and sustained relationship built on geographical proximity, and we share a head of state, Queen Elizabeth II. Indigenous communities around the world—what Māori refer to as *iwi taketake*, or the long-established people—have similarities in terms of our relationships to our environments, and how our cultures are sustained by intergenerational connection. Despite a sense of solidarity in these shared values and the dubious honor of having experienced colonisation, however, we reject a simplistic view of global Indigenous homogeneity. We are not the same and cannot speak for one another; what we can do is speak with adjacency.

This is something I consider when approached to write about an Indigenous culture that I don't *whakapapa*—have a kin connection to: I mustn't oversimplify our similarities, nor overstate the closeness of our connections. Instead, I want to focus on what is most compelling to me about the Karrabing Film Collective's work: the way they tell their histories, unashamedly from their own perspectives. They have what I would call *mana motuhake* in their approach, *mana motuhake* being self-determination of your future.

Karrabing's most recent film, *Day in the Life* (2020), charts a day, presumably like many others, in which the authoritative hand of the government is a constant, shadowy presence over the community. The film comprises five satirically titled vignettes—'Breakfast', 'Play Break', 'Lunch Run', 'Cocktail Hour', 'Takeout Dinner'—illustrating the ways in which the community's everyday lives are shaped by external influences and constraints, in the form of state agents policing their behaviour or private mining companies stealing resources and polluting their lands. In the work, the perspectives of the Karrabing cast are always central, creating an empathetic viewing experience that flips mainstream assumptions about Aboriginal communities on their head.

The film's dialogue is interspersed with a rap soundtrack composed by younger members of the collective and audio clips from radio and television programmes—sourced predominantly from the Australian Broadcasting Corporation—repeating deficit statistics about Aboriginal communities. These samples mention community impoverishment, overcrowded housing, and, most tellingly, the amount of

money provided by state and federal governments, illustrating how the mainstream media and Australian politicians perpetuate negative stereotypes about Aboriginal communities squandering government aid. The effects of one particularly damaging stereotype—that Aboriginal parents are unable to care for their children—are highlighted in the 'Play Break' segment of *Day in the Life*: two women enjoying an idyllic afternoon playing outdoors with their kids are abruptly interrupted by the arrival of government authorities.

It is in these mothers' fear that the effects of governmental oppression are felt most keenly. Fear accelerates their movements as they seek to hide the children. The segment reveals the double-edged sword of living under a government that provides significant welfare: it also determines what 'good' parenting looks like and will enforce that model accordingly. When the authorities ultimately take one woman's children, she morphs from close kin to pariah. The fear and stigma surrounding her make her repellent to others: will the events that befell her rub off on the community? This is a victory for *colonisation*: Indigenous families turning on each other in order to protect themselves.

The mother's fear is an inherited one, evident in a refrain repeated throughout the film: 'We're gonna do what our old people did, we're gonna hide our kids.' This is one of many references Karrabing filmmakers make to the Stolen Generations, the thousands of Aboriginal and Torres Strait Islander children who were forcibly removed from their families between roughly 1905 and the 1970s. The effects of these removals are everywhere in Karrabing films, regardless of whether they are explicitly mentioned. The consequences are seen in the dependence on welfare, the overcrowded housing, and the fear of government authorities. They are also evident in the quest to reclaim traditional knowledge and relationships to Country. As Karrabing films increasingly circulate internationally, perhaps their focus on the social inequity experienced by Indigenous people will compel audiences around the world to examine how their own governments legislated the assimilation of 'dying' Indigenous peoples into dominant settler power structures. After all, knowledge is a collective responsibility.

One scene in *Day in the Life* follows a young man who wakes to find he is unable to cook breakfast and have a shower, as the utilities in his house have been cut off. As he walks from house to house along seemingly deserted streets, it becomes evident that other households are in the same impoverished predicament: pipes are blocked and the residents are waiting for assistance, or the electricity has gone out. A refrain from the accompanying rap soundtrack lodged itself squarely in my brain: 'Forward to the bush, but where's he going to go?' There is a popular belief, even among Indigenous people, that we know best how to live harmoniously, symbiotically, with the environment. Frankly, it's a romanticised view. The reality is that as Indigenous individuals, we don't inherently hold that knowledge. Because of colonisation, which systematically removed Indigenous people from their lands and subsequently stripped them of their languages and cultures, we don't all know how to survive on our own land. One of the most devastating pieces of legislation passed in Aotearoa was the Tohunga Suppression Act (1907), which outlawed Māori cultural and spiritual practices, dismantled our traditional *wānanga* teaching systems, and led to the eventual banning of our language in schools. As with the Stolen Generations in Australia, it is impossible to quantify how government interventions have contributed to shorter life expectancy, lower quality of life, and Māori overrepresentation in prisons. So, forward to the bush, but what's he going to eat, and wear, and where's he going to live?

My *iwi* (tribe) are bush people from the Te Urewera mountains, and many of my family members are hunters, a role that feels completely entwined with who we are as Māori. However, the animals that we hunt in the twenty-first century—wild pigs, deer, tahr—are all animals that were introduced by European settlers in the eighteenth and nineteenth centuries. There are no mammals (apart from bats) endemic to Aotearoa: native birds, which would have traditionally been hunted, are now protected species. Knowledge of edible flora, another traditional food source, has eroded due to violent disruptions to our cultural well-being such as land confiscations, postwar migration from tribal homelands into urban centres, and the convenience of the supermarket. Meticulous crafting of bird snares and spears has been eschewed in favor of guns. As is likewise seen in Karrabing films, displacement from land and the removal of younger generations also disrupts another foundation of Indigenous life: intergenerational living. If this way of life is interrupted, so too is the ability to pass knowledge down.

This predicament is portrayed in the 'Takeout Dinner' segment of *Day in the Life*, wherein an elder is taking a younger family member on Country to teach him the ways of the land when they are distracted by the discovery of a lithium extraction site. Both the elder and his protégé question how they're meant to learn from and protect their land if it's being dug up and poisoned by white people. As portrayed here, the health of the land and the health of the people are inextricably linked. But, as is often the case in Karrabing films, the rather depressing storylines in *Day in the Life* are saved when Indigenous people's own stories and ways of life are asserted. In the film's closing scene, the protagonists initiate a *corroboree*, creating a swirl of time in

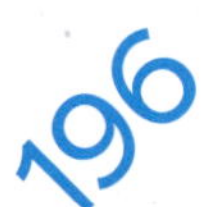

which the ills of the past are undone. Karrabing stories become powerful catalysts for survival itself.

One Karrabing film, *Night Time Go* (2017), addresses the past directly, posing as a documentary depicting an alternative history of Australia's domestic experience of World War II. Combining archival newsreel footage with grainy, black-and-white reenactments staged by Karrabing members, the film narrates the wartime experiences of Karrabing ancestors who were forcibly relocated to inland internment camps in anticipation of an imminent Japanese invasion, lest their 'simple minds' be manipulated by Axis influences to undermine the Australian government. The Karrabing ancestors escaped from the camp in September 1943 and returned to their homes on foot, a journey of more than two hundred miles. A title card at the beginning of the film states, 'No record of their journey, or others like it, exists in the settler archive.'

This film is an intervention into what mandated truth looks like, speaking back to the settler government's portrayal of official history. Researching the Katherine internment camp depicted in the film, I came across the following description on the government-run Northern Territory Tourism website: 'The Mataranka Aboriginal Army Camp was established by late 1943 comprised of 350 Aboriginal workers who were supporting the war effort by working for the Army.'[5] 'Supporting the war effort' and 'working for the Army' is an interpretation of events far different from the one portrayed in *Night Time Go*.

The government voice in the film, represented through archival clips, presents a picture of Australia that is pastoral and patriotic: the government is the benevolent patron of Aboriginal peoples, who are enjoying their 'simple lifestyle ... under the shelter of our great nation'. But Karrabing subverts this government archive, bringing historic photographs to life in reenactments. Settler histories have often ignored the fates of the people depicted in these images, but the film shows them as fully fledged individuals on a mission to re-chart their futures. In the process, Karrabing members also rewrite history, imagining an alternative course of events in which their ancestors not only escape the internment camp but expel the *whitefulla* from their lands on their journey home. At the end of *Night Time Go*, the 'Karrabing Free Broadcast System' announces: 'Australian North Falls. Army Retreats to Brisbane Line. Indigenous Peoples Celebrate Freedom.' Though the film borders on mockumentary, its satire isn't done for the sake of humour. Rather, Karrabing's re-creations elicit hope for what an alternative, *mana motuhake*, future would look like for Karrabing members and their

5 'Katherine in WWII', *Northern Territory Tourism*, northern-territory.com.

families. It also illustrates that for Indigenous peoples living in settler states, participation in the World Wars meant turning attention to fighting external enemies at times when their own freedom was still under internal threat.

The Karrabing Film Collective has shown me that hope lives and dies on belief. For Indigenous peoples, this belief is tied to knowing our land, our kin, and our stories. To believe in ourselves is to unlearn much of what is told to us by the dominant media, and to escape all the tentacles of government that find their way into our schools and homes. The swirling circularity of history that Karrabing so deftly foregrounds in their work reminds us that our story has not yet ended.

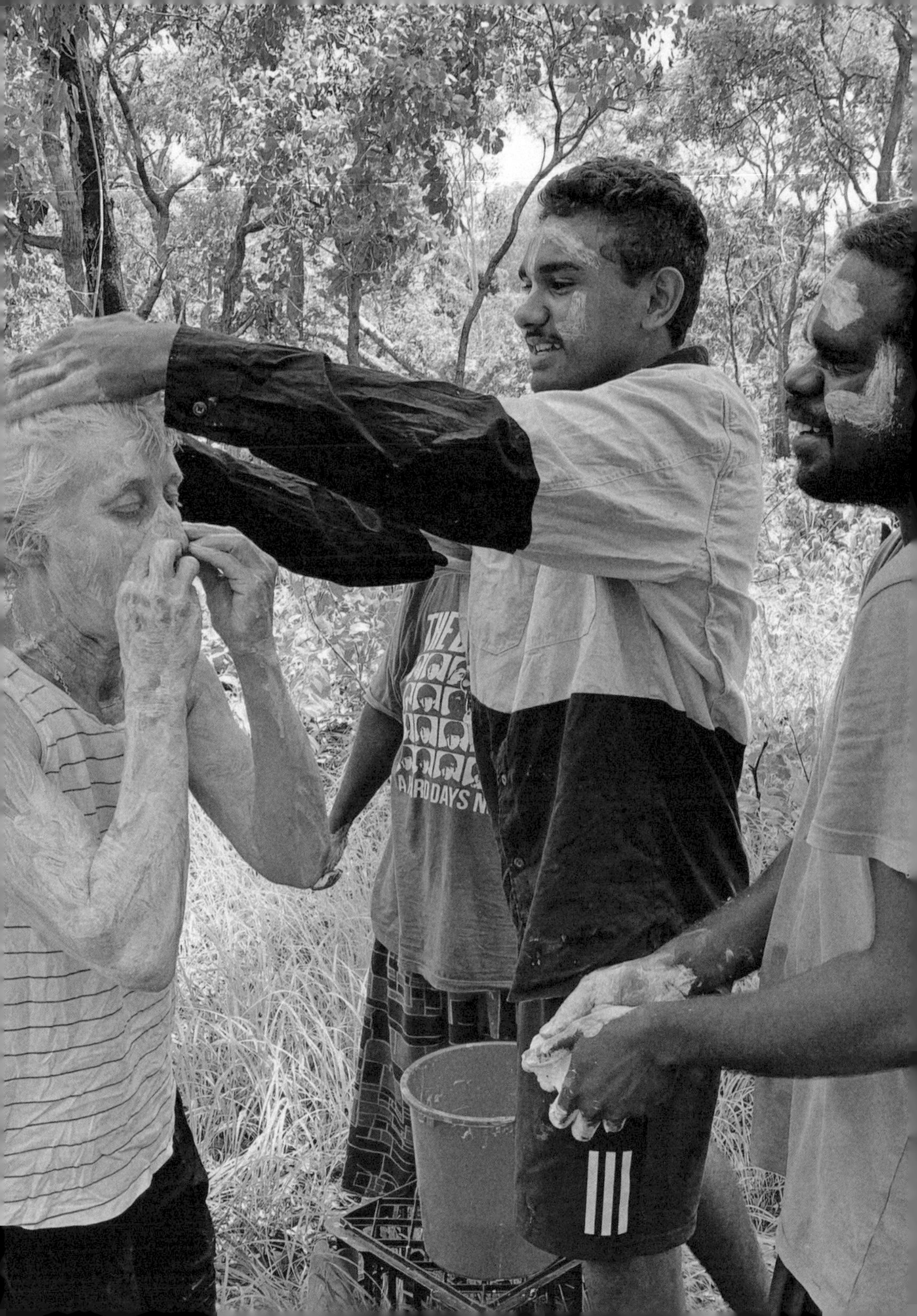

Biographies

Dr Paola Balla is an artist, curator, academic, and writer. Her practice-led research situates the ways Aboriginal women artists and activists disrupt artistic *terra nullius* by speaking back and 'Blak' to patriarchal and colonial narratives. Paola teaches Indigenous studies, education, and art at Moondani Balluk Indigenous Academic Centre, Victoria University, and co-founded the Indigenous Arts and Cultural Program and Wominjeka Festival at Footscray Community Arts 2010. Her essays and creative nonfiction works are published in *Etchings Indigenous, The Lifted Brow, Peril Magazine, Weather Stations, Victorian Writer, Going Down Swinging, frieze, SBS online, Artlink, NITV online, Oceania, Metro Magazine, Art + Australia*, and *Cordite Poetry,* amongst others. She and co-edited *Blak Brow, Blak Women's Edition* (2018) and *Indigenous: Visualising Sovereignty with Ali Gumillya Baker* (Artlink, 2021).

Curatorial projects include *Executed* in Franklin Street, City Gallery, Melbourne (2014), *Sovereignty* (2016) and *Unfinished Business: Perspectives on Art and Feminism* at the Australian Centre for Contemporary Art (ACCA, 2017)..

Richard Bell (b. 1953) lives and works in Brisbane, Australia. He works across a variety of media including painting, installation, performance, and video. One of Australia's most significant artists, Bell's work explores the complex artistic and political problems of Western, colonial, and Indigenous art production.

He grew out of a generation of Aboriginal activists and has remained committed to the politics of Aboriginal emancipation and self-determination. In 2003 he was the recipient of the Telstra National Aboriginal Art Award, establishing him as an important Australian artistic figure. Bell is represented in most major national and state collections, and has held a number of solo exhibitions at important institutions in Australia and America.

Kirsty Howey is Co-Director of the Environment Centre NT. She was a native title, land rights, and environmental lawyer for over a decade, including acting as instructing solicitor for traditional owners in landmark legal proceedings challenging the approvals of McArthur River Mine. Howey has a PhD from the University of Sydney investigating the intersection between Indigenous institutions, the environment, the state, and development in northern Australia, and has published widely in these areas. She was a board member of the Environmental Defenders' Office (NT) from 2013 to 2019, including three terms as Chair. She is an adjunct research fellow at the Northern Institute at Charles Darwin University, and on the editorial board of the Australian Environment Review. Howey's research interests include Indigenous land rights and native title law, environmental law, development theory, and discourse (particularly as it relates to developing northern Australia), the materiality of development, postcolonial studies, and the anthropology of law, institutions, and policy.

May Adadol Ingawanij / เม อาดาดล อิงคะวณิช is a writer, curator, and teacher. She works on Southeast Asian contemporary art; de-westernised and decentred histories and genealogies of cinematic arts; avant-garde legacies in Southeast Asia; forms of future-making in contemporary artistic and curatorial practices; aesthetics and circulation of artists' moving image, art, and independent films belonging to or connected with Southeast Asia. She is Professor of Cinematic Arts at the University of Westminster, where she co-directs the Centre for Research and Education in Arts and Media. Recent curatorial projects include *Legacies, Animistic Apparatus*. Recent writings have been published in *Afterall, Screen, Southeast of Now, New Left Review,* and MIT Press.

Begun circa 2012, the **Karrabing Film Collective** uses the creation of film and art installations as a form of Indigenous grassroots resistance and self-organisation. Oriented to maintaining ancestral relations to Karrabing coastal lands in northwestern Australia, the intergenerational collective of some thirty people opens a space beyond binaries of the fictional and the documentary, the past and the present. Meaning 'low tide' in the Emmiyengal language, 'karrabing' refers to a form of collectivity outside of government-imposed strictures of clanship or land ownership. Shot on handheld cameras and phones, most of Karrabing's films dramatise and sati-

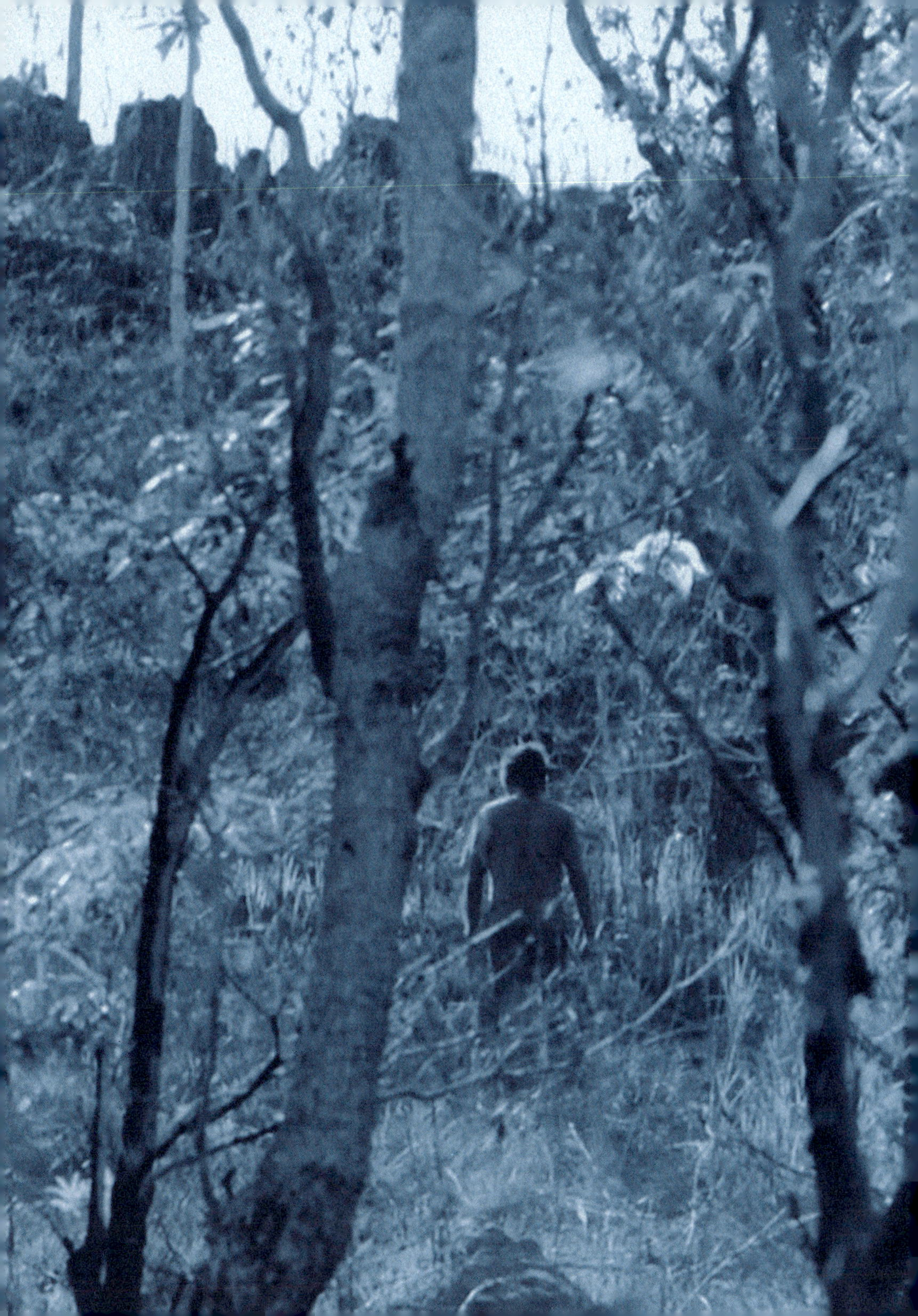

rise the daily scenarios and obstacles that collective members face in their various interactions with corporate and state entities. Karrabing have been the recipients of numerous prizes including the Visible Award (2015); the Cinema Nova Award Best Short Fiction Film, Melbourne International Film Festival (2015); Special Mention, Film Victoria Erwin Rado, Award for Best Australian Short Film, Melbourne Film Festival (2018); Eye Prize, Eye Film Museum (2021). They have shown at MoMAPS1, New York; Tate, London; the Serpentine, London; Palais de Tokyo; Madre, Naples, and numerous other places. Their works are held in permanent collections of Kadist, San Francisco; Van Abbemuseum, Eindhoven; and the Museo della Civiltà, Roma.

Professor **Tess Lea** is an anthropologist who specialises in the cultural life of policy. Her fundamental interest is with issues of (dys)function: how it occurs and to what, whom, and how it is ascribed. Looking at everyday militarisation, extraction industries, houses, infrastructure (e.g. plumbing and roads), schools, and efforts to create culturally congruent forms of employment and enterprise from multiple perspectives, her work asks why the path to realising seemingly straightforward ambitions is so densely obstacled. She is also exploring how, using new ways of intervening in policy, a wicked place like Sydney might become a beacon of cycling and pedestrian friendly amenity. She is the author of *Bureaucrats and Bleeding Hearts* (2008), *Darwin* (2020; fp 2014), and *Wild Policy: Indigeneity and the Unruly Logics of Intervention* (2020), which introduces new ways of thinking about policy as something that can be acted upon, but also shapes our everyday environments in chaotic and unequal ways.

Damian Lentini is a curator at Haus der Kunst München. He obtained his doctoral degree on contemporary art, curation, and museum studies at the University of Melbourne and lectured extensively on the history and theory of modern and contemporary art. After permanently relocating to Germany in 2014, he worked on various exhibition projects in both Berlin and Munich, including being awarded a Goethe Fellowship to contribute to the landmark exhibition project *Postwar: Art between the Pacific and the Atlantic, 1945*–1965 (Haus der Kunst, 2016). Since then, Lentini has been extensively involved in major exhibitions and publications featuring El Anatsui, Phyllida Barlow, Kapwani Kiwanga, Dumb Type, Sarah Sze, Sung Tieu, Harun Farocki, Jörg Immendorff, Khvay Samnang, and Raqs Media Collective, among others.

Elizabeth A. Povinelli is an academic, artist, and filmmaker. She is Franz Boas Professor of Anthropology at Columbia University, New York; Corresponding Fellow of the Australian Academy for the Humanities; and one of the founding members of the Karrabing Film Collective. Povinelli's writing has focused on developing a critical theory of late liberalism that would support an anthropology of the otherwise. This potential theory has unfolded primarily from within a sustained relationship with Indigenous colleagues in north Australia and across eight books, numerous essays, and eight films with the Karrabing Film Collective. Povinelli's individual artworks have been show in a number of galleries including Prometeo Gallery, Milan, and the Museo delle Civiltà, Rome. Her recent publications include *Geontologies: A Requiem to Late Liberalism* (2016), which won the 2017 Trilling Prize, and the graphic memoir, *The Inheritance* (2020). Povinelli lives and works in New York and Darwin.

Matariki Williams (Ngāi Tūhoe, Ngāti Hauiti, Taranaki, Ngāti Whakaue), is Pou Matua Mātauranga Māori | Senior Historian, Mātauranga Māori at Manatū Taonga | Ministry for Culture and Heritage, a curator, writer, and editor. Prior to this role, she was a Curator Mātauranga Māori at the Museum of New Zealand Te Papa Tongarewa. She is the co-author of the award-winning book *Protest Tautohetohe: Objects of Resistance, Persistence and Defiance* (2019) and co-editor and co-founder of *ATE Journal of Māori Art*. Her writing has appeared in various print and online publications including *frieze*, *Art in America*, *Art Zone*, *The Pantograph Punch*, and *e-Tangata*. She is a Trustee for *Contemporary HUM*, and a former board member of Museums Aotearoa and the National Digital Forum.

Vivian Ziherl currently serves as Research and Programs Manager at Kunstinstituut Melly in Rotterdam. She previously founded the Frontier Imaginaries art foundation and has presented projects with documenta 14 (Athens and Kassel), e-flux and Columbia University (New York), the Institute of Modern Art (Brisbane), the Jerusalem Show and Qalandiya International (Jerusalem), the Stedelijk Museum (Amsterdam), and the Van Abbemuseum (Eindhoven). She has served as curator with If I Can't Dance I Don't Want to be Part of Your Revolution, and is a PhD candidate in curatorial studies at Monash University.

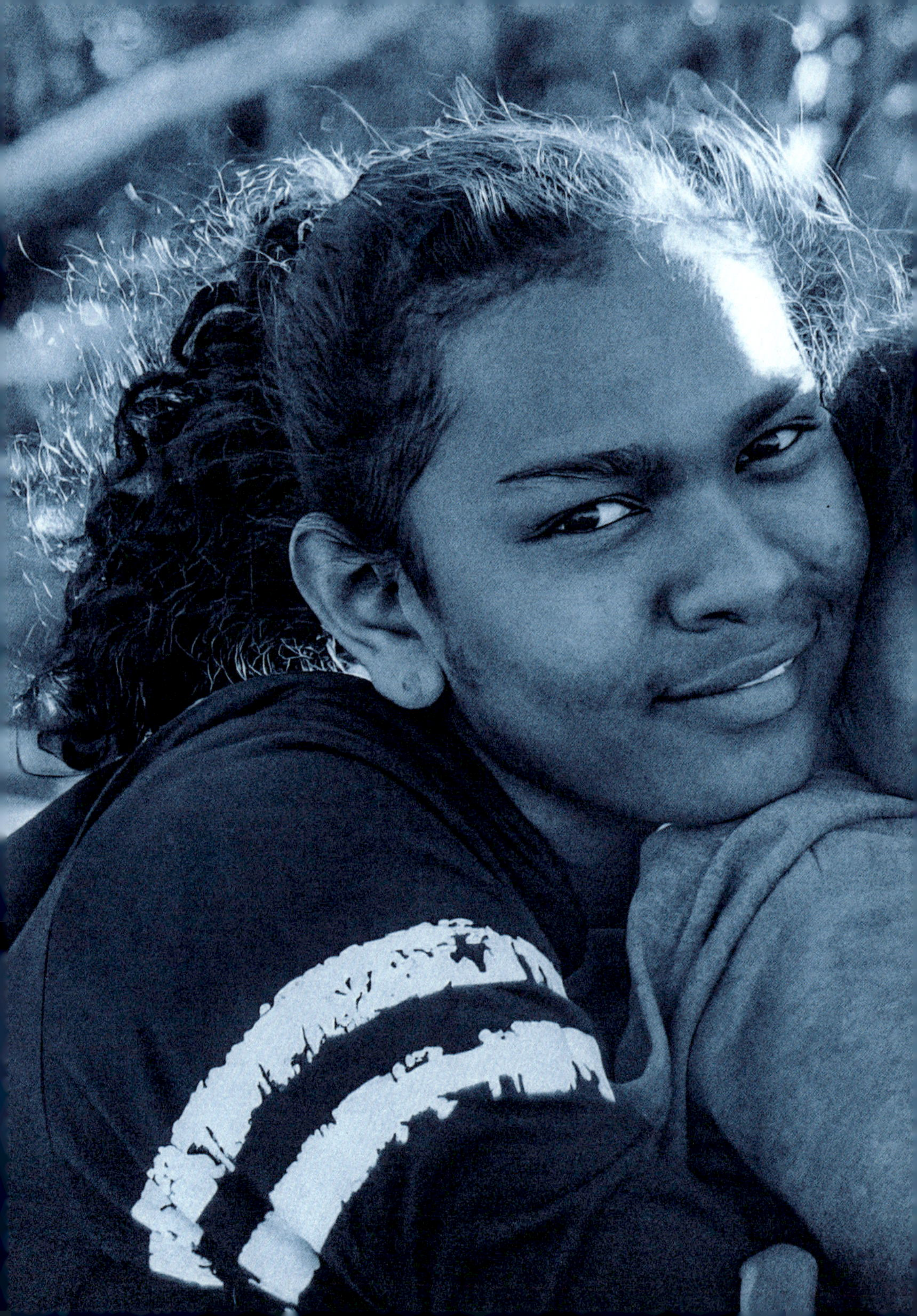

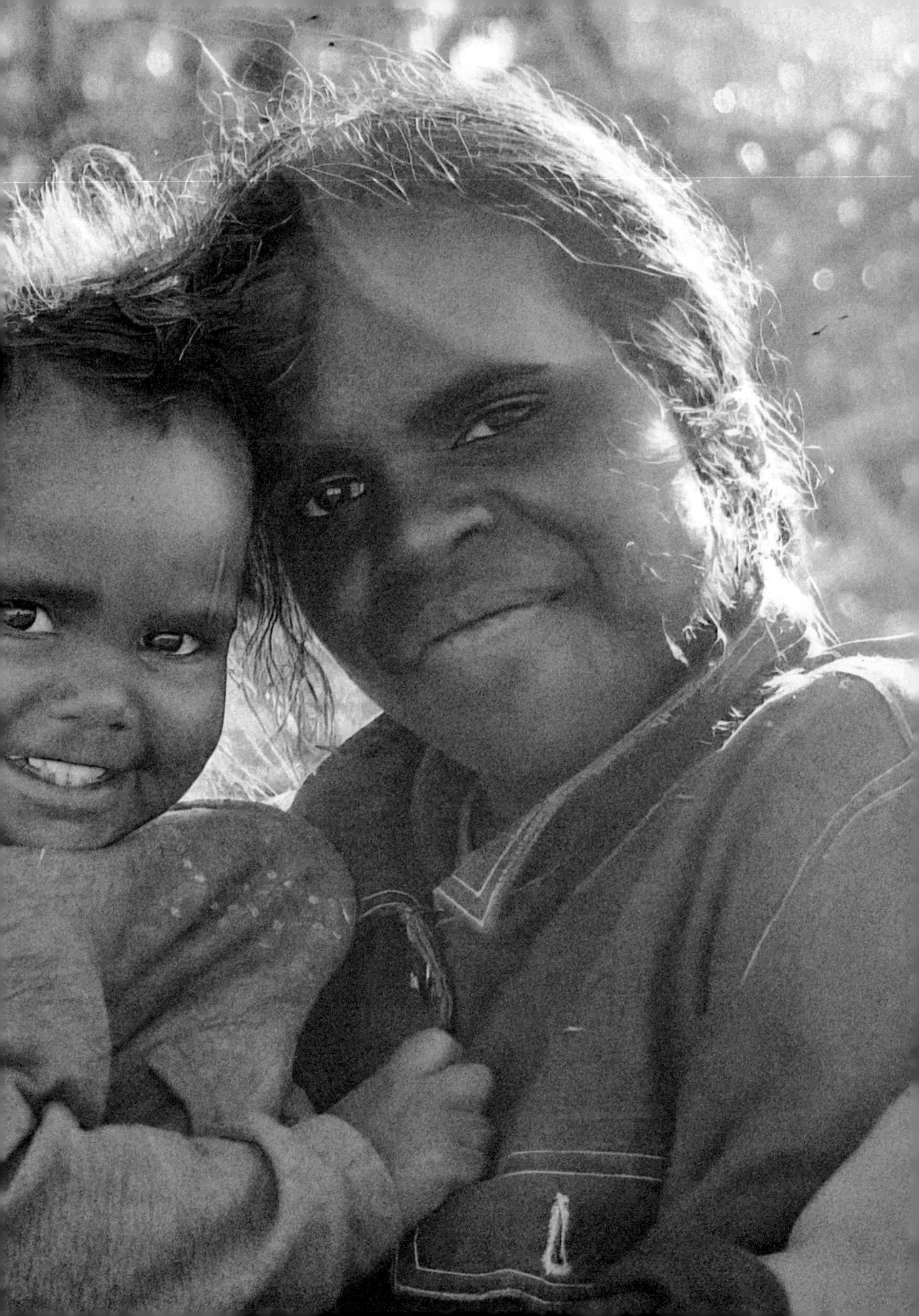

Selected Bibliography

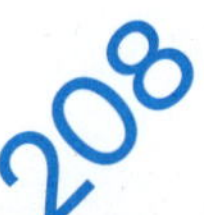

2022

Rebecca McLaren, 'From Belyuen to Berlin: the Karrabing Film Collective share stories around the world', *ABC Darwin Radio*, Broadcast Sunday 12 Jun 2022: https://www.abc.net.au/darwin/programs/sundays/karrabing-film-collective/13926118

2021

Ferial Nadja Karrasch, 'Toxischer Liebesbrief an eine Göttin', *Monopol*, 2 November 2021: https://www.monopol-magazin.de/luckenwalde-e-werk-power-nights-toxischer-liebesbrief-eine-goettin

Elizabeth A. Povinelli, 'Divergent Survivances', *e-flux journal*, Issue #121, October 2021: https://www.e-flux.com/journal/121/424069/divergent-survivances

Afifah Tasya and Sam Hewison 'Interview with Elizabeth Povinelli', *Sipakatuo*, 8 September 2021: https://www.sipakatuo.com/research/interview-with-elizabeth-povinelli

Daniel Fisher and Aidan Seale-Feldman, 'Filmmaking and Worldmaking: An Interview with the Karrabing Film Collective', *Visual and New Media Review*, 18 March 2021: https://culanth.org/fieldsights/filmmaking-and-worldmaking-an-interview-with-the-karrabing-film-collective

Elizabeth A. Povinelli, Elizabeth, Daniela Gandorfer, and Zulaikha Ayub, 2021. 'Mattering-Forth: Thinking-With Karrabing', *Theory & Event* 24 (1), 2021: pp. 294–323

2020

Elizabeth A. Povinelli, 'The Ancestral Present of Oceanic Illusions: Connected and Differentiated in Late Toxic Liberalism', *e-flux journal*, Issue #112, October 2020: https://www.e-flux.com/journal/112/352823/the-ancestral-present-of-oceanic-illusions-connected-and-differentiated-in-late-toxic-liberalism

Karrabing Film Collective, 'Displacing Displacement. Filmmaking against Neocolonialism: An Interview with Karrabing Film Collective', *Nero*, 13 July 2020: https://www.neroeditions.com/displacing-displacement

Mike Hoolboom, 'The Mermaids, or Aiden in Wonderland', blog post, May 2020: http://mikehoolboom.com/?p=20937

Matariki Williams, 'Karrabing Film Collective Tackles the Cultural and Environmental Devastation of Settler Colonialism', *Art in America*, 6 May 2020: https://www.artnews.com/art-in-america/features/karrabing-film-collective-day-in-the-life-1202686183

Adam Pugh, '49th International Film Festival Rotterdam', *Art Monthly*, 434, March 2020: p. 36

Maggie Wander, 'The Karrabing Film Collective: "Talking Back" to Ethnographic Media and Mineral Extraction in Australia', *Media Fields Journal*, 29 February 2020

Ben Eastman, 'Karrabing Film Collective', *Art Review*, 1 January 2020: https://artreview.com/ar-january-february-2020-feature-karrabing-film-collective

2019

Jason Farago, 'Can We Start Appreciating Indigenous Art on Its Own Terms?', *New York Times*, 20 May 2019

Martha Schwendener, 'Karrabing Film Collective Reflects a Disturbing Reality at MoMA PS1', *New York Times*, 15 May 2019

David Giles and Melinda Hinkson, with Elizabeth Povinelli, Lorraine Lane, Linda Yarrowin, Cecelia Lewis, and Sandra Yarrowin, 'Elizabeth Povinelli and Karrabing Film Collective', *Conversations in Anthropology*, podcast, Episode 18, 2019: https://soundcloud.com/anthro-convo/ep18-povinelli

Elizabeth A. Povinelli and Rex Edmunds, 'A Conversation at Bamayak and Mabaluk, Part of the Coastal Lands of the Emmiyengal People', *L'Internationale online*, 3 October 2019: https://www.internationaleonline.org/people/elizabeth_a_povinelli_and_rex_edmunds

May Adadol Ingawanij, 'Comedy of Entanglement: Karrabing Film Collective', *Afterall* 48. Autumn/Winter 2019: pp. 26–37

David Boarder Giles, Melinda Hinkson, Timothy Neale, and Karrabing Film Collective, 'A Conversation with the Karrabing Film Collective', *Commoning Ethnography*, vol. 2, no. 1, 2019: pp. 166–94

Eduardo Álvarez, 'Documentando La Resistencia Indîgena', *Madrid Art Process*, 3 April 2019

Gabrielle O'Brien, 'Keeping Country Alive: Dreaming, Decolonization and the Karrabing Film Collective', *Metro*, Issue 199, January 2019: pp. 108–113

2018

Maggie Wander, '"It's Ok. We're Safe Here": The Karrabing Film Collective and Colonial Histories in Australia', *Commonwealth Essays & Studies*, vol. 41, no. 1, 2018: pp. 53-62

Matteo Lucchetti and Judith Wielander, 'Indigenous, Not Homogenous: An Interview with Elizabeth A. Povinelli', in Nico Dockx and Pascal Gielen (eds.) *Commonism: A New Aesthetics of the Real*, Amsterdam, Valiz: Antennae Series, 2018: pp. 269–280

Tess Lea and Elizabeth A. Povinelli, 'Karrabing: An Essay in Keywords', *Visual Anthropology Review*, vol. 34, no. 1, 2018: pp. 36–46

Zoénie Liwen Deng, 'On "Trade Markings": Frontiers as Interfaces, Imaginaries with Responsibilities and Responsibilities', *Leap*, 13 July 2018: http://www.leapleapleap.com/2018/07/on-trade-markings

Maria Walsh, 'Karrabing Film Collective: Saltwater Dreams', *Art Monthly London*, 412, December/January, 2017/18: p. 35

Sumugan Sivanesan, 'Marking Histories' Discontents: Frontier Imaginaries Edition No. 5, Trade Markings', *un Projects*, 24 May 2018: https://unprojects.org.au/article/marking-histories-discontents-frontier-imaginaries-edition-no-5-trade-markings

2017

Colin Perry, 'Truth to Tell', *Art Monthly*, Issue 408, July/August 2017: pp. 1–5

Karrabing Film Collective, 'Growing up Karrabing, a conversation with Gavin Bianamu, Sheree Bianamu, Natasha Lewis Bigfoot, Ethan Jorrock, and Elizabeth Povinelli', *un Magazine*, vol. 11, no. 2, October 2017: http://unprojects.org.au/magazine/issues/issue-11-2/growing-up-karrabing

Karrabing Film Collective, 'Australian Babel: A Conversation with Karrabing', *Specimen, The Babel Review of Translation*, October 2017: http://www.specimen.press/articles/a-conversation-with-karrabing

Elizabeth A. Povinelli, 'Geontologies: The Concept and Its Territories', *e-flux journal*, Issue #81, April 2017: https://www.e-flux.com/journal/81/123372/geontologies-the-concept-and-its-territories

2016

Nicola Gray 'Themes of Return, Exile, and the Sea Trickle Through a Palestinian Art Festival', *Hyperallergic*, 16 December 2016: https://hyperallergic.com/345689/themes-of-return-exile-and-the-sea-trickle-through-a-palestinian-art-festival

Vivian Ziherl, 'Karrabing Film Collective Wutharr, Saltwater Dreams', *Vdrome*, October 2016: http://www.vdrome.org/karrabing-film-collective-wutharr-saltwater-dreams

2015

Martina Angelotti, 'Karrabing Film Collective', *domus magazine*, 18 December 2015: http://www.domusweb.it/en/interviews/2015/12/18/visible_award_2015_the_karrabing_film_collective.html

Aodhan Madden, 'Making Batteries: Interview with the Karrabing Film Collective', *un Magazine*, 9.2, November 2015: https://unprojects.org.au/article/making-batteries-conversation-with-the-karrabing-film-collective

Jeremy Elphick, 'Low Tide Turning: An Interview with the Karrabing Film Collective', *Melbourne International Film Festival*, 5 August 2015: http://fourthreefilm.com/2015/08/low-tide-turning-an-interview-with-the-karrabing-film-collective

Elizabeth A. Povinelli, 'Windjarrameru, The Stealing C*nt$', *Supercommunity, e-flux contribution to the Venice Biennale*, 21 May 2015—Day 12: http://supercommunity.e-flux.com/texts/windjarrameru-the-stealing-c-nts

2014

Karrabing Film Collective, 'Holding Up the World, Part I', *e-flux journal*, Issue #58, October 2014: https://www.e-flux.com/journal/58/61145/holding-up-the-world-part-i

Elizabeth A. Povinelli, 'Holding Up the World, Part II: Time/Bank, Effort/Embankments', *e-flux journal*, Issue #58, October 2014: https://www.e-flux.com/journal/58/61147/holding-up-the-world-part-ii-time-bank-effort-embankments

Lauren Berlant and Elizabeth A. Povinelli, 'Holding Up the World, Part III: In the Event of Precarity ... A Conversation', *e-flux journal*, Issue #58, October 2014: https://www.e-flux.com/journal/58/61149/holding-up-the-world-part-iii-in-the-event-of-precarity-a-conversation

Audra Simpson, Elizabeth A. Povinelli, and Liza Johnson, 'Holding Up the World, Part IV: After a Screening of When the Dogs Talked at Columbia University', *e-flux journal*, Issue #58, October 2014: https://www.e-flux.com/journal/58/61151/holding-up-the-world-part-iv-after-a-screening-of-when-the-dogs-talked-at-columbia-university

Colophon Exhibition

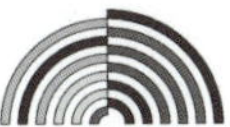

Stiftung Haus der Kunst München
gemeinnützige
Betriebsgesellschaft mbH
Prinzregentenstraße 1
80538 München
www.hausderkunst.de

DIRECTION

Andrea Lissoni
Artistic Director

Wolfgang Orthmayr
Commercial Director

Biljana Gligorić
Executive Assistant / Business Affairs

Christian Brockschläger
Student Assistant Administration

CURATORIAL DEPARTMENT

Emma Enderby
Chief Curator / Head of Programme and Research

Isabella Kredler
Assistant to the Chief Curator / Head of Programme and Research

Jana Baumann
Senior Curator

Damian Lentini
Curator

Sabine Brantl
Curator Archive / History Department

Anna Schneider
Curator

Sarah Theurer
Curator

Teresa Retzer
Assistant Curator

Anne Pfautsch
Curatorial Fellow

Manuela Hillmann
Curatorial Fellow

Hanns Lennart Wiesner
Curatorial Fellow

Lorena Harauzek
Project Assistant Curatorial Department

Sylvia Clasen
Team Assistant Curators

EXHIBITION COORDINATION

Hanna Kriegleder
Head of Exhibition Coordination/Production

Martin Oster
Assistant Exhibition Coordination/Production

Cassandre Schmid
Registrar

Margarita Shabaeva
Registrar Fellow

Felicitas Fendel
Student Assistant Registrar

Markus Brandenburg
Exhibition Construction

Tanja Eiler
Depot / Continuity

COMMUNICATIONS

Tina Anjou
Marketing / Head of Communications

Claudia Illi
Press / Relations

Judith Bodendörfer
Assistant Press Relations

Saskia Müller-Bastian
Digital Communication

Manuela Illera
Video / Audio Producer

Iris Ludwig
Team Assistant Communications

Veronika Lutz
Student Assistant Communications

EDUCATION LEARNING EVENTS

Pia Linden
Head of Education / Learning

Camille Latreille
Learning and Engagement

Andrea Saul
Events

Thomas Ludwig
Visitor Service

FACILITY MANAGEMENT

Anton Köttl
Head of Facility Management

Roland Roppelt
Janitor

Robert Szabó
Janitor

Konstantin Kamponeski
Mail Office

FINANCES AND ADMINISTRATION

Thomas Kirst
Finance and Controlling

Cora Szabó
HR Manager

Jessica Fuhrmann
Assistant HR

Moritz Peterson
Procurement Manager

Niels Osthorst
Visitor Services

Birgit Klerings
Head of Accounting

For their annual support of the program, we would like to thank our shareholders

Freistaat Bayern, Gesellschaft der Freunde Haus der Kunst e.V.

ALEXANDER TUTSEK——
—STIFTUNG

and our major supporter the Alexander Tutsek-Foundation.

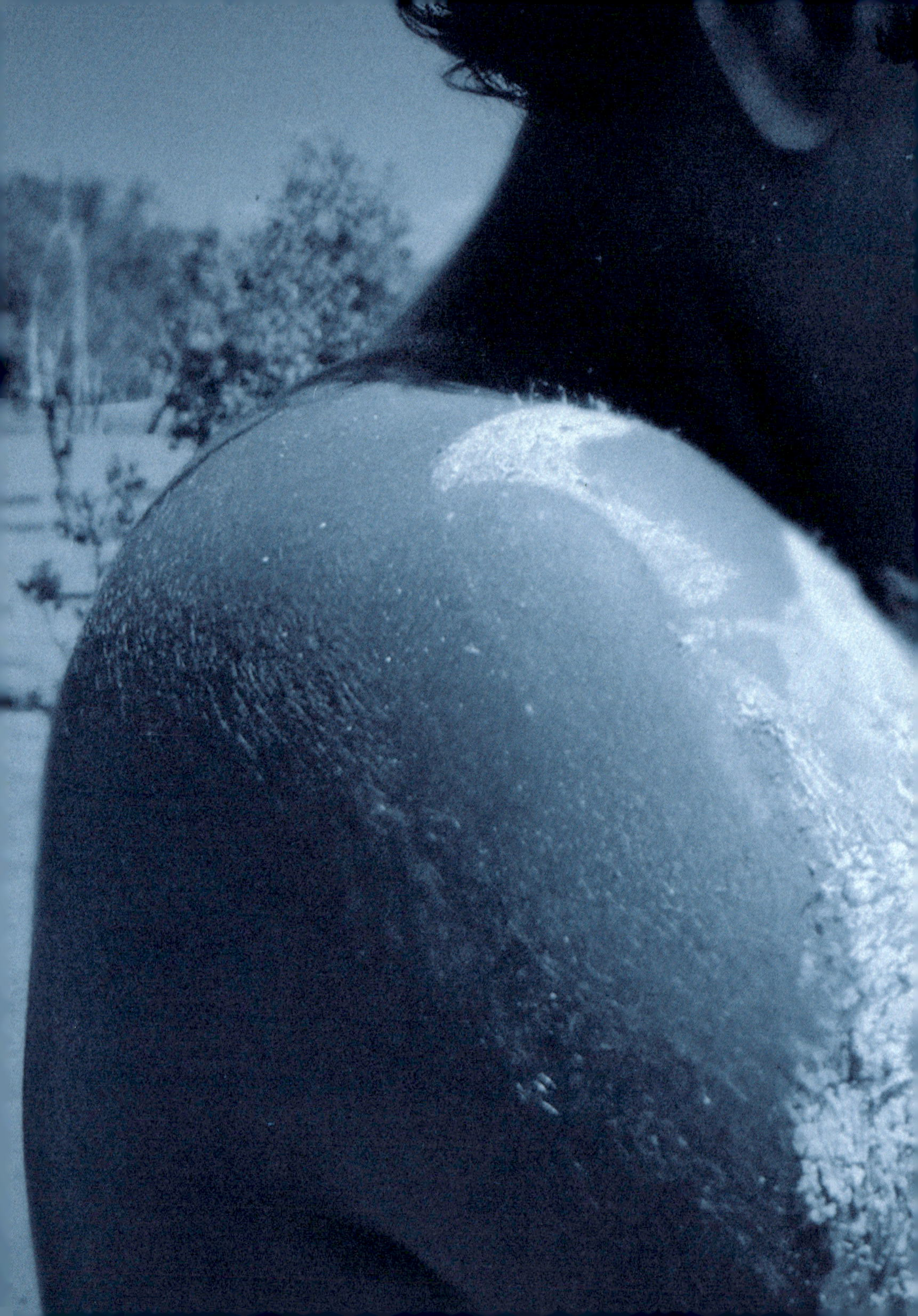

Colophon Publication

This reader is published on the occasion of the exhibition

Karrabing Film Collective. Wonderland
Haus der Kunst München
27.1.–30.7. 2023

Curator
Damian Lentini

Curatorial Fellow
Anne Pfautsch

PUBLICATION

Editor
Damian Lentini

With contributions by
Paola Balla
Richard Bell
Kirsty Howey
May Adadol Ingawanij
Karrabing Film Collective
Tess Lea
Damian Lentini
Andrea Lissoni
Elizabeth A. Povinelli
Matariki Williams
Vivian Ziherl

Graphic Design
Eva Schlotter, DISTANZ Verlag

Copy Editing
Olivia Parkes

Image Editing
Reproline mediateam, Unterföhring

Printing and Binding
Druckhaus Sportflieger, Berlin

Distribution
Edel Germany GmbH
www.edel.com
international-books@edel.com

Published by
DISTANZ Verlag
www.distanz.de

PHOTO CREDITS
© Karrabing Film Collective
6–7, 23, 26–27, 37, 48–49, 51, 57, 59, 61, 63, 65, 67, 69–71, 73–75, 77, 79, 87, 129, 147, 161, 199, 203, 214–215

© Damian Lentini
14–15, 16, 19–21, 24–25, 29–32, 34–35, 38–39, 41–42, 44–45, 47, 52–53, 80, 95, 143

Photographs Alana Branch, 2012
107, 152, 155, 171, 183, 191, 206–207

© Karrabing Film Collective
for all art works

Bibliographic information published by the Deutsche Nationalbibliothek
The Deutsche Nationalbibliothek lists this publication in the Deutsche Nationalbibliografie; detailed bibliographic data is available in the Internet at dnb.de

ISBN 978-3-95476-554-6
Printed in Germany

REPRINTED TEXTS

Paola Balla, "Across Australia, Artists are Disrupting the Colonial Mindset", *frieze*, 31 October 2018: www.frieze.com/article/across-australia-artists-are-disrupting-colonial-mindset

Richard Bell, "Bell's Theorem: AB-ORIGINAL ART – It's a White Thing!", originally published in November 2002 on the webpage: www.kooriweb.org/foley/great/art/bell.html

May Adadol Ingawanij, "Comedy of Entanglement: Karrabing Film Collective", *Afterall*, 48, Autumn/Winter, 2019, pp. 26–37

Karrabing Film Collective, "Growing up Karrabing: A conversation with Gavin Bianamu, Sheree Bianamu, Natasha Lewis Bigfoot, Ethan Jorrock, and Elizabeth Povinelli", *un Magazine*, 11.2, October 2017, www.unprojects.org.au/magazine/issues/issue-11-2/growing-up-karrabing

Tess Lea and Elizabeth A. Povinelli, "Karrabing: An Essay in Keywords", *Visual Anthropology Review*, vol. 34, no.1, 2018, p. 36–46

Elizabeth A. Povinelli, "The Ancestral Present of Oceanic Illusions: Connected and Differentiated in Late Toxic Liberalis, *e-flux journal*, Issue #112, October 2020: www.e-flux.com/journal/112/352823/the-ancestral-presentof-oceanic-illusionsconnected-and differentiated-in-latetoxic-liberalism

Elizabeth A. Povinelli and Rex Edmunds, "A Conversation at Bamayak and Mabaluk, Part of the Coastal Lands of the Emmiyengal People", *L'Internationale online*, 3 October 2019, as part of the e-book *Living with Ghosts: Legacies of Colonialism and Fascism*, edited by Nick Aikens, Jyoti Mistry and Corina Oprea: www.internationaleonline.org/people/elizabeth_a_povinelli_and_rex_edmunds

Matariki Williams, "Karrabing Film Collective Tackles the Cultural and Environmental Devastation of Settler Colonialism", *Art in America*, 6 May 2020: www.artnews.com/art-in-america/features/karrabing-film-collective-dayin-the-life-1202686183
Copyrighted 2020.
Penske Media Corporation

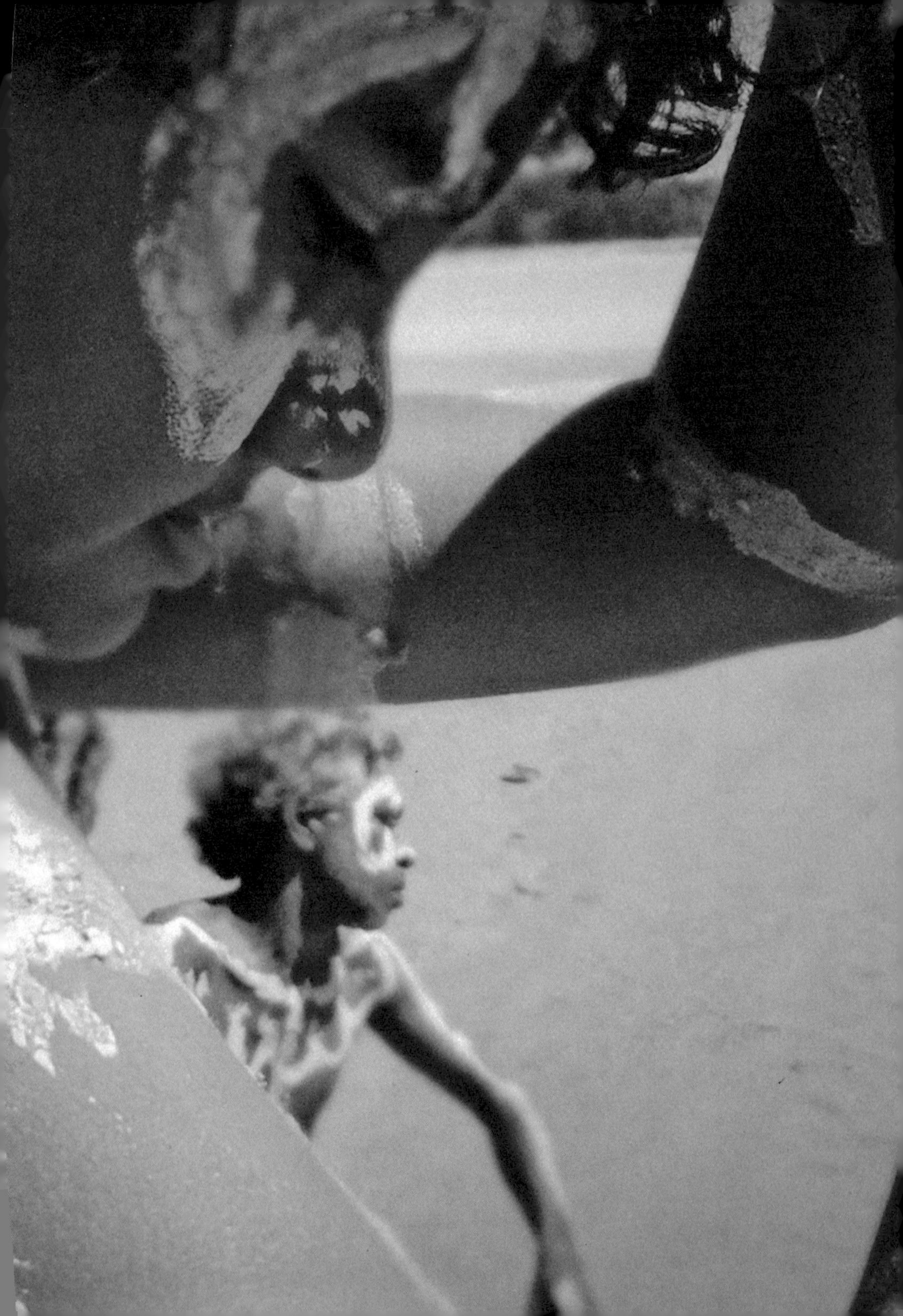